A

Made and Printed in Great Britain

A HISTORY OF
POSTAL AGITATION

A HISTORY OF
POSTAL AGITATION

FROM EIGHTY YEARS AGO TILL THE PRESENT DAY

A NEW AND REVISED EDITION
(IN TWO BOOKS)
BOOK I.

BY

H. G. SWIFT

I have eaten your bread and salt,
I have drunk your water and wine ;
The deaths ye have died I have watched beside,
And the lives that ye led were mine,

. . . . . .

I have written the tale of our life,

. . . .

—KIPLING'S *Departmental Ditties.*

Printed and Published by
PERCY BROTHERS LTD.,
MANCHESTER AND LONDON
1929

FOREWORD

BY

GEORGE MIDDLETON,
Editor of *The Post.*

I HAVE been acquainted with Swift's "History of Postal Agitation" ever since I have known the postal movement. Of late years I have come to appreciate it more and more ; and, insufficient though it is in some parts, it nevertheless presents on the whole a fair conspectus of the " movement " as it was born, and as it developed in the latter half of the nineteenth century.

I have long been convinced of the necessity of a complete picture of the movement, and it has for years been in my mind to persuade someone to do for the period 1900 down to date what H. G. Swift has done for the period covered by his book. I have also felt that it would be a good thing if Swift's book could be strengthened in certain places, particularly on the provincial side of the movement. Unexpectedly a meeting with Mr. Swift himself helped to settle the matter. Fortified with the historical resources of the Union of Post-Office Workers, I was able to induce Mr. Swift—even at his age—to undertake the task not only of revising his own work, but of accepting the task of bringing the picture up to date.

In regard to the latter part of the task the Union of Post-Office Workers hopes to publish a second volume covering the period opening with the Derby Congress down to the present time.

G. M.

AUTHOR'S FOREWORD TO THE NEW REVISED EDITION.

HOW THE HISTORY CAME TO BE WRITTEN.

THE struggle for improved conditions of work and pay amongst the great army of Post Office employees forms one of the most remarkable chapters in the whole history of British trade unionism. It is now nearly ninety years since the precarious birth of postal agitation and first efforts for reform, and for over fifty years the growth of combination has been marked by incidents of outstanding importance to the Labour Movement generally.

Just as the spreading tree from tiny seedling grew, so the history of postal agitation, like the great postal movement of to-day, has gradually unfolded itself. The wider postal movement, starting from obscure beginnings, and flourishing and growing in strength with advancing age, will soon have attained ninety years. This will come as a surprise to many who to-day sit under its sheltering branches, and perhaps few will realise that its history dates so far back. Yet, as we shall see, though it quickened into life amidst hardship, it withstood many a storm ere it became the towering landmark in the trade-union world that it is to-day.

So in a measure with the written history of it. What was at first intended to be a simple record of a single postal association—the record of a few years—expanded itself into a history of wider achievement and greater promise. For, as I proceeded to survey the prospects, and traced back postal efforts for betterment through the years, I was amazed at the interesting features revealed. Instead of a mere single field of local endeavour, I discovered, as it were, a strange and hitherto forgotten land. Till now there had been no attempt to survey in detail the ground that lay behind or to place on record in sequential order the discoveries that might be brought to light. Many, if not most, of the happenings of the previous half-century lay buried in oblivion, while even the dramatic incidents of a nearer time were only in the lingering memories of old men in the Service, or veterans long retired.

My quest, then, was for the origin and development of the desire for combination, the growth of organisation, and trade-union principle. The men who prepared the soil, who planted the seed and tended the sapling, at the call of the historian emerged from the past, though long since accounted dead, and from them, in no little degree, the narrative of the first period of Post Office agitation—the lean years of strenuous struggle—was pieced together after due verification. To reconstruct the old story of the early fight for liberty in the early days it was necessary to interview all sorts of people— old politicians, ancient pensioners,—to disinter and wade through hundreds of musty and defunct newspapers of the various periods, in the British Museum and elsewhere.

For over nine months the writer engaged on his sleuth work before assembling the necessary material for writing the first portion of the original edition. Then, when the time came to deal with the time and incidents with which I had had personal experience, the task became easier, and a labour of love was in due course completed. Completed, that is, for the time being. For during the interval of nearly thirty years since the book was published in 1900, many things have happened. Many new developments have taken place, much ground has been covered, and much of permanent value has been accomplished. What has taken place now these improvements have been gained, what is due to the fearless and brilliant men from the ranks of the postal workers, remain to be recorded in a permanent form later.

Now that a history of this later period is to be provided it has been decided also to reproduce the volume. As the historian of the first fifty years of economic struggle, I am privileged to have been asked to revise and amplify the original work, and, further, to complete the narrative by bringing it up to date.

H. G. SWIFT.

1929.

CONTENTS

CHAPTER VII

CHAPTER VIII

CHAPTER IX

CHAPTER X

CHAPTER XI

CHAPTER XII

CHAPTER XIII

CHAPTER XIV

CHAPTER XV

CHAPTER XVI

CHAPTER XVII

CHAPTER XVIII

CHAPTER XIX

CHAPTER XX

CHAPTER XXI

CHAPTER XXII

CHAPTER XXIII

THE 1890 POSTMEN'S STRIKE.

A contemporary picture of the police keeping a clear way before the G.P.O. for the evening delivery.

A HISTORY OF
POSTAL AGITATION

(FIRST PERIOD.)

CHAPTER I

INTRODUCTION : EARLY CAUSES OF DISCONTENT—
RISE OF POSTAL AGITATION.

THE history of industrial progress offers no more curious and
interesting anomaly than that the greatest profit-producing
Department, the Post Office, should have been the scene of
over half-a-century's arduous struggle amongst State servants
for the principle of a living wage and the elementary rights
of labour.

At one period the long continuance of disaffection in the
postal service seemed to justify the public in assuming that
the Post Office was an institution where the Englishman's
privilege, which is to grumble, was systematically indulged
in as a recreation. The spirit of unrest at last, finding
expression in organised agitation, had so long been in evidence
that the Post Office came to be regarded by many as not
merely a necessary convenience of life, but incidentally a
hot-bed of discontent.

In strange contrast to that serene contentment which
distinguished the rest of the Civil Service, the Post Office
continued for years to stand out with its familiar declaration
of workers' grievances, a single discordant note in the harmony.
The Temple of Mercury in St. Martin's-le-Grand had been
found so often the scene of angry discord that the caduceus
of the messenger of the gods, with its twining snakes, received

a new significance as a postal emblem. The ground about, that was expected to yield a perennial golden harvest for the Exchequer, too frequently produced also a crop of nettles. In the earlier years, discontent in a Government Department was regarded as a form of moral disease, and agitators were hunted as assiduously as the Colorado beetle. Yet it was not so much the workers as their conditions that were to blame, as events will show.

Beyond the fact that discontent with labour conditions was almost chronic in the postal service, the public knew almost nothing of the inner workings, or of the causes producing the symptoms. Probably the postman, being such a familiar, and, to the majority, a more or less welcome figure, filling the public eye as he did, shared with the P.M.G. the distinction of representing the biggest business in the world. It was principally the man in uniform who was given credit for keeping the whole machine moving. What lay behind the outward and visible working of the vast and complicated machinery hardly concerned the man in the street or his peers, because it was hidden from view. The public got its letters regularly—that was enough, and the press was apathetic. The swarming army of working bees which comprised the indoor staffs—those who sorted letters and despatched the mails—were as little thought of as the unseen crew of stokers below the water line, engaged in their inglorious, but none the less useful, task of keeping the furnaces going, and the vessel under steam.

So far, the history of labour in the Post Office for the most part was a history of restrictive discipline and resistance to claims on the one side and of almost hopeless efforts for redress on the other. But the early awakening of the trade union spirit, and the manifestation of discontent, so long as it confined itself to a few London letter carriers and indoor assistants in the first instance, was hardly formidable enough to cause anxiety, or to be taken too seriously. Discontent, unorganised, sporadic, and as yet almost inarticulate, could for the time remain ignored, or be dealt with individually as one would swat a troublesome fly.

It was not until about 1857 that agitation began to spread more widely from within outwards, and showed a disposition to organise. This soon aroused such apprehension and hostility that in itself it helped to aggravate those very evils which the permanent officials of those days aimed at suppressing. Time and again the authorities, while complaining of the heat, yet added fuel to the fire.

Unionism among the rank and file from that time onward was to be regarded as something to be discouraged and stamped out where possible, something impertinently out of place in a Government office, and its leaders fit only to be treated as breeders of mild sedition. And this was the official attitude for years after the principle of trade unionism outside had been reconciled to respectability and sanctioned by popular approval. Very slowly, step by step, labour in the Post Office had earned something of a recognition of its value, but before it gained any permanent advantage it had been forced to fight its way with official handicap and tape-tied feet.

Happily, however, the story of postal agitation and the spread of combination throughout the postal service is not made up entirely of failures, contumacies, inflictions, and punishments. That combination in this branch of the public service has had to fight hard for its very existence from the beginning is perfectly true. It has been uphill work throughout, but in its struggle against the forces of bureaucracy it has snatched a triumph here and there ; it has received rebuffs, and even now and again courted defeat, but it has had its exultant moments of victory too. And, on the whole, there is little to regret that the fight so far has been fought ; for where men have a principle at stake perhaps, to paraphrase a great dead poet, 'tis better to have fought and lost than never to have fought at all.

But, as a rule, as little heed as possible was paid to the claims of postal servants, and far less sympathy shown. Generally speaking, in earlier years especially, it has been the experience that a public department's niggardliness towards its employés has been in inverse ratio to its capacity for producing profit. A public institution like the Post Office, run on the conventional lines of commercialism and routine, and for the most part in the leading strings of a watchful Treasury, could never spontaneously better the conditions of its vast body of servants. Their very number supplied a convenient argument against such an innovation. Though the same held good of the relations between Capital and Labour or between private employers and their hands, it was more particularly so in a Government Department. It was too often proved that any improvement among the working staffs had to be insistently demanded from the ruling powers of the day by every legitimate method which agitation could devise, by persistent petitioning, by deputation, by public meetings, and getting M.P.s to beard the P.M.G. and the Treasury heads in their official lairs, or by tracking them down in the House of Commons. And even then, after all the expenditure of force, there was often little but disappointment in return.

That it is not always the administrators of a public department who are to blame so much as the rule and the method which usage and convention have fixed, must in all fairmindedness be allowed. It is easy to believe and understand that the various heads of departments, though never guilty of the unpardonable indiscretion of showing the smallest sympathy for agitation as such, none the less do often deplore the necessity of enforcing certain rules and regulations which act to the detriment of the men or which are productive of individual cases of hardship.

In such a situation, however, the responsible chief has to consult another tribunal besides his own conscience. It is always fairly safe to refuse concession, but it is dangerous to grant it before one is compelled to. When the public, the press, and Parliament, agree that such demands may at last be safely conceded, then it is time to take the credit—not till then. You bow with a good grace and say, " Am I not my master's servant ? " And the public and the press and Parliament think none the less of you for your firmness, interpreting your stubbornness as zeal for the public service, while they would have turned to rend you for your incompetence had you given way sooner. Such to some extent is the trying position of those in authority in public departments ; they needs must move only when the devil drives, and not a moment before. They are more or less in the position of a constable whose duty it is to keep back a clamorous crowd testing a right of way ; zeal and duty and anxiety for his position keep him firmly at his post till his superior and the law give him the nod and he has to fall back.

It is, therefore, perhaps not surprising that Government officials have steadfastly pursued a policy of resistance to all claims for reform emanating from the subordinate staff. And this policy has been rendered the easier by such resistance being shown through that abstract entity known as "the Department," which may mean one man or twenty, removing as it does the necessity for any particular individual, from the Secretary downward, to show his hand or reveal his identity. This was the system which made possible Dickens's famous piece of satire anent the "Circumlocution Office." It also provides a justification for Sydney Smith's equally famous dictum regarding corporations, and, of course, Government departments—that they "have neither a body to be kicked nor a soul to be damned."

Certainly, it holds generally true as an important and significant fact of postal history, at any rate, that the authorities have never allowed a claim except grudgingly. And a due appreciation of this fact will conduce to a better understanding of the events which follow.

That this species of official obstinacy is not altogether peculiar to the postal service may be abundantly proved by reference to the records of other public departments. The postal authorities have sinned in very good company ; and, to be fair to both sides of the question, let it be said that on the whole the sins of omission and commission have doubtless been dictated as much by a virtuous desire to save the public funds as to enhance their own credit. That at least is a saving virtue which is always conveniently placed to the credit of every permanent and public official, even when he has carried his zeal to excess. Allowing such a defence to stand without questioning, the fact remains that in their zeal for the public service the rights, the privileges, the convenience, the creature comforts, the health, and, it might be said, the very lives of many of the staff under their control have often been sacrificed in the past. Yet there have been exceptions, and it will be seen that the tens of thousands of the rank and file of the lower grades of the service have some reason to hold in grateful esteem the memory of one Postmaster-

General at least—Professor Henry Fawcett. The high-souled qualities of Henry Fawcett, the blind Postmaster-General, are even now as familiar as is the recollection of that lamentable infirmity which only roused him to " wrest victory from misfortune."

Generally, however, there had been two opposing principles at work throughout. And with two such positive and negative principles—the desire of the postal workers to assert those rights already accorded to almost every other class of labour, and the determination of the officials that such aspirations must be suppressed—it was only to be looked for that open discontent would manifest itself sooner or later, and presently assume a more or less definite shape.

In those days especially, the psychology of the departmental head or permanent official was peculiar to the time and circumstance. He was not as other men exactly. He might not devoutly thank the Lords of the Treasury, but he knew what was expected of him. He had to be true to type, and as his official ambient moulded him.

Consequently, the policy of departmentalism was generally a most conservative one. Its failure to move with the requirements of the times, its too reactionary refusal to allow for the universal tendency to combine, as manifested among all classes of labour outside, its cheeseparing system of economy, carried into the question of pay and prospects, accentuated the feeling of unrest and uncertainty, which culminated in resentment, open discontent, and organised agitation. Yet these growing symptoms only further stiffened the authorities in their attitude towards such extravagant claims as a living wage, fair payment for overtime, and the abolition of Sunday labour. In any case, they were not to be moved by the murmurings of malcontents who had become infected with the absurd ambition to better their conditions, who asked for the same advantages as factory workers, and who had the audacity to aspire to the princely sum of two pounds a week and the status of skilled mechanics ! It was too soon to have met such radical demands in a spirit of conciliation and compromise. So early in the day, it would have seemed like pandering to treason and subverting every workable tradition of departmentalism.

The fact that a Government job of any sort was some guarantee of permanent employment, so long as they did not complain, should, it seemed, be sufficient in itself to induce the rank and file to accept any humiliation and the poorest wages. In its desire to govern according to its own conception of a benevolent despotism, the Post Office had to keep its subordinates under and at their lowest market value, while it too commonly provided its employees with a grievance, or a succession of grievances, arising from its attempt to shape their workaday lives by rules of military discipline and restrictive regulations better fitted for a penal settlement than for free men and citizens of selected character and intelligence.

Such was the attitude of the Department and the general conditions of postal servants when the earlier would-be reformers essayed to urge their plaint, and, in the most legitimate manner, to strike a blow for freedom. The men who have been alluded to as those who were first to engage in agitation and the first to incur the as yet unknown danger of arousing the resentment of officialdom against such daring innovations, it must be acknowledged, made up in moral fibre what they lacked in experience and methods of organisation. At any rate, they deserve to be remembered kindly by those who afterwards benefited by similar efforts. They were the first to cut away the undergrowth, and to make the straight and solid path possible. If fault be found with their methods, it has only to be said that their mistakes were such as usually come in the experimental stage of almost every enterprise.

If it be thought that the happenings and incidents with which they were connected or of which they were the authors are here invested with undue importance, it will be recollected that the men who were identified with those happenings were among the first actors in an interesting little industrial drama. It will perhaps not be lost sight of that the incidents themselves, though insignificant if taken singly, none the less are important links in the chain, and necessary parts of a whole. Some acknowledgment is due to these men if only that they were the humble pioneers of an industrial movement of a special character, and because they kept abreast of the tide of progress when it was nothing less than dangerous to do so.

If it be objected that every grievance complained of— the conditions of service, insufficiency of pay, prospects and promotion, deprivation of civil liberty, and the right of combination reduced to a meaningless farce—have had their counterparts in every other department of the State, that objection in itself scarcely lessens the justification for the action taken by the agitators. The reasonableness or otherwise of their methods is another matter, which it is proposed to deal with later on as this narrative proceeds. If it be urged that the policy of attempting to force concessions from a Government department has been a more or less selfish one, it must be conceded also that principle has always entered largely into it. That their sole consideration was not to get the greatest material benefit at little cost, and that it was not with them entirely a question of more bread and butter and less work, is pretty well proved by the risks which postal agitators have run and the sacrifices they have cheerfully made. It had never been an easy matter for a man to demand his just dues in a Government office. The attitude of mind towards the subordinate staffs in the Post Office had not essentially altered since the days when they publicly hanged men for letter-stealing. That was only a little more than sixty years before, and if the asperities of administration were somewhat softened later, it was only through the force of public opinion, and because the men had learnt lessons of appeal which rendered it almost impossible for officialdom to persist in methods of repression for any length of time. It was because the liberty of the working-classes had been so enlarged that there could no longer be withheld a modicum of it from postal servants. But there was not wanting the evidence to show that something of the same spirit which sent working-men to the hulks and penal servitude for attempting to band themselves and their mates together for the purpose of safeguarding their few interests from a greedy and rapacious employer, was alive until comparatively recent times.

The postal servant seeking to better his position labours under far greater disadvantages than the mechanic or the handicraftsman. A postman, a sorting-clerk, or a letter-sorter, if he be dismissed from his employment cannot pick up his bag of tools and offer himself to the next workshop, for the simple reason that he has no tools, and his trade is one of such a peculiar nature that it is wanted nowhere outside the Post Office. Nor is a telegraphist much better off in that respect. Dismissal from the Service has generally meant very much more to the postal official than to the ordinary artisan. He not only lost his immediate source of livelihood, but his future prospects, his hopes of a pension, towards which he had contributed; his character and everything were gone, and he had to face the world afresh and take his stand in the battle of life against those with every advantage over him. And dismissal was particularly easy in the earlier times, when a suspicious officialdom could construe the smallest sign of disaffection into insubordination.

Thus it will be seen it was no child's play to engage in agitation forty or fifty years ago, and the men who did so evidently did not enter into it for the love of the game altogether. There must have been something very rotten in the State of Denmark when men were goaded into what was to them desperate methods, with so many odds against them, just for the sake of improving the conditions of their servitude. It shows that they must have felt their grievances keenly; it shows that in some degree at least that spirit of resistance to wrong and injustice, to which we owe so much, animated and sustained them throughout. In those days postal agitators stood almost alone, receiving very little sympathy from the press or the public, and equally little assistance from the various trades unions, simply because postal grievances, which have always been difficult of understanding, were much more so then, and because it was difficult then to make people believe that men in permanent Government employment could have grievances of any kind. That the trade unionists of the country were slow to rally to their assistance or to proffer them practical sympathy is now better understood, for postmen and letter-sorters were not readily recognised as a separate craft by the various unions of artisans; they could claim no trade kinship with them; they were neither this nor that, but a sort of ugly duckling in the legitimate brood of artisanship.

Fortunately, a more intelligent understanding and a better feeling now exist, and have existed for some years past. But even to gain this simple recognition that a postal official with a grievance battling against wrong was a man and a brother entitled to admittance into their ranks was not easily obtained, even when they sought it. Many of the men themselves were chary of accepting the position of professed trades unionists, and it was some years before the objections associated with declared trade-union principles and methods were waived by the men of the Post Office. The fact is, they remained for long uncertain as to their exact relationship to the general industrial and labour movement. There was some amount of mutual distrust between outside trade organisations and combination in the Post Office, and both parties failed to see distinctly what there was in common between them. It must be admitted that, despite their awakening so far, the postal agitators still preserved something of that reserve which may have been easily mistaken for pride or, perhaps, snobbishness ; and some felt that an open connection with trades unionism might damage their chances of redress, and alienate the support and sympathy of the few public men on whom they relied. Besides, it had to be considered that the trades union doctrine was not sufficiently accepted to be yet accounted respectable. But all that is long past ; it has been rendered both respectable and respected by almost universal acceptance, and postal agitation owes not a little to it. And if postal agitation owes more to the spirit of trades unionism than the latter does to any postal effort, then, to claim no more for it, perhaps trades unionism has no reason to feel ashamed of its poor postal relations, who fought a battle in its behalf years ago. They maintained its principle within that most unlikely and unpromising of places, a Government office, against hostile officials who were backed up with inexhaustible reserves and the best artillery.

That the solid advantages gained through agitation have not even up to the present day fully compensated for the sacrifices made, the time, the trouble, the energy, and the money expended on it, can perhaps be acknowledged. Yet the same holds good of every other movement of higher pretension, social and political. Men with a purpose count the moral advantage as well as the material gain. If only considerations of this nature had always weighed in the past, our Merrie England would to-day be divided into slaves and slave-owners.

To its credit be it said, then, Postal agitation has not been altogether confined to capturing the enemies' cattle, or to striving for yet a bigger share of the loaves and fishes. It has only had to discover its duties and responsibilities immediately to lay claim to them, and strenuously to assert its right to fulfil them. It has always maintained the principle of combination as a principle, while it has long and persistently protested against the exclusion of postal servants from the full enjoyment of civil rights and the untrammelled exercise of the franchise. It has lost few opportunities of championing the cause of the weak against departmental intolerance, and silently and unseen it has often stayed the hand of official injustice at the very moment it was raised to strike. It has triumphed ultimately where often it has seemed to have failed. It has fought for and won the one right accorded to every free-born British citizen who was not a postal official— the right of free speech and open public meeting.

When, as an unpretentious little organisation, numerically weak and modest in its programme, it was first started by a few London postmen and letter-sorters, it was doubtless prompted principally by the very human desire to improve their own workaday lives and to benefit their wives and children. It need not be claimed that they were animated by a much loftier or nobler motive than securing the living wage, though some may have visualised the better day, and dreamed dreams, as most reformers do.

To their successors, as time went on, " new occasions taught new manners," and as the sphere of their operations almost insensibly widened, so they readily accepted the responsibilities attaching to their character as the wing of a forward movement.

CHAPTER II

THAT the spirit of discontent in the Post Office manifested
itself so far back as over eighty years ago will probably
somewhat surprise most people outside the postal service
itself. Possibly even farther back than that some traces of
discontent and effort at agitation might be found ; but in
those obscure days, however the working conditions of the
service may have justified it, all such effort must have begun
and ended with a few individual insubordinates, whose
names are buried in oblivion and the official records. But
it has to be remembered that in the earlier days of the Post
Office the very conditions under which the members of the
working staff were introduced into the service almost precluded the possibility of organisation for the redress of
grievances. Indeed, it may be well understood that in the
pastoral days of the good old times—when life went slower,
and when there was an absence of that feverish rush and
hurry so characteristic of the present everywhere, and of the
Post Office in particular—postal officials were the happy
inhabitants of a sort of Sleepy Hollow. In a word, probably
there was little discontent in the earlier days, owing to the
system of appointment by patronage. At least there could
have been very little open and avowed discontent, and much
less could it have been organised.

As a survival of the system in vogue in the old twopenny-
post days, the greater part of the working staff—that is to
say, those subordinates who afterwards came to be described
as the manipulative part of the machinery—were for many

years after the introduction of the Penny Post in 1840, recruited from those in whose behalf some influence had been exercised or invoked. Many were the sons of old servants of the aristocracy, others the sons or relatives of the dependants of M.P.s, of Justices of the Peace, of lawyers, and public men more or less eminent. Every notability who could exercise any influence with the postal authorities had his nominees. It was then next to impossible for a mere outsider, whatever his merits, to obtain employment under the Postmaster-General without this golden talisman. This system, so general in the earlier days, has been adverted to only in order to show one reason for there being so little discontent openly manifested, and to explain why agitation did not assume an organised form till later in the century. For however slow may have been the times, doubtless the conditions of the postal service were not even then so Arcadian as to stifle entirely the feeling of discontent in some. But the system of nomination by influence and patronage, and what in these days might be called by the uglier name of nepotism, was better calculated to foster a feeling of dependence in the majority, and one of grateful loyalty in many. This, too, it has been already pointed out, was in the days when the principles of trades unionism were little studied and little understood, even so far as they had taken root in the minds of the working-classes. Combination in any shape or form was in fact little sympathised with by those whom it sought to benefit, and in Government offices particularly would have been anathema to the authorities, or, at any rate, received with fear and aversion.

While the good old principle of " looking after Doub " prevailed extensively in every other Government office, it was almost paramount in the Post Office ; and this being so, it would be surprising to find anything but a state of stagnant contentment existing among the working staff. If not exactly a state of stagnant contentment, the readiness to assert a principle, and to resent encroachment on existing rights and privileges, would certainly not be forcibly in evidence. Whatever official wrongs, if any, they may have been subjected to at the hands of their superiors, they showed no willingness to be awakened to a sense of them. The tide of Chartism beat in vain against the grim walls of the Post Office ; the fluctuations of trade disputes, strikes, and lock-outs interested them only in a casual way, if at all ; while the bare idea of organised opposition to the wishes of the authorities, however arbitrary, would have spelt downright treason. They were recruited from a class of men who, if they had not always been brought up in the paths of virtue, had always gone along the line of least resistance, which was that of conventional respectability. Once in the Post Office, they had a character to keep up, and they were not as other men who had to work for their living with dirty hands. They felt that their Queen and country had reposed a confidence in them by selecting them for the responsible position they held. They were something midway between lawyers' clerks and menials of the royal household. They doubtless felt they were very superior persons, though their wages were meagre and their uniform scanty ; but the authorities were like unto little gods to them, and so they took it for granted that Heaven had established a natural gulf between them. Still they were the children of patronage, and of fathers whose only ambition was to see their sons settled in a Government situation ; for a Government situation was for their sons the Mecca of those people who always kept good and paid proper respect to the parson and their rent regularly to the squire. And when the sons got there they felt they were a chosen few, invested with a caste and a distinction which entitled them to hold their heads a little higher than the people living in the same street. The consciousness that his neighbours occasionally pointed him out as the " gentle-man who works in the Post Office " more than atoned for his inability to wear fashionable clothes and a top-hat like his superiors.

This system of patronage as a means of rewarding the deserving relatives of old servitors and sworn retainers by drafting them into the General Post Office, though it would not be tolerated in these democratic times, yet is reminiscent some-what of the good old days when such things were only right and proper in every department of the State, and when it was taken for granted that Government situations were only the just reward of faithful service rendered elsewhere to the heaven-born men of power and influence in the State, and created for them to prove their generosity. Such a system is perhaps therefore saved from utter condemnation by just a suggestion of poetry about it, recalling the earlier coaching days, when the bond between master and servant was often one of intimacy and mutual obligation ; and perhaps it would not be difficult to say a good word for it. It showed at least that whatever the failings of those in power and those in high places, whatever their attitude towards the working-classes generally, however they may have sniffed contemptuously at any suggestion of Chartism, or at all attempts at combination among the masses, they were not always unmindful of their moral duties towards their own dependants. Willingly enough, they paid their obligations, and rewarded services rendered by quickly pushing the applicants into the service of the State. They felt that they had discharged the whole duty of man when they had done this ; they had provided the son of a deserving old family servant, of an influential constituent, or of a good paying tenant, with a berth for life in a Government office, and, what was more, had proved their importance in being able to do so.

Still, whatever may have been the abuses attaching to such a system, the State was to an extent the gainer in getting men of good character, with a good certificate of family respectability, and, moreover, men who were guaranteed to go for any length of time without winding up, who were warranted never to become discontented, but always to remain faithful and loyal, well satisfied with the position in which it had pleased God and their patron to place them.

With the rank and file of the postal service composed of such men, brought in under such conditions, it is not surprising that discontent never raised its head, and that many a grievance went unredressed because it was silently endured. Nor is it surprising that the Post Office, garrisoned by such an army sworn in in this manner, was almost the last citadel that it attacked with any degree of success. It would have been too dangerous for any man to have attempted to bell the cat in those days, and however strong may have been the desire in some, without the support and confidence of their fellows, it would have been sheer official suicide to have taken the first step. They were men calculated to endure much. Petty official tyranny to such men meant no more than mild discipline. A grievance with them was but an evanescent thing, felt to-day, forgotten to-morrow; for they had a stake in the Post Office. To express discontent would be to court certain dismissal, and that would have meant much to them, while it would mean the betrayal of the good, kind patron, their father's master or landlord, whose powerful influence had placed them there. Indeed, it is easy to understand that no man would have felt himself either a spy or a renegade to principle in secretly or openly denouncing the rash fool who would endeavour to organise a meeting of protest against his superiors.

Such were the conditions and such the temper of the men of the postal staff that must have long obtained prior to the 'fifties and 'sixties. From the introduction of the Penny Post in 1840, which practically organised the Post Office on a new basis, there is no evidence of combined discontent worth recording till the early 'fifties, though through that period of eighteen years or so the leaven of discontent was slowly but surely working, till a desire to make their wants known at last became manifest.

Yet only a few years after the institution of the Penny Post the indoor working staffs and the letter-carriers were both given grave cause for dissatisfaction by the extension of Sunday labour. Whatever protest they may have made of their own accord counted for little; but it is interesting to find that so early as 1848 an influential and public-spirited section of the community took up the matter of compulsory Sunday labour on behalf of the aggrieved postal servants, the sorting-clerks, and others, and publicly expressed that dissatisfaction which Government servants dared not themselves utter too openly.

At that time it was contemplated by the authorities to compel two attendances on that day as on other days of the week, and to abolish entirely for postal servants in London the distinction between the Day of Rest and ordinary working days. This was the origin of that question of compulsory

Sunday labour in the Post Office which was to continue for thirty years and more as one of the prevailing causes of dissatisfaction to thousands of men. On the 8th October, 1849, a great mass meeting was called at Exeter Hall to protest as strongly as possible against this desecration of Sunday. The meeting was convened in the interests of postal servants themselves as much as in furtherance of the Sabbatarian principle, and there is little doubt that the men of the Post Office who were the principal objectors to the new regulation, were behind the scenes aiding and abetting in the success of the movement.

A writer in the *Patriot* newspaper of that year, and one evidently familiar with the Post Office machinery, drew a vivid picture of the possibilities of Sunday labour in the Post Office. This article in the *Patriot*, probably from the pen of the first avowed discontented postal servant, did not a little to further the memorial for the cessation of the practice, which was afterwards drawn up by the Sunday School Union and forwarded to the Lords of the Treasury. The action of the authorities was denounced as sacrilegious, arbitrary, and tyrannical, by a number of clergymen and others speaking for the aggrieved men, while Rowland Hill, the postal reformer, the " Father of the Penny Post," came in for a large share of hostile criticism, his name being repeatedly hissed at the Exeter Hall meeting.

If the audience hissed Rowland Hill, they as loudly cheered the postal servants on whom this new official imposition was to be put, directly it became known that, to their honour, they had respectfully but firmly declined to submit, and that when the sheets for their signature went round the large establishment only two men could be got to sign away their birthright for the little extra pay. The name of the Queen was invoked to prevent this iniquitous violation of the " Pearl of Days."

The memorial was forwarded to the Treasury ; and the request for an interview with Lord John Russell to support the prayer of this memorial, met with only a curt refusal through his secretary. There the matter ended, so far. The Post Office had its way, and compulsory Sunday labour in the Post Office became an established, and in the minds of many

c

a disgraceful, fact ; to prove, however, a source of further trouble later on, and to provide one of the most substantial excuses for agitation during the next thirty years. Yet the comparatively feeble agitation by proxy, set on foot then in 1848, did produce, nevertheless, some little result ; and on March 18, 1850, a Parliamentary paper was issued to show the "results of the measures recently adopted for the reduction of Sunday labour in the Post Office."

CHAPTER III

FROM about 1854 it seems a new class of men were gradually being introduced. By the operation of what was known as the Elcho Scheme, there was a large reduction of the clerical class who had hitherto usually discharged the duties of letter-sorting, as well as the despatch and receipt of mails. But the authorities, beginning to awaken to the fact that the Post Office was becoming a splendid source of revenue, decided to cut down expenditure by introducing a more poorly paid class to take up the duties of those who had been in receipt of a much higher salary than it was proposed to offer the new entrants.

The work of sorting letters, for example, which had hitherto been performed by clerks, was now to be entrusted to men of an inferior grade. And the "Report Upon the Post Office for the Year 1854," in which this innovation is first announced, expresses the hope that such persons on an inferior salary would be able, as necessity arose, or on "occasions of any extraordinary pressure," to take a share also in the duties of the clerks. This is perhaps one of the earliest indications of that policy of cheeseparing and depreciation of the value of official work, which, if it has not always justified discontent and agitation, has proved a fruitful source of it. From the introduction of the Penny Post, and probably from a long time before, the public correspondence was treated tenderly and disposed of conscientiously. So high was the importance attached to it that none were deemed worthy of being entrusted with it who were not servants belonging to the " major establishment." Both the sorters of letters and those who despatched the mails belonged to the clerical staff, while only the work of " facing," stamping, tying, and the work of conveyance and porterage, was entrusted to the class of minor officials who afterwards came to constitute the main bulk of the force.

From this period the clerks, who had been the only ones entrusted with the high responsibility of sorting and despatching letters, gradually became a restricted and exclusive class, while the lesser officials, who formerly had been scarcely allowed to touch the correspondence, were now trained to those superior duties, but without a corresponding increase of remuneration. It is worthy, however, of bearing in mind that the despatching of mails was still deemed of such responsibility and importance that mere letter-sorters were not yet allowed to perform such duties, only clerks on a salary rising to £400 a year being thought worthy of that honour, although a few years later, when such duties became several times heavier and correspondingly more responsible, the inferior class of letter-sorters were compelled to take them up. It was the continuance of this anomaly for some length of time, indeed, which constituted one of the main elements of discontent, and came to be regarded as a distinct grievance among the letter-sorting staff especially.

As the growth of the Post Office business necessitated a larger staff to cope with it, so a new class of men were being slowly introduced. The Penny Post was a reform so much appreciated by the public by this time that it had become even now, in 1854, the most flourishing business in the world. And Rowland Hill was not slow to take every advantage of his discovery that the Post Office contained greater possibilities than to remain a cheap public convenience. The founder of the Penny Post was now Permanent Secretary, and a greater power in the land than the Postmaster-General, not a little of a bureaucrat, and one who had trained himself to regard his postal domain as a sort of family preserve. He saw no harm in introducing cheap labour ; he discovered a new way of cutting down expenses by relegating the work which had been paid for at a salary of from £200 to £400 a year, to this new class of minor officials, mostly salaried at less than a fourth that amount. There was one new element introduced with the new-comers, however, which probably was never taken into account at the time—and that was that they were drawn from a better educated and a more enlightened body of men than those hitherto engaged on inferior duties. The educational tests for admission into the Post Office had previously been very meagre, and almost nil where special influence had been used. The old system of patronage and nomination was maintained as long as it was convenient, and as long as it worked satisfactorily, and for some considerable time longer. But at length, owing to the expansion of postal business, even patronage could not of itself keep up an adequate supply of qualified recruits. And it was impossible to go begging to lords or distinguished commoners for poor relations or cast-off dependants, as that might be putting a premium on dishonesty, and cheapening still further good recommendations which were already in some cases too cheap to be genuine. Besides, the growth of democratic ideas among people outside was making them inquisitive.

There was the beginning of a feeling that nomination by aristocratic influence was not of itself recommendation enough for a Government post, however humble ; though, perhaps, this was shared most largely among those ever ready to make a mark of public departments, and by those who had failed themselves to invoke such influence, or who envied those who had succeeded. Again, the claims of education had never been sufficiently recognised in filling these subordinate positions, and now was the opportunity to get a better value for money. Accordingly, by slow degrees the old system of nomination by influence alone came to be not insisted on as the highest qualification—which was certainly a step in the right direction. Instead, a suitable educational test, coupled with ordinary certificates as to character, was the principal introduction required.

Patronage was still allowed to exercise its influence where it desired, and continued to do so for many years afterwards, but it was no longer held to be the only " open sesame " to a berth in the Post Office. And so there were drawn from almost every rank in life, men of a better educational standard, men who knew the world better, and men who in many instances fostered a feeling of independence, more or less, by having some knowledge of a trade, or the experiences gained in a former occupation. In any case, they were not drawn from any particular class. They were not all the sons or relatives of sworn retainers—of humble and obedient family servants grown grey in bowing and scraping to superiors,—nor from a stock always warranted by such circumstance to remain quiet in harness. Doubtless some still were ; but the majority were not. If, on entering the Post Office, they had to share the lot of all postal officials in those days, of being deprived of the franchise, they were as free as, or freer than, their predecessors to influence members of Parliament secretly and indirectly through their relatives or friends who had votes to give, or, may be, to sell. Though there is no reason to think that any number of them at that time attached any very serious importance to the loss of civil liberty in this respect which entry into the public services entailed, still members of Parliament, and intending Parliamentary candidates having influence in high quarters, could not altogether refuse their good offices on behalf of a letter-carrier or a sorter, whose case, or whose individual claims, might be represented by a friend who was a constituent suffering no such electoral disability. One postal employé might influence half a dozen votes in a constituency.

At first this new departure in economy had been attempted very gingerly, only about twenty selected men of the minor establishment being introduced into the sorting department for this purpose. The class from which they were drawn comprised the letter-carriers, messengers, doorkeepers, etc., who were originally intended to remain in those inferior positions as long as their service lasted. These twenty men were accordingly brought into the Inland Letter Branch, where for a time they were exclusively employed in the first stages of those duties for which their superiors, the clerks, had been drawing three times the highest salary they could ever hope to obtain. This work of primary sortation, dividing and sub-dividing the correspondence at the general sorting and divisional tables, necessitated no great intellectual strain, and required no educational ability beyond that of reading the addresses on the envelopes. But, as will be seen, the

" experiment " was bad in principle, inasmuch as whatever the inducements, whatever the promises, the new sorting staff got no improvement in pay or prospects. It was a too flagrant and sudden depreciation of the standard of work hitherto regarded as of such exclusive importance that none but clerks rising to substantial salaries had been thought capable enough or trustworthy enough to deal with it. The experiment, for the best of reasons, was pronounced satisfactory, and then after a while new responsibilities were heaped upon these twenty expectant scapegoats, whose expectation proved to be their only comfort. They were eventually put to " despatching," and other highly responsible duties were vacated by the clerks ; others, letter-carriers, etc., being brought in to perform the primary sortation. And so this system of replacement continued year after year until eventually the whole of the Inland Letter-sorting Office was manned by minor establishment men. This was a piece of official cozening that was complete in its success. That from £200 to £400 may have been too big a salary to pay for such work in those days especially, may be readily granted; but it certainly might have been expected that some improvement in position corresponding to their new duties and heavier responsibilities would have been granted the new class of sorters. As it was, they were left to remain on their old status as letter-carriers and messengers. In the face of this—that Rowland Hill and the authorities had found out a new way to get the public's correspondence dealt with at somewhere about one-third the original in salaries—it seems difficult of belief that absolutely nothing was done for this badly treated class of men until fully twenty-five years later. Yet such is the fact. It was not that the men felt they had no cause for complaint ; it could not have been because they did not realise that they were a disgracefully sweated body of men. Many, indeed, left the Post Office in disgust after remaining only a few months. But whatever discontent may have shown itself, and however justified, there were none in Parliament yet who could be induced to take up their cause as a body. Doubtless, individual representations were made by the score, but while they may have been pretty well agreed by this time that they were being duped more or less, there was still a lack of unity among them. Besides, they were a small and obscure body, about which the general public knew next to nothing, and cared less ; they were as yet without any means of making known their plaint, even if they so desired. They were without influence as without votes. They were not only without influence and without votes, but those who by circumstances were compelled to tolerate the conditions of their service felt that the rigorous rule against communicating with the press or approaching M.P.s directly was looked upon as having all the sanctity of law by those outside. Even the organs of the public press were not to be trusted, it was felt ; while to communicate directly and privately with any M.P. would have been not only useless, but dangerous. They could have taken a ready revenge for being pestered by men with grievances but no votes. Consequently, there was never, till a few years later, discontent open enough or of such a nature to draw public attention.

At this period the London letter-carriers were principally confined to the chief office, St. Martin's-le-Grand, and as the grades of stampers and sorters were mainly drawn from this body, and as both were located in the same huge building, the relationship between them was of a close connection. Whatever grievances were felt by one class were felt or sympathised with by the other. If there was no movement among them answering to combination as it came to be understood a little later ; if they did not set their faces in one particular direction by common impulse ; if they as yet had no thought of gathering in public meeting and attempting to break the silence imposed on them by official restraints, it was not because they were not agreed that they were an ill-used body of men. The awakening was beginning ; the signs of discontent were scarcely concealed, but the authorities saw no reason to inquire further.

Already the most daring among them directed their eyes to Exeter Hall, and some talked of the possibility of a public demonstration. As was very natural, the majority hesitated about taking a step which had scarcely before been attempted. It was like exploring an unknown country, and they could only guess at the difficulties and dangers ahead. No one was certain, either how the public would receive any demonstration of aggrieved postal servants. It might be regarded as an exhibition of downright disloyalty by those without, and as rank mutiny by the authorities within. It might even be looked on by the public at large as the beginnings of a postal strike ; while it was feared that the press would prove anything but friendly. If it did not hold their puny efforts up to scorn and ridicule, it might hamper them in no small degree, and alienate any little sympathy they might be able to command among a few influential public men who had quietly promised to assist them to get the matter looked into. It was such considerations as these that caused the proposal to hang fire for a period.

About 1855, however, the discontent among the London letter-carriers began to express itself in something like organised effort. A committee was formed, and small subscriptions were collected to defray the expenses of hiring a hall in which to hold public meetings. The principal ground of complaint was, as usual, the smallness of salary as compared with the high price of provisions and increasing house-rent, and the withdrawal of payment for extra duty. It appears that while the men had been allowed the opportunity of adding to their slender wage by making sixpence an hour for overtime, they bore with the conditions of the service uncomplainingly. But they very justly regarded the withdrawal of this payment for extra duty as incompatible with the increased pressure of work imposed upon them. The meanness which few private employers would care to be found guilty of was unblushingly practised by a State monopoly upon its poorest and most defenceless menials even at this early period. But the letter-carriers were not without spirit, and not without spokesmen to protest on their behalf. On the 13th January, 1856, a meeting of letter-carriers was for the first time convened to ventilate their grievances and prepare the terms of a memorial to the Postmaster-General. The memorial was accordingly drawn up, but the memorialists—who principally consisted of the fourth or lowest class of letter-carriers, and therefore the poorest paid—committed the fatal mistake of allowing its publication in the press before presentation to the head of the Department. This fact was seized upon by the then Postmaster-General, the Duke of Argyll, as in itself sufficient ground for refusing their claims, and it was intimated to them that the step was so improper in the circumstances that even had the memorial been found reasonable in itself, his Grace would have found it difficult to take it into favourable consideration. In the second annual report of the Postmaster-General the " misconduct " of the agitators was severely animadverted on, but his Grace in conclusion expressed his willingness to make allowance for " misconduct arising out of excited feeling," and desired to take as lenient a course as was consistent with due regard to the discipline of the office. He therefore satisfied himself with reminding those who had shared in these " objectionable proceedings " that henceforth no annual increment would be granted without a certificate of continued good character from their superiors.

Having regard to the circumstances and the times, perhaps they had some cause for congratulation that their offence had been passed over so lightly. Certainly it must be said that the Postmaster-General of 1856 showed an example in lenity which a successor of twenty years after would have done well to copy, and which would have shown him in more consistent accord with the growing and expanding spirit of reform.

Undoubtedly there was ample justification for the discontent which centred in the recent memorial from the letter-carriers. The conditions of the service for them and the lower ranks of postal operatives especially were perhaps not what they should have been, a recent slight improvement notwithstanding. But they were better off than they were to be a year or two later. Things were bad in the Post Office ; but if the plain truth be told, probably the position of the letter-carriers rather favourably compared with the lot of those outside whose occupation and calling bore the nearest analogy to theirs. For, though the Department had committed itself to a policy of rigid economy and profit-making, and had definitely assumed a position of subserviency to the Treasury, it had not yet fully entered on that policy of parsimony at the expense of its humblest workers which was later on to characterise it the more as it became wealthier and mightier in its operations and its ambitions. It had assumed to think its servants well paid on a starvation pittance, but presumably it still felt some little concern for their bodily comfort. And this was something in those days when labour had few rights and no privileges. With a curious inconsistency, while it kept the letter-carriers on a wage too low to enable them to live decently, and deprived them of a means to add a shilling or two to their incomes, it actually expressed a philanthropic concern about the manner in which their poor pay and prospects compelled them to house themselves. The dwellings of the letter-carriers became for some time the object of the authorities' benevolent attention ; apparently on the assumption that a slave-owner may consistently pose as a good, kind master, it at least pretended to take a paternal interest in the domestic welfare of these humble public servants still complaining of too little pay. It was suggested that some sort of postal barracks for letter-carriers and their families should be erected near to the General Post Office. It was thought that they would enjoy a greater immunity from sickness, but more especially would it be convenient to the Department to have them within easy reach, so that they might summon them by bugle-call, and shepherd them in one big drove whenever big mails arrived from abroad. Doubtless, also, it entered into the calculations of the authors of this proposed pretty little postal commonwealth that they would be better able to keep an eye on the morals of their employés, and preserve their good characters. The authorities, however, shrank from the responsibility of erecting and maintaining such barracks at the cost of the Government. They did not trust their pet scheme so far as that. The Duke of Argyll, whose original idea it was, thought the prospect one more suitable for a public company, but it was stated in his report that the Department might afford aid by " securing to the company its rents, deducting the same from the wages " of the letter-carriers. The Postmaster-General of the period may have been animated by the best of motives ; but it is observable that no part of the cost was to be borne by the Department, nor were the men, already poorly paid, to be assisted in paying for the extra convenience to the Department. The report of the medical officer on the matter discloses the conditions which the low wage of the letter-carriers compelled them to live under. A perusal of this report alone, it seems, provides sufficient excuse

for the letter-carriers' claim to better pay as servants of the
State.   And the Duke of Argyll, by the publication of the disgraceful facts, provided an unanswerable indictment against
his own judgment.   It has to be remembered that these were
the days before workmen's trains, when the neighbourhoods
around the city were almost as congested as at present,
and much more squalid.   The medical officer's report
showed that the great demand for house-room, and the convenience of living near their work, obliged these men to live
in single apartments, for the most part low, imperfectly ventilated, and " in many cases totally unfit for habitation." " In
some of them the officers who have lodged there have taken
smallpox, scarlet fever, and similar contagious complaints.
. . . All the cases of smallpox and fever that have come
before me during the last six months have occurred to officers
living in such tenements."

And yet the public servants compelled to live amidst such
surroundings were reprimanded for their " misconduct " and
" objectionable proceedings " in daring to ask for that slight
increase of pay which would enable them to improve the very
conditions which his Grace of Argyll so deplored.   The Postmaster-General's dream of a contented little postal Utopia
nestling under the shadow of St. Martin's-le-Grand was, as a
matter of course, never attempted to be realised ; nor was
the slightest compensating advantage given to the neglected
men.   Yet it must be stated, to the credit of the authorities of those days, that though they refused any improvement in pay or prospects, they offered the men good
investment for their money in the way of an insurance scheme
for their benefit.   If they could not better provide for their
employés while living, they made amends to them when
dead.   The Post Office was willing to provide a decent
funeral cheaply for any of its servants whom death from ill-
nutrition and overwork had saved from becoming State
pensioners.   It was a happy stroke and a bold one in the
direction of economy, for which the Duke of Argyll was to
be eminently commended.

Still, when all is said, and when all allowance is made for
the times, the Post Office as an employer was no worse than
many a factory and many another huge workshop.   It was

certainly no worse than it was itself destined to become on the departure of the ducal pseudo-philanthropist from St. Martin's-le-Grand. If there was one thing in postal administration during this time which called for praise it was the earnest solicitude after the health of the staff. The earlier reports from the medical officers of the Post Office are examples of completeness, and display a patience, a research, and a suggestiveness, as well as a desire to improve the sanitary conditions and working environment of the staff, which are all the more creditable seeing that the Post Office then employed only a tithe of the vast army which to-day toil within its walls.

Yet, painstaking and conscientious as these annual reports on the health of the staff continued to be for the first few years of their appearance, they were by virtue of their very quality calculated to mislead the public as to the inner conditions of Post Office life. For one thing they referred principally, if not wholly, to the staffs of London ; occasionally Edinburgh and Dublin and other large centres came in for observation, but generally speaking too little attention was paid to the conditions of the provincial offices and other places. Extensively quoted and commented on as all such reports were likely to be, they helped, despite the good intentions of their authors, to convey a lasting impression that the Post Office was the best-managed and best-regulated department of the State, second only to the army in point of immunity from liability to disease in sanitation and general healthful surroundings. They conveyed the idea that the authorities were on the whole so solicitous about the health and comfort of their lesser subordinates that they would temper the wind to the shorn lamb, and were only too eager to stand between a postman and a draught even while they resolutely refused him proper boots and a winter overcoat. They conveyed the notion that while it was good for his moral welfare to underpay him and put temptation in his way, they none the less themselves endured sympathetic pains each time an epidemic of diarrhœa swept through the office. They might be found guilty of many things, but it could never be urged against them that they neglected to regulate the number of microbes in the drinking-water. Altogether such regard apparently was paid to the health of the postal staff in these earlier reports that they gave a suggestion of an abiding humanitarianism in postal administration which should cause postal officials generally to regard themselves as fortunate indeed.   Only the timidly uttered discontent among the letter-carriers gave indication of that newly imported spirit of profit-mongering commercialism which in a few years was to weaken that leavening principle almost beyond recognition. Not that there was any conscious hypocrisy as yet in official-dom.   Through all the changes that ensued, the authorities acted according to their conception of their moral duty. For, up to the present, no responsible minister had risen to accuse the Government of being the model employer.

Rowland Hill, the Permanent Secretary, who by this time had become petted and praised and honoured as the greatest reformer of his or any other age, was nevertheless beginning to be found out by his humbler subordinates.   Among them at least the " Monarch of the Penny Post " was anything but a living embodiment of all human virtues.   These, the little army of obscure minions about the footstool of his gilded throne, had discovered that the idol had feet of clay.   While the crowd worshipped without, the servants within the temple dedi-cated to his fame could not seal their eyes to his imperfections. They were the menials on whose humble shoulders was borne the weight of that throne and footstool on which he rested ; and they most of all knew that their worshipful master's clay foot was one that could crush most mercilessly.   Such was the feeling under the surface, while the great postal reformer himself never dreamed that those so low down would dare to question either his wisdom or his benevolence in finding em-ployment for such a class of men as they.   If he ever dreamed that menials could prove so ungrateful for his inventing the Penny Post, which gave them their livelihood whatever the conditions, it is probable he did not care.   Had he been curious to find out, like another Al Raschid, how his servants regarded him, he would have been surprised.   But suddenly, one day, in the summer of 1858, there was circulated broadcast among the members of the London postal service a stinging piece of satire in verse, which purported to represent the esteem in which he was held by the rank and file of the working staff. There is not the slightest doubt that means were taken to ensure his getting a copy, even if his own cherished Penny Post were used as the medium. If Rowland Hill ever saw it, history is silent as to how he took it. Possibly he only smiled contemptuously; certainly he was not the man to wince because the sting of an insect had found a loose joint in his armour. Needless to say, the author never came forward to claim his laurels, nor was his anonymity discovered. The verse, which was printed on a small handbill, convenient for secret distribution, is almost a literary curiosity now after all these years. It read as follows :—

THE WHITE SLAVES

To the Magnate of St. Martin's-le-Grand.

The author presents his compliments to Mr. Rowland Hill, and begs his acceptance of the accompanying lines as a mark of the respect in which he is held by a numerous and hard-working class of which the writer is one, as

A POST-OFFICE FAG, *alias* WHITE NIGGER.

O Rowland Hill! O Rowland Hill!
Thou man of proud imperious will!
Forbear to crush, with iron hand,
The drudges under thy command;
And strive to purify thy fame
From stains that now defile thy name.
Hast thou all sense of justice lost,
Great Monarch of the Penny Post?
Thou takest care, O Rowland Hill!
Thy own big-bellied purse to fill;
But woe betide the hapless wight,
If thou canst nibble at his mite.
Is not thy service rather dear,
At fifteen hundred pounds a year?
Thy brother, with a thousand too,
Methinks is pretty well to do:
And then thy Son, that hopeful sprig,
Five hundred hath to laugh and jig.
So thou hast feathered well thy nest,
And now canst giggle with the best.
But sometimes, Rowland! cast a thought
On those by labour overwrought;
Nor crimp them of their scanty pay,
That thou mayst revel with the gay;
Invoke their blessing, not their curse,
And thou wouldst never fare the worse.

There is reason to believe that the lines were produced by the printers of the *Civil Service Gazette*. They gave an immense amount of secret satisfaction among the class of men to whom the poet was supposed to belong. But better was in store. Following almost immediately on the publication of the verse, the *Civil Service Gazette* announced its early intention to ventilate the grievances of the " Fags " and " White Niggers " of the postal service. Great was the jubilation among the aggrieved men, for each confidently expected to borrow a copy from his neighbour when it came out. The *Civil Service Gazette* was a luxury few could afford in those days, costing, as it did, fivepence, principally owing to the paper duty, not yet repealed.

It was the very first time that any public organ had shown the courage and independence to take up the little-known case of the sorters and letter-carriers. They were naturally delighted, devoured the articles, and looked for more. Now that their grievances had at last found ventilation in all the glory of print, surely the day of their deliverance was close at hand.

But the articles fell short of the mark. They were forcible and telling enough—as all such articles of the *Civil Service Gazette* in those days were—and they showed no small justification for the discontent prevailing. Yet they convinced nobody but the aggrieved men themselves ; the authorities were scarcely impressed, except with the impudence of it, while they were read with only a qualified sympathy by the other members of the Civil Service who chanced to see them. The only effect the publication of the articles had on the heads of the Department against whom they were more or less directed was to provoke an inquiry into the authorship of what they chose to regard as a gross literary impertinence. The usual voluntary spies and amateur detectives were set to work secretly to discover by their own methods who could have been guilty of communicating the facts, or, better still, who was the actual author, and if he had any connection with the service. If the men knew anything at all, they kept the secret loyally. The authorities never got beyond suspicions, which they failed to justify, and so the matter blew over. If ever there was a postal Junius in connection with the

case, none but a few and the *Civil Service Gazette* knew his
identity.

Before leaving the matter of these articles, of which such
high hopes and expectations were raised, it may be worthy
of mention as a curious item that the interest and enthusiasm
of the men were for some time before kept alive by
the surreptitious distribution inside the office and elsewhere
of handbills issued from the publishers. Let the handbill
speak for itself, and break the silence of over seventy years :—

READ THE " CIVIL SERVICE GAZETTE "
Unstamped 5d.—Stamped 6d.

July 24th, 1858,

ROWLAND HILL'S LAST UKASE !

BREAK DOWN OF THE GAGGING SYSTEM !

WHITE SLAVES OF THE POST OFFICE.

31st,

ROWLAND HILL'S JOB FRUSTRATED :

HIS GREAT REVENGE :

The Screw and Gagging System of the General Post-Office.

POST OFFICE REFORMS

AND THE WAY TO GET THEM :

HOPE   FOR   THE   LETTER-CARRIERS.

Coming Emancipation of the White Niggers. .

August 7th.

POST-OFFICE   MANAGEMENT :

OUR MISSING LETTERS AND OUR LATE DELIVERIES

THE LETTER-CARRIER'S " BILL OF FARE."

14th.

POST-OFFICE REFORM BY MERIT :

REVELATIONS FROM ST. MARTIN'S-LE-GRAND.

HOPE FOR THE OPPRESSED.

THE POSTMASTER-GENERAL AND THE LONDON LETTER-CARRIERS.

D

These handbills with the articles were all that remained as sad mementos of a new experience and a great disappointment.

The day of postal deliverance was not yet. There were many hills of difficulty to climb ere they could hope even to catch a distant glimpse of the Promised Land.

CHAPTER IV

GROWING DISCONTENT AMONG LETTER-CARRIERS—PROHIBITION
OF PUBLIC MEETING—THE FRANCHISE AMONG POSTAL SERVANTS
AND ITS HISTORY

For another ten years practically the authorities allowed the
malcontents to stew in their own juice.

There was, however, some slight attempt on the part of the
letter-carriers again to bring their grievances under notice in
1858 by holding another public meeting in the south-western
district of London. This meeting, in the newspaper reports
of which the names of the speakers were concealed, for that
reason principally, incurred the serious disapprobation of the
authorities, and it was honoured with special reference in the
Fifth Annual Report of the Postmaster-General. Therein
the letter-carriers were severely rebuked for not adopting the
same regular course which had hitherto failed to bring them
satisfaction. One or two passages are instructive. Instead
of the proceedings being " conducted in an open, manly, and
respectful manner, the meeting referred to was held away
from the ordinary place of employment, and speeches were
made containing statements which the men who uttered them
must have known to be false, but from the consequences of
which they endeavoured to screen themselves by concealing
their names." Lord Colchester, the then Postmaster-General,
took the opportunity to warn the letter-carriers " against the
machinations of discarded officers who, reckless of the ruin
they may bring upon others, strive to spread disaffection in the
Department from which they themselves have been removed.
Coupled with this warning there was a half promise that,
though their position was, as was maintained, a very enviable
one, their grievances would be further looked into—providing
they complained no further and held no more meetings.

A year or so later, in 1860, owing to the persistent representations made by the various bodies comprising the circulation department, in which they complained of insufficient
remuneration and other grievances, an Inter-departmental
Committee of Inquiry was held, composed of the principal
authorities, assisted by the Assistant-Secretary of the Treasury.
This committee occupied itself with the subject-matter of
the memorials which had been presented. The result was a
report in which they recommended a slight increase of force,
and a small increase in wages. Whatever the increase of force
that was recommended, it was not before it was needed. As
for the increase of wages, it was not only insignificant, but the
manner of its application betrayed it at once as only a temporary stop-gap hesitatingly offered by a parsimonious Department anxious to obtain the most credit out of the transaction.
Before the public the letter-carriers were represented as
coming in for another Departmental legacy, but the microscopic benefit was still further diminished by being confined
to the " men now in the Service," so that " men newly
appointed to the minor establishment would come in on
the old and lesser rates of pay." Even this slight improvement in the conditions of the service therefore was to be
confined to the men who had agitated and put the Department and its Inter-departmental Committee to some little
trouble and expense.

In the year 1866 Lord Stanley of Alderley, then Postmaster-General, felt constrained to prohibit all outside public
meetings which were called for purposes of promoting agitation among discontented postal officials. Lord Stanley issued
an order prohibiting such open meetings on pain of dismissal.
However it may have been justified at the period of its introduction, it is interesting to note that successive Postmasters-
General allowed it to remain practically in abeyance for the
next twenty-five years. Either Lord Stanley's order was forgotten, even in the most stormy periods between 1871 and
1874, or the different public heads of the Department felt a
reluctance to reintroduce it. It was not till 1890 that a
definite prohibition of the right of public meeting based on
this order was issued by Mr. Raikes.

The London letter-carriers at this period of 1866 were in a

highly dissatisfied state, notwithstanding that on March 22, 1865, there had been a slight revision in the scales of pay for sorters, stampers, letter-carriers, and supplementary letter-carriers. The latter were in receipt of eighteen shillings, while two classes of letter-carriers went from twenty shillings to twenty-five, and from twenty-six to thirty shillings a week. In introducing this improved scale of pay in a circular memorandum, the Postmaster-General did not forget to impress on the lucky recipients that " the benefit of their places is by no means confined to their bare wages, and that this is especially so in the case of the letter-carriers." They were also once more reminded of the amounts they received from the public " in gratuities at Christmas—a sum which, if divided equally and spread over the whole year, would produce on an average 5s. a week to each man."

Yet though a beneficent and paternal Department gave sanction to the indirect taxation of the public to bring up the wages of the letter-carriers, the letter-carriers themselves still found cause for complaint. On March 1, 1866, a small meeting was held in a public hall to decide on the best means of letting the public and the authorities know of the chronic discontent prevailing, and the adoption of the most effectual means of agitating for the purpose of obtaining a higher wage. The prime mover of this was a letter-carrier named Padfield, in receipt of twenty-five shillings a week, and his principal coadjutors were Sinfield and Booth. Some strong comments were made regarding the decisions of the Postmaster-General and upon the replies of the Chancellor of the Exchequer in the House of Commons, which utterances, as reported, were objected to by the authorities as exceeding the bounds of official licence. Padfield, who called the meeting and filled the chair on this occasion, had been an active agitator for some years, and the fact was remembered to his detriment when this particular meeting was taken into account. The Postmaster-General thought it would be against the interests of discipline to retain such a man in the service, and directed that he be dismissed, in the hope that this single example would serve as a sufficient warning to the others. Padfield was accordingly dismissed in the thirteenth year of his service, his defence that he merely took the chair to enable the meeting to express an opinion, which he in no way directed, being of no avail. The two minor sinners, Booth and Sinfield, were dealt with more leniently, and escaped with a severe admonition and a warning as to their future conduct. Booth, however, was to reappear as a more important character later on.

It was this meeting called by Padfield which induced the Postmaster-General, Lord Stanley, to put down with a strong hand these public expressions of discontent among postal servants. He had already expressed disapprobation of such meetings, and could no longer think that there remained any grievances unredressed.

On March 13, 1866, Lord Stanley issued a minute dealing with the practice of holding meetings in public, and the privilege was withdrawn. The decision come to by Lord Stanley was that he was " determined no longer to tolerate a system of agitation which is got up by a few turbulent men, and which tends to create a spirit of discontent and restlessness among the whole of the lower body of the Post Office servants. With this view he forbids, on pain of dismissal, the holding by officers of the Department of any meeting beyond the walls of the Post Office building for the discussion of official questions."

The Department by this time had whetted its appetite for economy ; it had at last wholly committed itself to a policy of save-at-any-price. Had not the great oracle of reform, Rowland Hill, himself shown the way ? It was easy to effect this by reducing postal servants' pay in proportion as their work became harder and their responsibilities increased. It. was also easy of accomplishment by compelling those employed and paid for performing inferior duties to take up those of their immediate superiors who had been in receipt of nearly double their wages. Not that this was altogether a new shuffle in the game of economy, but it had never been so effectively applied. The stampers, therefore, who were regarded as an inferior grade of letter-sorters, were forthwith made to take up despatching duties, those same duties practically for which only a few years before clerks at £200, £300, and even £400 a year had been almost exclusively employed. Thus was the dignity and responsibility of postal duties depreciated still further ; thus were the men given fresh causes for complaint ; and thus were the seeds of future agitation further sown. The stampers resented it in the only way possible, by petition, verbal and written, and by every means of respectful protest that remained to them. The Department had not yet even learnt how to be diplomatic—it practically left them without an answer ; not even one of those characteristic replies which have so often protracted the struggle by referring it to their successors for interpretation. They thought that appealing to the men's vanity would remove their discontent ; that by giving them a new designation they would feel they were not so hardly worked after all. They thought that by calling a man something else he would consent to regard himself as less of a white slave than he was in reality. They very magnanimously altered his official description from that of a stamper to sub-sorter, but without the smallest difference in point of pay or prospects in return for the newly fixed responsibilities. The malcontents were still ungrateful enough to remain unconverted to the Department's point of view. They did not mind being called anything that would befit them—a rose by any name would smell as sweet ; but if they had to do more work of a higher responsibility, they wanted correspondingly better pay.

The Department had yet a deal to learn, but it played the game with a sublime indifference to the rules of fairness, and wondered when it was detected cheating. It had not yet learned how to cheat with grace, and by means of forced cards, without the subterfuge being exposed on the instant. That was to come later. It had been so used to submissiveness on the part of the force that it could not think the men would have the courage to persist in their objections now. So it thought to compromise the difference by giving the men yet another title, that of " assistant-sorter," and putting them on the sorters' scale, but with a reduced maximum when they should reach the top. Now the only advantage the Department could afford the men as a solatium in their disappointment was to offer them a maximum more easily attained to by being reduced by five shillings. This was the result of a "revision " made in September, 1867. The highest wage a man could now receive was 45s. a week instead of 50s., and the only compensation offered for his deprivation of prospect was an increase of 6d. in the yearly rise, and a very slight increase on the lower scale. So that instead of taking nearly half a lifetime to reach 50s. by twenty-seven yearly instalments, it now took sixteen years to reach 45s.

Then after a while they were given the option of remaining on the 50s. maximum at 1s. increments, or the 45s. at 1s. 6d. annual increments. In either case it was like the promise of a copyhold in the moon ; at least so the men regarded it, especially as the immediate outlay to the Department meant only a dozen shillings or so. But they were compelled to accept the conditions and to take up the duties none the less.

Even with an unblemished character it took perhaps half a lifetime to reach a respectable salary. Consequently many —the stampers, sub-sorters, postmen, and others—had to eke out their meagre income by working at an alternative trade, such as bootmaking, watchmaking, or other odd jobs, in the intervals which should ordinarily have been given to sleep and leisure. One man who used to engage in " moving jobs," he having a little greengrocer's business, was constantly late for the afternoon duty. When called on to explain, he gave as his reason that the Post Office gave him his bread, and he had to employ his spare time elsewhere looking for his cheese. It is a trifling incident, but the reply would have equally well fitted hundreds of others in similar positions.

As has already been pointed out, the bond of relationship between the letter-carrier and the stampers and sorters was becoming a most intimate one, and one body scarcely moved without the other. The letter-carriers complained of poor pay in proportion to the value of their work, and bad treatment generally. The stampers and the sorters had their own distinct grievances, but there was to an extent a common ground of action between them. They had as yet no right of public meeting ; indeed, that right, conceded as such, did not come till twenty-five years after, when it was granted expressly by Mr. Gladstone. There appeared to be a total absence of instruction on the matter, but it was generally taken for granted that postal servants who were debarred the simple privilege of recording their votes at election times, except under most dreadful pains and penalties, most certainly would not be allowed to convene meetings or to hire halls for purposes of " agitation." It had always been thought that postal officials courted official outlawry by attempting to do so. The withholding of the franchise from them encouraged the belief, even among themselves, that they were not fit and proper persons to engage in anything but their own business, which was that of serving the State and the public as faithfully as they knew how on their scanty pay. Yet it was not till 1866 that there was any direct official pronouncement on the matter, and it is probable that nothing but the events happening previously provided the warranty for it.

The greater portion of the Civil Service at this period were up in arms to claim their right to the franchise, and the Post Office, as represented by the clerical staff particularly, played its part. The Post Office clerks took the lead, and joined with the rest of civil servants in the general demand to be treated as loyal and intelligent citizens. Many meetings were held, at which M.P.s and influential speakers attended. Postal servants of the lower grades gave sympathetic support, but it must be confessed that they were as a body less impressed with the importance of the principle than were their superiors in the service. With them it was more a question of more bread and butter than votes ; and only a proportion of the more discerning saw how the exercise of the franchise would directly affect them and their position.

On the whole, the credit for agitating for the franchise for postal servants must be given to the clerical staff of that period. It is not, however, to be supposed that they were animated by any democratic desire to extend political privileges to such people as letter-carriers and letter-sorters. They, as was only natural in the circumstances, played principally for their own hand ; but they helped to win the game, and the thanks of those who afterwards shared in the spoils were due to them.

And here it is perhaps allowable to point out as a noteworthy fact that it was the clerks of the Civil Service themselves who originally were responsible for the withholding of the franchise from all Government servants. They it was who relinquished their birthright, and were the indirect means of depriving future generations of it. This happened so far back as 1782, and it was actually done at their own request and petition. Nor was there anything particularly reprehensible or blameworthy in their taking up such a position, as it was done entirely for their own protection. The possession of a vote in those days had proved more of a curse than a blessing ; and an election period meant a time of coercion and anxiety about the security of their position under Government. In an election they could not please both parties, and their votes being solicited by rival factions, woe to them if they did not vote on the lucky side. At this time the existing Government, through the votes of public servants, controlled no fewer than seventy seats in the House of Commons. Just before a General Election, Lord North, who had been in power for twelve years, took a high hand by sending notices to those constituencies where the votes of Government servants were likely to turn the scale, that unless they voted for his party it would go very hard with them in the event of his being returned to power. This was a threat and a warning serious enough in itself, but it was rendered more so by the opposite party retaliating in a like fashion by also sending out notices to the effect that there was a likelihood of their coming into office, and that if they did not give their vote, such Government servants would find themselves in a very awkward predicament.

A strong petition was sent up pleading for disfranchisement, and a Bill was introduced shortly after the formation of Lord Rockingham's administration, which was to deliver ministers from temptation to tamper with civil servants, and the better to secure the freedom of election. It is a somewhat surprising fact, looked at in these days, that this Bill was warmly contested in all its stages through the House of Commons. But it was eventually passed by considerable majorities, though in no division were more than 110 members present. At that time it was regarded as a very necessary precaution to have passed this Act (22 Geo. III. c. 41), as it was computed that the Revenue officers formed nearly twenty per cent. of the whole electorate. While the Government of the day wielded such power over the destinies of civil servants because of the possession of these votes, and in point of fact they could by this means influence no fewer than 140 votes in the House of Commons, it was perhaps far better that civil servants should be disfranchised. But the natural consequence was that all Post Office servants, whatever their rank, high or low, were excluded from the use of their votes ; and this in course of time gave rise to a very grave injustice.

While citizen liberty was everywhere expanding, and the greater majority of the artisan and labouring classes were being gathered into the widening folds of the British electorate, those who happened to serve the Crown in any capacity had to pay for the privilege by the sacrifice of their vote. From allowing too much liberty to Revenue officers and those serving under the Crown, the Government rushed to the other extreme, and an Act was passed in the pre-Reform days (7 & 8 Geo. III. c. 53, s. 9) by which the provisions of former Acts were amended and extended still further by increasing the penalty to be inflicted on any Revenue officer (including postal officials) for voting at election times while still in his Majesty's service, and for two months subsequent to leaving it. The penalty was increased from £100 to £500. An officer in the Post Office was not merely liable to this heavy penalty for recording his vote, which in the ordinary course was allowed him as a citizen by the law, but on conviction was declared to be for ever disabled and incapable of holding or executing any office of trust under the Crown if he committed the heinous crime of voting at Parliamentary elections. The great Reform Act of 1831, which came to be hailed with such joyous satisfaction by the whole community, afforded no relief to the Post Office official, and it was not till a quarter of a century later that they were thought worthy of being entrusted with a vote. However this deprivation of the franchise may have been justified in Lord Rockingham's time in 1782, times and circumstances had materially changed when the middle of the nineteenth century arrived.

Such was the paradoxical position taken up with regard to postal servants and all those who served the Revenue, that while they were invariably men of selected character and selected intelligence and education, generally introduced into the public service through the highest influence to vouch for their integrity, they were not thought trustworthy enough to use a vote with common honesty and discretion. The absurdity and injustice of the position could not fail to arouse in course of time the opposition of those affected. In those days the future brilliant critic and fighting editor of the *World*, Edmund Yates, and Anthony Trollope, the future novelist, were in the Post Office; and these, in co-operation with Messrs. Frank Ives Scudamore, Chetwynd, and Ashurst, threw themselves into a movement for the removal of such electoral disabilities. The Inland Revenue was represented by Messrs. Dalbiac, Jacobs, and Alaric A. Watts, and the Customs by Messrs. Dobell and Hamel. These, the representatives of the Post Office, the Inland Revenue, and the Customs, resolved themselves into a committee. A circular was issued to the members of the service, and the support of members of Parliament was obtained; among these were included Mr. Charles Buxton, Sir Harry Verney, and Mr. Charles J. Monk. The discontent with the existing political restraint placed upon them in a short time pervaded all ranks and sections of the Civil Service; and, feeling that the retention of the present disabilities was a slur on their intelligence, and a stigma on their character for loyalty, the agitation for their removal was entered into with earnestness. This was the first organised attempt to obtain the removal of the disabilities in respect of voting and taking part in Parliamentary elections, which invidiously differentiated all Revenue officers from all other civil servants of the Crown. But it was to prove nearly a nine years' hard fight before they were to take back what had been so hastily thrown away by a previous generation of civil servants. Beyond a few private members, no minister could be induced to give countenance to what had almost come to be regarded as an impossible demand.

When the Reform Bill of 1867 was passing through the House of Commons, Sir Harry Verney, who had warmly espoused the cause of the disenfranchised civil servants, proposed a clause enabling Revenue officials (who were otherwise qualified) to vote at elections, but, on the recommendations of both Mr. Gladstone and Mr. Disraeli, this clause was negatived without a division. Yet this part of the proposal, at any rate, vehemently opposed though it was by the Government of the day and the leaders of the Opposition, was to be within two years embodied in a statute of the realm. Each forward step taken by the friends of enfranchisement was contested by the occupants of both sides of the House; and every argument that could be devised for and against was imported into the discussion.

It was due to Mr. Charles J. Monk, the member for Gloucester, that the first breach in the Opposition was made. From the very first he had been struck by the unfairness of excluding educated and selected men in the Post Office, Customs, and Inland Revenue from the exercise of the franchise, while their brethren in all the other departments of the State could freely vote and take part in elections. The principal high official argument, used in its many variations, was that it would be an unsafe weapon to place in the hands of men who might use it for furthering excessive demands, and for general purposes of agitation. Mr. Monk's reply was in most cases to the effect that " if these officers have just cause of complaint it is far better that the grievance should be brought before the House by their Parliamentary representatives than that it should be left to seethe below the surface, or be brought to light through irregular channels." It was early in the session of 1868 that Mr. Monk introduced his Revenue Officers' Disabilities Removal Bill. Slowly and inch by inch it was carried through all its stages in the House of Commons, defeating the Tory Government of Mr. Disraeli, on the motion for going into committee on the Bill, by a majority of thirty-two. This was certainly a triumph for the friends of reform, considering that the Government had the support of the Leader of the Opposition in opposing the measure. Lord Abinger took charge of the Bill in the House of Lords, when the Lord Chancellor, Lord Cairns, much to the astonishment of the peers themselves and many others in the Lower House, supported the measure most strongly. This was sufficient to ensure its success, and it speedily passed into law (31 & 32 Vict. c. 73).

During the subsequent Parliament, 1868-1874, Mr. Monk made several attempts to complete the measure of enfranchisement by enabling officers engaged in the collection and management of her Majesty's revenues to take part unreservedly in the election of members to serve in Parliament. But he was invariably opposed most strenuously by the then Prime Minister, Mr. Gladstone, and it was not till another Parliament had been elected, in 1874, that he was enabled to accomplish that object by passing one other measure (37 & 38 Vict. c. 22) through Parliament, with the concurrence of the Chancellor of the Exchequer of the new Government, Sir Stafford Northcote.

The services of Mr. Monk in getting passed the measure of 1868 were still appreciated by the newly emancipated postal servants and others ; and Mr. Frank Ives Scudamore, Assistant-Secretary to the Post Office, on behalf of the Revenue Offices generally, presented him with an illuminated address, expressive of their gratitude to him for his skill and ability in carrying their " Bill of Rights " successfully through Parliament, " in despite of formidable opposition."

If it was the higher grade of civil servants who for their own protection threw away their right to the franchise, it was the same class who recovered it, and who were instrumental in procuring it even for their humbler subordinates in the postal service and elsewhere.

During the progress of the agitation among nearly all Civil Service bodies to obtain the franchise, discontent was becoming all the more acute in the Post Office. Doubtless the contemplation of practically the whole Civil Service engaged in furthering a united demand, in no small degree gave an impetus to the growing postal movement, and helped to develop the forces of discontent within.

CHAPTER V

FORMATION OF AN ORGANISATION—BOOTH, THE LETTER-
CARRIER—CONDITION OF THE LETTER-CARRIERS—PROPOSED
PETITION TO PARLIAMENT.

IT was scarcely to be expected that, with the spirit of discontent so widespread among every class and section, that discontent would remain altogether dumb and inarticulate. If
the authorities imagined that by putting their veto on the
right of public meeting discontent would in consequence
die a natural death, they were mistaken. It might have slum-
bered for a while, but that there were already a few active
spirits at work among the letter-carriers. Secretly and quietly,
and almost unrecognised even among those whom he was
slowly organising, one man particularly at this period was
actively at work. His name was William Booth, a City letter-
carrier. He began by convening little hole-and-corner meetings in all sorts of out-of-the-way places. And what was a
source of no little annoyance to the authorities, those smuggled
meetings of postal employés were more often than not reported
in the public press, though the names of the speakers were not
always given. Nor did it stop at smuggled meetings outside
the official domain ; for Booth called several meetings, with
the official permission as well as without, in the letter-carriers'
kitchens. Some were impromptu meetings, carefully planned by
the indefatigable Booth, and, as usual, reported next morning.
Such meetings were generally for the purpose of shaping a
policy, and for discussing the best means of drawing the attention of Parliament to their grievances. They were always well
attended, not only by the letter-carriers themselves, but by
every other class and section of postal employé in the Post
Office buildings. But spies and overseers were frequently present
to see that no one used a pencil to scribble a surreptitious

note. Yet, even with this precaution, to the chagrin of the authorities, the morning papers had accurate accounts of the proceedings. The invisible reporters were never looked for in the proper place, for they stationed themselves by one of the open windows of the underground kitchens which looked into the Post Office yard ; and through these windows every word of the speakers floated upward to be caught by the eager reporter in waiting.

Then, as if to test the existing official prohibition, Booth advertised that he would lecture on postal grievances at Cowper Street Schoolrooms, and the fact was announced by the distribution of some thousands of handbills. The lecture was delivered to a crowded and enthusiastic audience, and many of the public were present. The result of this was that the lecturer was next day called up before the Controller to explain why he held a meeting outside the Post Office building, the forbidding rule notwithstanding. Booth very adroitly won his case on a quibble, and was afterwards none the less proud of having done so. He maintained it was a lecture merely, there being no resolution of any kind discussed ; and there being no prohibitive rule against lectures, of whatever nature, he submitted that he had broken no regulation. The official Solon discharged him with a caution.

The agitators were by this time made aware in many unpleasant little ways that they were constantly under the surveillance of the Departmental informers. Both on duty and away from it they could scarcely move with freedom. Booth especially was regarded as such a dangerous firebrand that the Department felt it advisable to keep itself acquainted with his every movement while off duty, and for that purpose he was constantly shadowed to find out where he went and with whom he mixed. His house at Brixton was watched almost night and day, and several times the official touts got reprimanded by their superiors for reporting that Booth had not left the house after being seen going in, when as a matter of fact he was found to have addressed a postal meeting the same evening. For the sake of causing their discomfiture, and for the fun of the thing, he generally circumvented the watchers by getting over the back-garden wall and dodging through a neighbour's house into a side street.

In this manner principally he got together meetings of men whose co-operation he sought, and though such gatherings were often secret and unrecorded, they were largely the means of setting the agitation on the move along definite lines. The agitation from this period may be said to have been started in a little coffee-room off Gunpowder Alley, in Fleet Street, and from Gunpowder Alley, very appropriately, most of the squibs to be directed against the postal authorities were prepared and fired. It was here that the first conference of postal servants was held, when Booth, having called together a body of representatives from the various district offices, besought them to assist him to form an organisation of postal employés for mutual benefit and maintenance of rights. It was the ambitious aim to unite the whole of the Post Office and Telegraph employés, to assist in obtaining by legitimate means the abolition of Sunday work, increase of wages, and an honest and clearly-defined system of promotion without loss of pay, and generally to relieve cases of distress. The planks of the platform having thus been rough-hewed, it remained to nail them together. For this purpose a small preliminary public meeting was called in a schoolroom attached to the Borough Road Congregational Church, which was lent by the Rev. G. M. Murphy, a notable preacher of the day, who became an active sympathiser with Booth and his efforts. This inaugural meeting in the little schoolroom took place on May 17, 1872, when the society was formally constituted and members enrolled.

At the time the bare idea of a protective society of this kind within the ranks of the postal service was so novel and audacious, and the difficulties in the way of its complete success so numerous, that for some months it hung fire, and even many of those who had joined predicted an early demise. At any rate, the progress made was not very reassuring to Booth and his coadjutors, who were staking almost everything on the cast of the die. Nevertheless, the leaders worked with a will to pull the movement together and make it presentable before the public, and an enormous amount of work was quietly accomplished. An extensive correspondence was carried on with public men and others who were to be counted on as friendly, and who were likely to help and encourage them in the future. By this means they awakened an interest in their work among a numerous class of members of Parliament belonging to both political parties, and gave them that knowledge of postal wants which was expected to bear fruit when the time came.

It was not very long before the authorities were surprised to receive an application from the men to be allowed to hold a mass meeting inside the Post Office, and the loan of the Newspaper Branch was requisitioned. Whatever may have been the hesitation in giving official sanction to so large an order, the required permission was, nevertheless, granted after some delay. The object of this meeting was to discuss the terms of a postal petition to Parliament, and possibly it was the nature of the project which caused the authorities to deem it wiser to confine its discussion within their own walls than to drive it into the public arena.

And just here it is necessary to point out that at this time the fraternal feeling between the London letter-carriers and the letter-sorters was stronger than ever. The several public meetings and the encouragement they had received, with the numerous injunctions from outside friends and sympathisers to keep together, begot a spirit of comradeship which sank all petty distinction of class, and Booth's activity did much to cement them. The sorters were slightly better off than the letter-carriers in point of pay and status, but they had grievances much in common, and they had learnt more than ever to recognise that they were useful and necessary to each other in the fight for freedom, a decent wage, and better conditions of work. The army of discontented letter-carriers had been very much increased since 1860. In that year the levelling-down principle, first introduced in 1854 by Rowland Hill and a Commission which then sat, was carried one step further by the formation of an inferior grade to be known as auxiliary or assistant letter-carriers, originally a hybrid class, something between postal labourers and the ordinary letter-carriers. They were badly paid and worse treated ; they shared all the misfortunes and hardships of the letter-carriers without their advantages as to pay and prospects. They were a cheap class of labourers in the rich postal vineyard, for whom it seemed the authorities thought any treatment good enough, if only because they were cheap. Their working hours were spread over a greater period of the day even than were those of the full-blown letter-carriers. Their position in the service was most precarious.

Their wretched conditions of service soon impelled them to organise among themselves, but their organisation was as feeble as their funds were shallow, and though nominally they were a separate body, yet virtually they were to be counted in with the general army of malcontents. They gave and received whatever moral support was possible. They joined in where they could ; they attended the postal meetings, and assisted in some degree towards the general betterment of the service.

The condition of the auxiliary letter-carriers was so pitiable as to cause wonder that the heads of the Department could be so short-sighted as to set up in the persons of these men, many of them almost bootless scarecrows, such a damning and convincing proof of postal ineptitude and parsimony. With a class of men in the Government service working under such conditions, it is easy to see that they were not to remain unaffected by the prevailing epidemic of discontent. Almost from the first they sent forth ready recruits to swell the ranks of the disaffected. They were in themselves a reservoir of discontent, and provided the agitation with a fresh justification, enabling the agitators to make a stronger complaint than ever against the authorities. If anything were wanting to prove that the letter-carriers especially were a body of ill-used men, these auxiliaries supplied the last piece of material evidence. They presented a pathetic spectacle to the public eye. The idea of a man struggling to keep himself and a big family on fifteen shillings a week, the while to remain honest and irreproachable, was likely to awaken the public to it as a matter for its own concern. The auxiliaries had to attend, whenever their services were required, at a remuneration lower than that of a dock labourer, being threepence or fourpence per hour, and but for the fact that they were compelled to engage in other callings many of them might have starved.

The condition of the indoor staffs could not be so prominently brought under the public eye, but both letter-sorters and letter-carriers alike suffered from disabilities, and had

grievances which fully entitled them to an inquiry and a
hearing. It was not only that they were expressly forbidden
by rule to hold public meetings to discuss their grievances and
endeavour to enlist outside sympathy, or to take any public
action whatever for the purpose of removing the wrongs of
which they complained. To obtain redress of any grievance,
the only course officially open to them was to apply through
their immediate superiors ; but this, with the so-called right of
appeal to the Postmaster-General, more often than not begot
annoyance and petty persecution from those of whom redress
was sought. The right of appeal especially was rendered
nugatory by the exercise of the power of damaging endorse-
ment on the part of officials through whose hands such an
appeal would have to pass on its way upward to the chief of
the Department. Indeed, their experience in the matter of
petitions to the Postmaster-General had up to the present
amply proved that the authorities were intended to serve as a
breakwater or a barrier to resist all such appeals, and provide
the public head with ample excuses for refusal or an ignoring
of the claims of all humble subordinates. As has already been
noted, it took many dreary years of waiting or slow climbing to
reach what is to-day regarded as a decent living wage. The
rules of the Department did not insist that a man should work
more than eight hours in the twenty-four, but owing to the
increase of work they were more commonly extended to ten
and sometimes eleven hours in the working day, while these
duties were usually divided into two, three, and four separate
attendances, the intervals barely leaving time for meals and
going to and from the office. All that the sorters had ventured
to ask for was that these abuses should be removed ; that
their pay should better correspond to their heavier responsibilities, and the increased cost of living ; that their hours should
be confined to eight in the twenty-four, and adjusted more
humanely.

The letter-carriers joined with the sorters in complaining
that their pay, thirty shillings a week after fifteen or twenty
years' drudgery, was not a fair wage ; that promotion was not
only unequal, but too slow. A peculiar grievance with them
then, as it has always remained, was that the fact that letter-
carriers were given Christmas-boxes by the public had

invariably been made a pretext for paying the men badly. Letter-carriers who were formerly eligible for sorterships had all such promotion closed against them ; and practically they were left without any hope of ever getting beyond their thirty shillings a week, even if ever they got so far. A great and widespread source of dissatisfaction, too, was the way in which men who had been induced to enter the service with a fair promise of promotion had been bilked by subsequent alterations in the establishment.

There were other causes of discontent not so broadly defined, but poor pay and lack of promotion were the main features. Man cannot live by bread alone, but the Post Office made it its business to see that its servants never became lazy through over-feeding. It sealed their lips and prevented a public voicing of their grievances, and it almost dared them to open their mouths too widely either for talking or eating.

CHAPTER VI

BOOTH THE LEADER OF THE AGITATION—A MASS MEETING IN THE GENERAL POST OFFICE—A PETITION TO PARLIAMENT.

So the wave of discontent gathered force. By 1871 the agitation for better pay, better-adjusted hours of duty, and better prospects had assumed some appearance of an organisation, though without a recognised leadership. But the man was to come when the hour demanded him. The forces were ready ; an army of volunteers, enthusiastic and confident in their cause, but as yet undrilled. They were not undisciplined though, for the rules and restrictions by which they were bound kept them in order, and strengthened their self-control. An army of discontented Government servants thus almost of their own free-will, and spontaneously brought together without an acknowledged leader, without even as yet an accepted plan of procedure, is, from this distance of time, not a little curious to contemplate. It at once affords an evidence of the existence of very real grievances as the impelling cause of the men's sincerity and of their self-command. So far, there is not one single case of enthusiasm carried to excess ; the movement had been orderly in its growth, and in no case had their grievances caused them to forget the respect due from them to those who ruled over them ; nor to diminish their loyalty to the public service. It is as gratifying as it is remarkable.

Here, then, at this period were the forces, two contingents of them, ready and eager to test their strength in any manner that was legitimate and lawful.

They would not shrink from the displeasure of the officials ; they knew that the frown of the Postmaster-General was already upon them. Who then was to be the leader of these irregulars ? The man came forward when the moment arrived, and henceforth for a few years Booth was to assume the leadership. He was not particularly eloquent, and had no gifted fancy, nor a tongue to form choice periods ; but he had a full-throated voice with a ring in it, a head well poised on thick-set shoulders, and every comrade knew him for one who was not afraid. Every comrade knew him for a man who meant what he said, and could say it pointedly, if not elegantly. Experience of him had taught them that what he put his hand to he carried through ; they knew that he could formulate a petition as easily as he could knock a man down.

Up to this time petition after petition had been laboriously drawn up by committees and meekly presented by the men, only to be ignored by the authorities, or returned as informal. Months had been wasted in this manner, till the aggrieved men, letter-carriers and sorters alike, got weary of waiting. They wanted to be on the march, but none knew whither. It was now that William Booth came to the front. The forces of discontent were not to dwindle away for want of a man. There was work to be done ; there was a road to be made, and here were the willing hands and the implements ready. Booth sprang out of the ranks, and put himself at the head of them, and facing them addressed them.

His first word of command was short and decisive. " To the House of Commons ! " said he. The very audacity of the proposal for a moment almost unnerved them, but the fact itself went a long way to convince them that their leader had come at last. Too long had they wasted their energies and their time on fruitless effort, and too long had they contented themselves with standing still, or progressing slowly over the same beaten track provided by officialdom. " To the House of Commons ! " There was something original in the idea, and its very daring after a while recommended it. From the armoury of the franchise they had been provided with a new and efficient weapon ; and St. Stephen's should provide them with a shooting-range.

Forthwith, under the recognised leadership of Booth, they set themselves in this direction. The first difficulty that presented itself was the discovery that Parliament was guarded by the skirts of the Department, and that therefore it was necessary first to obtain permission of the magnates of St. Martin's-le-Grand to draw up a petition to Parliament at all. The liberty of the individual was more restricted than they imagined. The franchise had been extended to them ; a weapon had been put into their hands by the Constitution ; but the authorities reserved to themselves the right to overlook their powder and shot, and fix the firing distance for them. There was no help for it ; not even the originality of their leader could circumvent the Department in this respect. The House of Commons, free of approach to every working-man in the kingdom, was as yet barred to postal officials by an inquisitive and mistrustful bureaucracy to prevent their being too rash in their importunities. They might think themselves very fortunate in having obtained the liberty to use their vote ; but to dare approach openly the sacred persons of those who represented them, without first submitting their intention, was not to be thought of.

Accordingly the necessary petition to the Controller of the London Postal Service, asking the liberty and the indulgence of being allowed to draw up and present a humble petition to the people's representatives in Parliament assembled, was prepared and sent in. The humble petitioners waited with bated breath, and wondered what would become of Booth when it was realised that he was the moving spirit of the daring enterprise. With more than usual discretion, too, they obtained this official permission to hold a meeting to consider and discuss the terms of the proposed petition to the House of Commons. After some little delay, and a few further inquiries, thought more or less appropriate and necessary, the permission sought for was granted. But there was to be no outside public meeting this time. Whatever they had to say must be said within hearing of the officials and under the official roof. And there were to be no strangers present ; and journalists and newspaper reporters were so strictly prohibited that any one might have shot them on sight as interlopers without incurring Departmental displeasure.

The meeting was interesting, if only from the fact that it was the first meeting of this nature ever known to have been held in the Post Office. It was quite a new departure, and the men halted between satisfaction and suspicion. They felt that whatever the advantage in other respects, they were muzzled to an extent. They felt that the Department was treating them like children who could not be trusted beyond the playground for fear of throwing stones in the street. Still, they determined to accept the situation, and to make the best of it.

The meeting was called for the 28th June, 1873, to be held after the duty, at eight o'clock in the evening, and the Newspaper Branch at the top of the building was placed at their disposal. For in those days, in this particular branch at least, there was a cessation of duty after this hour. The conditions were bad ; but the Post Office was not always at work during the whole round of the clock ; it was not exactly the ever-panting, ever-working, never-ceasing, never-sleeping monster it is at the present day. The floor of the branch would be capable of accommodating over two thousand men ; but it was necessary to make some preparation. A platform was extemporised from two or three of the facing or stamping tables, each almost of the dimensions of a respectable platform in itself, and round this a number of chairs and seats were ranged. The seating accommodation was, however, principally made up of bundles of disused mail-bags and baskets, while a considerable number, perhaps the majority, stood. The success of the meeting from the first moment was beyond all expectation. If any had fears that the men would be too suspicious of attending a gathering of this kind within the precincts of the building, and under the shadow of the Department, they were mistaken. Almost directly the despatches were finished, and the duty done with for the night, they swarmed in from every part. From every other branch in the building—for the old G.P.O. was a nest of branches, like a Chinese puzzle-box—and from outside offices they swarmed up the stairs and through every means of entry. The men from the districts showed up in full strength, and provided a few spectators for the platform. The branch in its structure was admirably suited to such a meeting ; it was lofty, and there was a plentiful supply of gas-jets, depending in a long regiment from the ceiling. By half-past eight, the time for opening the meeting, the vast room was crowded. Every one was expectant and curious ; this was an auspicious occasion, and there was something of novelty in the circumstance

and the local surroundings. It was pretty well con-
jectured that spies would be present, as they were generally
to be looked for at all their open deliberations. They were
pretty well known, but it would have been impolitic, if not
impossible, to exclude them. Those who were among the
crowd could not very well on the spot take notes of what they
heard and saw without betraying the real reason of their
presence there. But if it was suspected there were official spies
there, it was more than suspected, it was known almost for a
certainty they had on their side a newspaper reporter, who had
been quietly smuggled in with the crowd of district men.
Thus was the prohibition of the officials evaded ; and it was
said that the *Standard* reporter avoided the scrutiny at the
entrance by borrowing a portion of a letter-carrier's uniform.
It was afterwards said that the enterprising reporter found
concealment in a recess beneath the great gallery clock, which
overlooked the whole of the branch. However this may be,
that there was an officially proscribed " chiel amang them
takin' notes " was sufficiently evidenced a few hours later,
when the morning *Standard* came out with a report of the
night's proceedings.

The floor of the branch, which when empty was like the
interior of an enormous barn, by half-past eight was black with
men. Not only did they completely cover the floor in a
dense, solidly-packed mass, but they perched themselves on the
tops of the sorting-tables ; they swarmed up the tall slim iron
columns which upheld the roof, and clung there, thirty feet
above those below. Others, more venturesome, by the same
means, found a resting-place on the higher ledges of the over-
stretching girders, smothered in dust, their heads in contact
with the shelving ceiling. Hundreds more had to content
themselves with catching an occasional glimpse of the platform
and its occupants through the tiers of empty pigeon-holes
rising from the middles of the sorting-tables into which the
newspapers were sorted. For every one came to see as much as
to hear. A very large number from distant districts had only
heard of him, and wanted to see Booth. They wanted to see
what kind of man it was whose audacity and whose organising
resource had so far overcome official objections as to make
this meeting possible, who had thus enabled them to beard

the official lion in his very den. The rostrum on the platform was contrived of big square mail-baskets and some wooden boxes covered over with mail-bags, touched up with a piece of green baize in the middle ; and by this there were sitting a few postmen and others. Some one rose to speak, but the tumultuous outbreak of applause kept him silent on his feet for fully a minute. This, then, was Booth ; and eyes and ears were strained to better take his measurement, and to catch his words—a rather short, sturdy man, with a full head and somewhat Gladstonian features. He spoke for half an hour or more, and if at fiist there were any waverers in the crowd, there were none when he finished. They would have stormed the Treasury benches that very night. Other speakers followed, and emphasised the necessity of laying their plaint before Parliament ; and in the end a provisional committee was elected to draw up the petition. The lines on which the petition to Parliament was to run were to ask for the appointment of a Select Committee to inquire into their grievances, and their claims for better pay and improved prospects of promotion, and the abolition of Sunday labour.

The petition was accordingly prepared, only, however, to be returned as not complying with the standing orders of the House. It was soon framed on more constitutional lines, and again being forwarded through the approved channel, the petitioners awaited the result with renewed confidence. There was a weekly subscription among the men ; there were letters to Parliamentary candidates ; there were bushels of circulars openly posted to sitting members, the folding and addressing being done by volunteers in their spare time in the official retiring-rooms. Further than this, Booth now sought the co-operation of the provincial men, and worked night and day, often depriving himself of sleep to prepare and send the necessary correspondence. No less a number than three-quarters of a million tiny circulars, it was said, were dropped in pillar-boxes all over London and elsewhere, and Booth and his assistants spent hours of their spare time in disseminating by this means the seed-corn of discontent. Then one morning the Petition Committee were sent for by the Controller of the London postal service, and informed that they had incurred the serious displeasure of the Department, as they were exceeding the bounds of a legitimate movement. They were informed that they had not confined themselves to formulating a petition to Parliament, but they had become active in fomenting an agitation throughout the entire service. They were forbidden to act as a committee, and they were to receive no recognition from their followers, and they were forthwith to disband themselves without calling any meeting. Whatever protest or appeal may have been thought necessary to save the situation was made, but without avail. There was no alternative but dismissal. The committee was therefore disbanded, the affairs wound up, and balance-sheets issued to the men, the reasons being given for this strategic movement to the rear.

CHAPTER VII

BUT it was not Booth's way to take a defeat so tamely.
Almost immediately the organisation was re-formed on a
more definite basis than ever, with the new high-sounding title
of the " United General Post-Office and Telegraph Service
Benefit Society." Rules were made and collections were
started ; Booth was appointed chairman, and a dismissed
agitator, named Hawkins, was engaged as secretary. After the
official rebuff the men felt it unsafe to join openly, but they
none the less joined secretly, and cheerfully responded to the
calls upon their purse. Booth animated the whole movement ;
and it is probable that but for him the officials would have
seen it crumble to pieces ; yet they probably saw that his
dismissal just then would only have strengthened his arm
against them. The authorities, however, went so far as to
suspend him from duty on some trivial pretext ; and Booth
was not slow to turn the fact to his advantage. He immediately set about organising a public meeting to be held at the
Cannon Street Hotel, July 16, 1873. The objects of this
meeting were twofold : it was to strengthen the hands of the
members of Parliament who were supporting the postal
petition, and it provided a means of protesting against the
leader's unjust suspension. But mainly it was intended as a
hint to the Government, and as a parade of strength to show
that their Parliamentary friends were well supported by a
following in the postal service. A few days previous to the
date of the meeting a conference had taken place in the tea-
room of the House of Commons, attended by nearly every

member pledged to their support, from whom the statement of grievances, made by Booth and several others, received a very attentive hearing. Among the members of Parliament who had interested themselves in the postal case were Mr. W. H. Smith, Mr. A. J. Mundella, Mr. Roger Eykyn, Mr. J. Locke, and several other influential members. And it was to give support to their friends in the House that this first Cannon Street Hotel meeting was called.

On the Post Office vote being taken on Monday, July 28, the claims of the aggrieved postal employees were strongly urged upon the attention of the Government by each of those members who had attended the tea-room conference, and the advocacy of Mr. W. H. Smith, Mr. Mundella, and others was particularly able. The reply of the Government was, however, unfavourable, or at least unsatisfactory.

The antagonism towards their claims, as voiced in the House by the Postmaster-General and other members of the Government on that occasion, caused Booth to decide on another public meeting. This meeting of protest against the decision of the Government was called also in Cannon Street Hotel, on Tuesday, August 5, and was to be presided over by Sir John Bennett. The forthcoming meeting was officially " proclaimed," and the men were warned against attending such public demonstrations; but it was looked forward to with enthusiasm. Elaborate preparations were made for the forthcoming meeting, and almost all the funds in hand were used to ensure its success. Five brass bands were engaged, and the procession of district men then off duty, marshalled by Booth, was to start from Finsbury Square so as to reach St. Martin's-le-Grand a minute or so before eight o'clock, the hour when the staff at the General Post Office would cease work. The district contingents turned out strong at the place of meeting, and by a quarter to eight the procession of postmen in uniform, followed by an enormous crowd of sightseers, moved in the direction of Cannon Street by way of St. Martin's-le-Grand. The five brass bands blared out some stirring marching tunes, and the procession was animated with all the enthusiasm of men anxious in defying authority. On reaching the General Post Office they were quickly joined by the letter-sorters, letter-carriers, and others, and, their numbers now swollen to a big battalion, they marched to Cannon Street Hotel as if to capture a fortress, the bands meanwhile keeping them in step with " The Postman's Knock " and " Rule, Britannia."

The huge hall of the Cannon Street Hotel was filled to overflowing within five minutes of the arrival of the procession ; and the utmost enthusiasm took possession of them. Sir John Bennett, who had already distinguished himself as a friend of the postal workers, was punctually in the chair. Sir John, with his snowy ringlets, his gold spectacles, his velveteen jacket and Hessian boots, and his fresh, clean-shaven, almost boyish features, which so belied his years, was a familiar public character, and the postal employés felt that in securing him for chairman they were favoured. Among those supporting the platform were Henry Broadhurst—not yet M.P., but a working stonemason ; George Potter, who then owned and edited the *Beehive* newspaper ; and Charles Bradlaugh, not yet either so notorious or so distinguished as he afterwards became.

The speeches were stirring, and the keynote of almost every speaker was that as postal employés enjoyed the right of every citizen to petition Parliament, they had no need to fear the petty restrictions of red-tape ; and this inalienable right should be their sheet anchor and their hope. At the same time the authorities were violently denounced for so meanly visiting their resentment on the leader Booth by suspending him without any assigned cause ; and, as may be surmised, the most capital was made out of the incident, the action of the officials being ascribed to his having dared to exercise his right as a free-born Englishman ; in which, on the whole, the speakers were probably not far wrong. Mr. M. C. Torrens, M.P., and other well-known friends of the movement graced the platform, and formed the necessary firing party. All the speaking from the platform was done by the public friends and sympathisers ; the postal employés themselves significantly remaining dumb. They had not yet the right of free speech, though they had asserted the liberty of holding a public meeting in this fashion ; that was to be tested later on. The public press noticed the meeting at some length ; and it acted as a splendid advertisement for the postal claims. The next day Booth was ordered back to the chief office, not, however, to receive his sentence of dismissal as was surmised, but to be restored to duty without suffering the loss of pay usual in such circumstances.

For the purpose of discussing ways and means of raising funds to keep the fire going and sustaining the enthusiasm of the men, there were also one or two meetings held at a little hall known as the Albion Hall, conveniently situated in London Wall, near to the General Post Office. Mr. George Potter took the chair, and Sir John Bennett, of Cheapside fame, ably supported.

Sir John Bennett had proved himself one of the staunchest and most industrious of their numerous public friends at this period. He has an especial liking for the postmen, and any one of them in uniform could purchase a three-guinea watch at his shop at something like thirty-five per cent. discount. But they were doomed to lose him in a somewhat peculiar manner. The postal volunteer corps, the then 49th Middlesex, had been formed on the occasion of the Fenian scare of 1868 ; and during a recurrence of a similar alarm from the same causes, a number of the postmen and others joined the corps in a body. Sir John Bennett was peculiar in his views of postal patriotism, and dropped the postmen and their agitation from that moment.

" If," said he, in his blunt fashion, " you who are agitating for better hours and a better wage can find time to go ' gallivanting ' about with weapons of destruction in your hands, you have no reason to ask my assistance."

It was scarcely a fair statement of the position ; but he was not to be moved further, and kept his word.

That, however, was a loss not to be sustained till later.

Not long after the great public meeting, and probably resulting from it to some extent, there was a slight revision in the scales of pay of the London town letter-carriers. But it was a very niggardly affair, and the entire benefit secured amounted to about £52 in a period of fifteen years, or a rise of one shilling and fourpence per week, no regular addition being made to the maximum or minimum, while even this small benefit was confined to a small class of about four hundred men only. This, in the circumstances, could not be accepted as a complete settlement of all their various claims. It was not only quite inadequate to meet the needs of the class it was intended to satisfy, but entirely ignored the claims of the suburban, auxiliary, and country letter-carriers, and also those of the sorters, assistants, and porters, many of whom stood in even greater need of an increase of salary than the limited number who received this slight benefit. This small unsatisfactory scheme was rendered all the more unsatisfactory by its giving to the inspectors a really substantial increase amounting to 8 per cent. on their minimum, 25 per cent. on the annual increment, and 20 per cent. on the maximum. The inspectors who thus mostly benefited were already regarded as comparatively a well-paid class, besides which they as a body had contributed neither funds nor sympathy to the agitation which had secured these benefits for them. What was intended as a sop was only another fresh cause for dissatisfaction ; and in any case it was deemed necessary to prosecute the agitation with renewed vigour.

Thereupon Booth and his associates, with a view of strengthening the Society and definitely proclaiming their character as trades unionists pure and simple, got the Postal Union affiliated to the London Trades Council. They hoped thereby to secure the co-operation of the various trade societies, should it at any time be deemed necessary or expedient to call for that assistance which they themselves were prepared to render to others.

Again, some little time after this great public demonstration, the leader of the agitation, Booth, found himself suspended from duty by order of the Controller. It was not that impending dismissal had any terrors for him, but he was determined to avoid if possible the humiliation of it. With his usual readiness he decided to take the bull by the horns in his own fashion. He conceived the idea that unless some such step as he contemplated were taken at once, his dismissal, which he knew had been recommended, would this time be certain. He hurried off to the printers who usually did such work for the movement in those days, but was told the men could not be prevailed on to work after the usual time. Booth said he had a job which would engage them all night, and being told that it was quite impossible, asked to see the men in a body. He came, he saw, he conquered, and

F

the men agreed to stop the night through for the production of a cartoon which had been roughly sketched out. It took three hours to prepare the lithograph-stone, three draughtsmen being simultaneously engaged on parts of the sketch. During the night and early morning four or five thousand copies were printed off, and by ten o'clock they were being sold like hot cakes in St. Martin's-le-Grand and all over the City. To ensure their sale and circulation they were virtually given away to the street-hawkers, who retailed them at a penny apiece. The first batch was soon exhausted, and before the day was over as many thousands more were sold. The pictorial lampoon had little of artistic merit to recommend it ; it was fearfully and wonderfully made ; the drawing was vile even for caricature ; but the letterpress, the scriptural quotations wittily applied, and the illustrations together, told. The broadsheet contained four or five separate illustrations, having reference to the recent great procession of postal employees to Cannon Street Hotel, " in defiance of official threats " ; the question of Sunday labour, hit off by the figure of a portly bishop offering a tract on Sunday observance to an overladen postman ; the recent postal petition to Parliament, and cognate matters. Booth, suspended from duty, was represented by a figure on a gibbet, intended as the mental vision in the mind of the official who had ordered it ; while disposed about in odd corners of the cartoon was a " spy-glass," " the bullet," " ye sack," labelled " Post Office persuaders." It did not bear criticism, but as the work of a single night it was interesting ; and, what was more, it had some of the effect intended. The suspended leader was restored to duty the day following.

What had now come to be known as the Postal Petition to Parliament was from that moment never lost sight of by its promoters and their followers. Booth and his little staff of lieutenants worked night and day and every hour that their official duties spared to them to keep the petition before the members of the House of Commons. One result of their persistent efforts in this direction was that they had soon quite a respectable number of Parliamentary friends who promised to support the motion for inquiry when it came to be raised on the estimates. And petitioners were not content merely with verbal promises of support, for where possible they obtained an autograph letter embodying the promise, which letters were put on record in the *Postman*, the organ of the movement. Booth during this time was untiringly ubiquitous. He was everywhere, and his hand was in everything, from getting out circulars to lobbying M.P.s. He undertook the duties of the orderly as well as those of the captain.

Among the petty annoyances to which Booth had been subjected by his zealous superiors was his being made to finish up his evening duty at the furthest possible point from his home, his last delivery of letters being by the Angel, Islington, he living at Brixton. But he now succeeded in getting on a walk by which he had to deliver the Temple, where eminent counsel and the élite of the legal profession most do congregate. He did this with a motive, knowing that he might make friends among those who could command influence. He soon found an opportunity of making himself known to every legal M.P. who had chambers in this vicinity, while those who were prospective candidates for Parliamentary honours no less escaped his attention. In addition to making friends for the movement by this means, Booth and his lieutenants—Hawkins, the secretary ; Haley, a fellow-sorter, and virtually second in command ; and others—interviewed eminent divines of every denomination on the sore question of compulsory Sunday labour in the Post Office.

Such were the number of promises of support they received from M.P.s, and such were their importunities, that at last it was resolved to hold another conference in the tea-room of the House of Commons to discuss the petition and decide on some action if possible.

Earl Percy took the chair, and among those present who had pronounced favourably on the postal claims were Mr. Mundella, Mr. W. H. Smith, and Mr. Roger Eykyn. A deputation of the aggrieved postal employés had been invited to urge the points of the petition for a Select Committee of the House, and these points provided arguments for better pay and improved prospects of promotion, and the abolition of the hated compulsory Sunday labour.

The conference listened attentively and sympathetically, as conferences always do when they are composed of politicians out of office. In the present instance the tea-room conference was composed chiefly of Tories who coveted the seats on the Treasury bench then occupied by the Liberals. There could be little doubt about the honesty of the intentions of Mr. W. H. Smith, of Mr. Mundella, or of Mr. Roger Eykyn ; they each proved it in every manner possible. Each by this time was well informed on the postal grievances, having been interviewed privately on previous occasions. But at this stage of the proceedings the agitators were not quite sure how far the good intentions of these gentlemen would be carried into practical effect. For it has ever been a common practice with the party in opposition, Liberals and Tories alike, just before the eve of a General Election, to gather up all the elements of discontent throughout the country and promise support to each in turn. But at length the men, having pleaded their various points, came away fully assured that in the Tory party lay their principal hope of salvation, though they were aware that some time must elapse before their petition could come to be considered by Parliament. Their one aim now being a Select Committee of Inquiry, their Parliamentary policy became more active than ever, every by-election being assiduously watched and every candidate approached by personal interview or by letter.

At this time, between 1872 and 1874, agitation was rife among all classes of labour throughout the country, and the feeling of discontent was principally due to the cost of the necessaries of life being out of proportion to wages. This was followed by a general rise in wages to meet the increased cost of living among the working population, many employers, to their credit, voluntarily raising the wages of their employés. This circumstance very materially strengthened the postal claim for an increase on their wretched pay ; but the Post Office as the greatest employer of labour would not concede one farthing until compelled by the public and Parliament. The officials, with characteristic obstinacy, defended the state of stagnation as to wages and promotion prevailing in the Post Office. On one occasion, about this period, when the leaders of the agitation had reason to interview the Controller on the matter, that official, who considered his wisdom was none too well paid at £1,200 a year, pointed to himself and reminded them even he had to cut down his luxuries. This provoked the retort from one of the poorly-paid men that in his, the Controller's, case it simply meant a denial of luxuries, but in their case it meant a denial of the very necessaries of life for themselves and wives and families. This might have been dismissed with an official frown as only a mild impertinence ; but the Controller, a thick-set, burly, overfed man, unwittingly growled out the brutal truth in his rejoinder, " WE don't engage your wives and families ; WE only want the men ! "

But the universal rise in wages everywhere outside the Post Office could not but provide them with a further justification for continuing the agitation for an inquiry. They obtained further funds to carry on the campaign, and more public friends rallied round them. Daily the postmen were becoming more than ever objects of sympathy. Subscriptions flowed in steadily from postal bodies all over the country, and a list of these subscriptions was published in the *Beehive* newspaper, which for some time past had opened its columns to the budding literati of the movement. The postal organisation had had for some time now an official organ of its own, the *Postman ;* but as it had not the weight and authority of a public organ, circulating, as it did, among postal servants only, the assistance rendered by the *Beehive* was not inconsiderable. Edited by George Potter, who of course was in full sympathy with the agitation, its columns placed at the disposal of the postal cause were several times contributed to by Lloyd-Jones.

One postal contributor to the *Beehive*, who was the literary champion of the movement, was one of Booth's lieutenants, a postman, who wrote under the *nom de plume* of " Silverstick." The contributions of " Silverstick " betrayed no small amount of literary merit, and were eagerly looked for every issue by the men.

The hospitality of the *Beehive* was fully taken advantage of at this time (the official organ of the movement, the *Postman*, having now fizzled out), and the agitation received no small support from its powerful advocacy. George Potter, whose name will always be associated with public reform, gave the postal advocates carte-blanche in the use of his organ ; and the secretary of the postal movement, Hawkins, who was employed on it, was assisted in every possible manner to bring postal grievances to the front. Besides the *Beehive* there had been the *Postman*, which exclusively devoted itself to the advocacy of their claims, and which, to an extent, rendered valuable service by being circulated among their outside public and Parliamentary friends. It may here be mentioned that the *Postman* had been started some few years before, being originally brought out as a small printer's venture. It was started at the instigation of a postman named March, who was associated with the small printer's business in question, situated in Clerkenwell Close, and he was principally instrumental in making the *Postman* the success it afterwards became. March, the postman agitator, was the same March who, when he left the postal service built up a flourishing business as a ballad printer, supplying hawkers and street singers with topical rhymes, coupled with the publication of more innocent toybooks and fairy stories for juveniles.

The *Postman* was almost wholly contributed by the leaders of the agitation, assisted by notes and scraps of interest from various correspondents of the different branches of the service. The circulation was kept going at this time principally by Booth and the others. It was never allowed to be openly sold in the Post Office, though means were found to evade the vexatious prohibition, and the condemned publication was all the more anxiously looked for when the day of issue arrived. Booth generally directed special attention to it among the postmen. He always managed to obtain advance copies, and, knowing the most important item of news, gave the word to be passed round directly he came on duty, " Look on page so-and-so of the *Postman*." Before the duty was over it had circulated all over the General Post Office.

In connection with this organ of the movement it may be of interest to mention that for a time it was machined at the same firm as was the *Court Circular* or *Journal ;* and there was a story to the effect that these pages of the two very dissimilar publications being of equal size, on one occasion two " formes " of type got mysteriously mixed, and to the amazement of the *Postman* readers the next issue informed them, after reporting some of the private doings of the Queen and Court, that her

Majesty had graciously seen fit to order an inquiry into the postmen's grievances.

The leaders now decided on a third big public demonstration. The same preparations as before were made, bands engaged and public men written to and interviewed to get their presence on the platform. Exeter Hall was chosen this time as the place of meeting, and when the date, November 18, 1873, arrived the principal anxiety of Booth and his lieutenants was as to where they should find room on the platform for all the brilliant notabilities who had promised to attend. The chair was this time to be taken by Mr. Roger Eykyn, M.P. for Windsor, while their old champion, Sir John Bennett, was once more to appear with his well-known and ever-welcome " So here we are once again, my postman friends ! " The district contingents as before met at Finsbury Square, and with brass bands playing and colours flying they marched to St. Martin's-le-Grand, where at eight o'clock they were promptly joined by the men of the chief office. Then, defiantly striking up " Rule, Britannia," they moved on towards Fleet Street, the authorities meanwhile crowding at the windows of the General Post Office to watch the procession as it swept round into Newgate Street. On reaching Fleet Street the greatest excitement prevailed, the traffic had to be suspended, and crowds from all parts joined in the congestion. The postal procession was this time preceded by two red mailvans, which, with the postmen in uniform, gave it a tone of local colour. The band, during its slow progress towards the place of meeting, improved the shining hour with " The Postman's Knock " and " Work, Boys, Work, and be Contented," a musical sarcasm in the circumstances much appreciated. Exeter Hall was not large enough to hold the immense throng who sought admission, and an overflow meeting had to be held in a side street. Exeter Hall platform presented a distinguished gathering of public men supporting the chair, which was filled by Mr. Roger Eykyn, the member for Windsor. Among those who crowded the platform was the midget-like figure of the redoubtable George Odger, president of the London Trades Council, who had brought with him a deputation of trade unionists. There were a large number of members of Parliament, and the principal labour leaders of the day, notably Mr. George Howell, who had already endeared himself to the postal servants by doing an enormous amount of work for them one way and another. The meeting was addressed by Sir Antonio Brady and several distinguished M.P.s, among the number being W. Williams, M.P., W. Fowler, M.P., and A. Stavely Hill, M.P.

It was at this meeting that Booth determined to test once and for all the right of postal servants to speak in public. He and one or two others spoke, and Booth took means to get their utterances reported among the speakers.

The result was as he had anticipated. He and the others were carpeted before the Controller. That official said that his attention having been drawn to the reported meeting, it was his duty to call on them to explain. There was nothing very objectionable in the language they were reported to have used, but the fact of speaking at all sufficiently compromised them as Government servants. Booth and his associates were called on for written statements, and they each defended their conduct on the ground that they were exercising a common citizen right in asking Parliament and the public for a redress of those grievances which the Department had refused to consider.

Within a few days they were again called up to listen to a severe reprimand from the Postmaster-General. There was some protest to a few public men, and Mr. Roger Eykyn interviewed the Permanent Secretary on behalf of the men ; but there the matter ended.

The men themselves, however, feeling that their speeches had been so studiously modest and moderate, could not but regard such notice being taken by the authorities as both arbitrary and unconstitutional, and opposed to the spirit of English liberty.

Based on the resolutions passed at this public meeting, a monster petition to the House of Commons was prepared on behalf of the letter-carriers, sorters, porters' assistants, rural messengers, and others employed in the minor establishment of the Post Office throughout London, suburban, provincial, and rural districts. Having regard to the increased cost of living and the rise in the value of most classes of labour, they submitted that the time had arrived when such an addition should be made to their pay as would constitute a more adequate remuneration for their arduous and responsible duties. A Commission of Inquiry was also strongly asked for to receive evidence on the questions of promotion, Sunday labour, and general grievances not specified but known to exist.

One of the principal planks in the platform of the postal movement at this time was the abolition of compulsory Sunday labour for letter-carriers ; and in furtherance of this end Booth and the other agitators interviewed the most eminent divines and religious leaders of the day. Among those whose assistance was sought to procure a free Sunday for postal workers was Cardinal Manning. A deputation of Booth and two other postmen waited on his Eminence at his residence. He was politic in discussing the question ; he sympathised with them in their laudable efforts to relieve Sunday labour ; but he hesitated to pledge himself to assist them ; he must have time to consider the matter. The deputation withdrew inspired with very little hope from their diplomatic reception. The truth was Cardinal Manning hesitated to assist in any way in hampering the Government while Mr. Gladstone was tackling the Catholic University question. They interviewed Dr. Parker at the City Temple, with a vague sort of hope that he might denounce postal Sunday labour from his own pulpit. But Dr. Parker did not prove the rigid Calvinistic Sabbatarian they imagined ; he thought that certain forms of labour were very necessary even on the Lord's Day, and it was desirable to receive letters from distant friends and relations at least once on Sunday. Even Professor Fawcett and Mr. Charles Bradlaugh both concurred in thinking this a weak plank in their platform, and tried to induce Booth to abandon it for a time at least. But Booth would not be dictated to even by two such men as these, and expressed his determination to try to carry it through in spite of all opposition.

This question of compulsory Sunday labour, as it affected the rural letter-carriers especially, was a very sore one. Some lines of verse written by one of their number were about this time freely circulated. The few lines selected will show that they possessed tolerable poetic merit.

THE POSTMAN'S DAY OF REST

We are toiling, we are toiling on each sunny Sabbath morn,
We are toiling when the dewdrops sparkle on the white-robed thorn,
We are toiling when the sons of toil have found a Sabbath blest ;
But for us no Sabbath dawning, no holy day of rest.

We are toiling thro' the dewy fields ere peeps the eye of morn,
When the mist on pastures hanging makes the aspect so forlorn ;
Thro' mud and mist, and mire, and rain we pick our toilsome way,
While fellow-men are warmly housed upon the Sabbath day.

If in the annals of the world your names unrivalled stand,
Then cleanse so foul a blot from the escutcheon of our land,
And a thousand hands shall cease from toil, and find a day of rest,
And the God of heaven shall bless you, as He has our country blest.

F. K. (*Letter-carrier*).

[An appeal from the rural letter-carriers of England, who are employed delivering letters, circulars, and newspapers on the Sabbath day.]

While this question of Sunday labour was being pushed to the front, Mr. Joseph Chamberlain, M.P., desiring to become Mayor of Birmingham, was approached by Booth, who promised him the whole postal support of the town if Mr. Chamberlain would in return direct his influence against Sunday duty imposed on postal officials. The promise was given ; Mr. Chamberlain became mayor, but he now found it would be inexpedient in the commercial interests of Birmingham especially to abolish Sunday labour in the Post Office.

Although the right to exercise the one privilege accorded to every British citizen, that of presenting a petition to Parliament, had up to now been their mainstay and the bulwark of their personal protection, the agitators constantly found that they were the objects of departmental attention. They had been particularly careful, for the success of their movement, to proceed along thoroughly constitutional lines, and nothing could have tempted Booth and his associates to depart from this. As has already been shown, the disappointment induced by the protracted methods of the Government, and the antagonism of the officials to the agitation, was such that it might easily have risen to the point of rebellion had the leaders been so inclined ; but they were not ; and as it was, they had frequently to exercise to the utmost their

restraining influence on the men. It was scarcely to be
supposed that the authorities would give them any credit for
this, and as was only natural, perhaps the leaders were held
wholly responsible for the strained relations between the
Department and its subordinates. Booth and his lieutenants
therefore had no mercy to expect from their superiors should
they commit themselves. The very surveillance, the constant
spying, and every manner of testing and trap-laying to which
Booth especially was subjected, would have caused any other
man with less fortitude and with a more sensitive temperament
to have given up long before he did. But for all the
insidious influences to which he was exposed Booth never
showed the least concern, but went about his work as though
there were never an official to dog his footsteps even to his own
door, nor a band of the permanent officials anxiously waiting
and watching for the moment when they might reasonably
dismiss him with humiliation and degradation. In the official
mind in those days, whoever lent themselves to agitation within
the walls of a Government office could be little better than
desperadoes and conspirators, disloyal alike to the service and
the public. It was not to be wondered at, then, that they were
regarded as playing a desperate game, which, to go no further,
even as yet almost brought them within the clutches of the law.
The agitators were not blind to the position in which they
stood, nor ignorant altogether of the desire of the authorities
to encompass their destruction. Already Booth had been
most unpleasantly made aware that his private correspondence
had been tampered with in its passage through the post ; that,
before reaching his hands, the letters addressed to him had
been watched for and " Grahamed "—to use an expression
which signified the secret methods of opening and overhauling
suspected people's correspondence then, as a survival of the
" Espionage Room," more or less in vogue in the Confidential
Inquiry Branch of the General Post Office. While the Department had such a piece of machinery as this at its disposal, it
was not going to confine its use to such men as Mazzini and
political personages disagreeable to the Government, and allow
the postman Booth, and others of its own household, to
escape. He had had cause to suspect that his letters,
addressed to those who were assisting the agitation, had been

intercepted, and their purport conveyed to the authorities who had ordered it. To evade the prying curiosity of official detectives and the " Grahaming " process, the letters exchanged through the post between the leaders, and touching on questions of policy, were thereafter directed to a fictitious " Mrs. Harvey " at various convenient addresses.

Nor did Departmental antagonism, both open and concealed, to the principle of combination rest here. That the ringleaders of the agitation had all along pursued purely legitimate and constitutional methods to obtain redress for their grievances, affording so few technical loopholes through which they might be made answerable, was almost sufficient in itself to cause the Department to look on them as mischievous breeders of wholesale contumacy and discontent, and agitators of the most dangerous description. They might have got rid of them one by one " on suspicion "—a process of dismissal which carried with it an implication of common dishonesty—only that the men had now too many powerful advocates, and, moreover, there might have been an outcry in the press against such an obviously hollow pretext. They were so far saved from such a fate as had befallen others of a lesser calibre. But they had, almost unknown to themselves, narrowly escaped losing their personal liberty for the part they had taken. It was only owing to an accidental hint dropped by an eminent member of the legal profession and a member of Parliament, who at the time was friendly disposed towards Booth and his movement, that the whole of them were not made the subjects of a Government prosecution under the odious law of conspiracy. Booth ferreted the matter out, and learnt that the brief was already prepared. The postal leader was given the comforting assurance that he stood to get two years imprisonment, and the others nine or six months apiece, and that the writs would probably be issued within a few days. Such, at least, was the information gathered, and circumstances made it extremely probable that the Government contemplated delivering one blow which would not only rid the postal service of a number of powerful agitators, but completely demoralise and disorganise their followers for years to come. If such was the motive, then the Government was checkmated in one simple move. Booth at the time was on the Temple " delivery," and it was due to this fact principally that he obtained the interest and assistance of several eminent counsel who had either already obtained or had an eye on a seat in the House. After piecing his information together, so as to be morally certain that some such *coup* was intended, Booth the same day hastily summoned a meeting of the executive of the postal organisation, and before night handbills were in circulation advertising the fact that Booth was now the sole official representative of the movement. Next day he learnt the contemplated prosecution was to be abandoned, for the sufficient reason that the Law of Conspiracy could not very well be made to apply to one man only, it taking three at least to become conspirators. After Booth's adroit manœuvre they could not with decency proceed against the agitators by legal action, and so nothing more was heard of the matter.

CHAPTER VIII

A TEST OF " THE LABOUR MARKET "—THE UGLY DUCKLING OF
TRADES UNIONISM—MR. GEO. HOWELL'S ASSISTANCE—FURTHER
DEMONSTRATIONS—THE DEPARTURE OF BOOTH.

NOTWITHSTANDING the numerous strong expressions of public
opinion evoked by the recent meeting of November 18,
1873, the Government showed no disposition to meet the
moderate demands put forward in the petition to the House
of Commons. The authorities particularly seemed bent on
resisting the claims of the men. Acting on instructions
contained in a Treasury Minute issued under the previous
Government, they extensively advertised for persons to fill
the places of the letter-carriers. Yet, as a matter of fact,
there were no such vacancies as alleged in the public adver-
tisements, unless the Department contemplated dismissing the
existing staff wholesale. The ostensible reason given was an
experiment to " test the labour market." There was a rush
of applications, but there was a cruel insincerity in the whole
business. A large proportion failed to pass the medical
examination, while others who had passed were so disgusted
at the neglect they received, and the time they were kept
waiting in suspense, that they refused to attend for final
approval. There had been something like twelve hundred
applicants originally, and of these only nineteen were finally
passed as suitable for the situations. The fact spoke for
itself, and confirmed the opinion, generally entertained, that
it was nothing more than an attempt to damage and discredit
the case of the men, and intimidate and discourage the
" agitators."

If this experiment to " test the labour market " did nothing
more, it tended to promote still further the feeling of misunderstanding in the minds of the general public, and assisted
to obscure the issue.

However, the aggrieved postal employés, as represented on the London Trades Council, were accredited trade unionists. The trade unionists of the Metropolis, little as they understood their case, were compelled to take them into partnership.

By this time the efforts made by the postal employés had attracted considerable attention from every quarter ; but trade unionists generally were almost as much at a loss to understand the precise nature of their claims as were most people, and there was much need for information. From the press reports and allusions to the matter in Parliament from time to time, a vague notion existed that postal employés were badly paid, and wanted better treatment, but little was known as to the real objects sought, or of the means by which they were to be obtained. The peculiarity of their position, the fact of their not being handicraftsmen in the generally-accepted sense of the term, caused their movement still to be looked on as the ugly duckling of trades unionism, and many were against allowing its claim for kinship. It was principally due to Mr. George Howell that this feeling of misunderstanding was removed. The condition of the postal employés and their battle for liberty was for the first time brought prominently before the trades unionists of the country at the Sheffield Trades Union Congress, January, 1874. Mr. George Howell was secretary of the " Trades Parliamentary Committee," and as a special delegate of the Postal Society, he read a paper which most clearly and convincingly showed that postal servants were in need of sympathy and moral assistance from the organised labour of the country. To the majority present it came as a revelation that those in Government employ were so restricted in the matter of civil rights. In thanking Mr. Howell for his valuable paper, they desired to express their sympathy with the movement of the postal employés for increased pay, better regulation of the hours of labour, the abolition of Sunday work, and a just system of promotion. The Congress recommended their cause to the trades societies of the United Kingdom, as well worthy of support.

The first General Election of 1873-4 had come and gone, and Mr. Gladstone found himself again returned to power, but with a majority of only forty. He immediately dissolved the House, and forthwith appealed to the country a second time.

The country was again in the throes of a General Election, and towards the fag-end, and before the result was certain for either party, another meeting of postal employés was called again at Exeter Hall. Meantime a written letter was sent by the Society's secretary, Hawkins, to every Parliamentary candidate, asking for support in their demands. Nearly one hundred of those who gave their pledge were eventually returned to the new Parliament.

When it became known that preparations were in progress for holding another meeting, the authorities issued an official edict threatening with the penalties of insubordination any one found attending. They liked the Cannon Street Hotel meeting but little for the unenviable publicity it gave the Department, but the prospect of the Exeter Hall meeting they liked still less. The meeting was again " proclaimed," but a full two thousand attended, notwithstanding. Again there was music and banners, and a procession through the streets, and two thousand or more filled the vast space confronting the historic platform. Mr. Mundella took the chair on this occasion, and was supported by several Tory M.P.s just returned triumphant from the poll. There were among them Mr. Ritchie, Mr. William Forsyth, Captain Bedford Pim, and Sir Charles Dilke. There were a number of eminent clergymen, among them the Rev. John Kennedy, D.D., and the Rev. Hugh Allen. The latter reverend gentleman generally prefaced his remarks at postal meetings with the words, " Those who distribute the correspondence of the country, distribute the wealth of the country, and their pay should be in proportion to their responsibility." This agreeable sentiment was at once appropriated as the motto of the movement, and it figured on the stationery, and more than once on their banner. There was also the Rev. John Murphy, well known at the time as the " Bishop of Lambeth," who had assisted right through the struggle till now. Altogether the platform presented a gathering of eminent men of almost every degree.

Mr. Mundella, as chairman, was just about finishing his address when the herculean form of Charles Bradlaugh was seen hurriedly pressing his way on to the platform. As the heretic agitator took his seat not far from that region of the platform sanctified by the presence of so many clerics of different denominations, there were some signs of dissent among some of the postmen in front. It almost immediately subsided with a wave of the chairman's hand ; and at Booth's request Mr. Bradlaugh was given fourth place among the speakers, as he had to leave early. The several other speakers spoke, and it came to Bradlaugh's turn. But immediately his huge form rose from the chair there was a hostile demonstration which gradually swelled in volume. Mr. Mundella requested the postal leader, who was sitting beside him, not to insist on Mr. Bradlaugh being heard. Charles Bradlaugh himself, always considerate in the interests of his friends and those whom he wanted to assist, thought his speaking might mar the success of the meeting, and made as if to leave the platform ; the " booing " and groaning continuing meanwhile. They had not till now been ashamed to listen to and take counsel from the freethought lecturer " Iconoclast," and many who now groaned at him had cheered him to the echo when it suited them. The hostile demonstration was probably only their way of paying a compliment to their reverend friends on the platform, though there were one or two, at least, among them who had come to assist in this good cause who would not have hesitated there and then to burn the heretic amidst a bonfire of his own godless pamphlets kindled with the light of sacred truth.

"You see, Mr. Booth, they will not hear him," said Mr. Mundella, rather testily. But " Bulldog " Booth, as he was now known among his intimates, was not to be beaten. " Then dissolve the meeting, sir," said he stoutly. " But they will hear him."

The chairman rose and succeeded in calming the storm ; and Mr. Bradlaugh essayed to speak. He had always been an active sympathiser with the postmen and the postal movement. It was not the first time he had stood before them. Once on his feet with a determination to make himself heard, he would not be denied. A towering figure, a leonine head, and huge, pale, clean-shaven face, with its mastiff's mouth, he looked as ugly as Mirabeau, and as tremendous. Yet there

G

was the charm of simplicity and a conviction of earnestness in his utterance, which made them feel ashamed at his reception. He spoke for four minutes, and adjured them to maintain the principle of combination ; to stick together, to exercise their rights as citizens, and to use their votes, and to support those who supported them. When he had finished, Bradlaugh received probably as loud an ovation as any who followed. A number of the clerical friends of the postmen naturally took the line of denunciation against forced Sunday labour, and their utterances for the most part were curiously reminiscent of those speeches on the self-same topic on that same platform twenty-five years before.

Among other eminent labour leaders and Radical politicians of the day there figured George Howell, who never failed the postmen in their need, and who had interviewed perhaps more members of Parliament and the heads of the Government than any other public man ; for at this period it had particularly fallen to Mr. Howell's lot to represent their case in this manner.

Shortly after this great Exeter Hall meeting the society published a balance-sheet, which clearly showed the enormous amount of work involved in the previous two years' crusade. During the two years of agitation, numerous meetings, both reported and unreported, had been held ; they had carried the war into almost every part of the kingdom, they had interviewed public men innumerable, prepared and got signed three monster petitions to Parliament, and attained to the dignity and importance of occupying the time and attention of the House of Commons more than once. The general correspondence of the society during the two years of its existence had involved the writing of no less than 2,546 letters ; while to the public press communications to the tune of nearly 2,000 had been sent out. But, altogether, during the two years nearly 14,000 communications were addressed to Parliamentary candidates, M.P.s, public men, and others. Truly, the Post Office had been made to direct its hand against itself. Among the list of subscribers were the names of several public men, including Canon Liddon and Sir Charles Dilke.

The organisation of combined postal servants was now being perfected in various ways. Interviewing members of Parliament, both privately and at the House, was now almost of daily occurrence ; and Booth and the various others were on terms of intimacy with most of the prominent men of the day.

It was this time a Conservative Government in power, and those members who wished to show a desire to redeem their promises convened a conference of the known Parliamentary friends to the postal cause. For the Exeter Hall meetings had had a marked effect on the press and the public. The conference was therefore called at the Westminster Palace Hotel, a stone's throw from the House itself. It was to be quite public, and reporters admitted. A deputation of the aggrieved men attended to urge their case once more. Mr. Roebuck was this time in the chair ; and Mr. Staveley Hill and numerous other influential and well-known M.P.s formed the self-appointed jury. Booth once more went over the old ground of their grievances ; and Haley, another postal agitator, also gave an able exposition of their simple claims, which appeared to impress them favourably. The immediate result of the conference was that Mr. Roebuck, on behalf of his colleagues, promised to do an indefinite something as soon as found convenient.

They so far redeemed their pledge and showed their confidence in the justice of the postal claims as to privately urge the Government to take up the matter. For a month or so there was a superficial quietude among the discontented men. There were no meetings, but the postmen and the letter-sorters were subscribing to the general fund. There was no further interference on the part of the officials, probably from the fact that they were now beginning to recognise that the movement was too strong, and rendered stronger by Press sympathy and public support. Eventually Mr. Roebuck—" Tear 'em," as he was called in reference to his pugnacity in the House—brought up the matter of the postal case for inquiry on the Estimates. Booth, Haley, and the rest of the leaders of the agitation were found a place under the gallery, by the side of Sir John Tilly, the secretary, and Mr. Scudamore ; for in some things the House is no respecter of persons. The debate was eminently interesting, and brought out all the points of the postal case in a marked degree.

The reply of the Government was unfavourable ; and the argument, which has done duty so many times since, that there was really no just cause for complaint, was then used for the first time, and set an easy precedent, which nearly all succeeding Postmasters-General faithfully followed.

After the debate the leaders of the agitation crowded round the members in the lobby, Roebuck particularly was besieged by the disappointed men ; but he shook himself free of them with the air of a man who had done his duty, and was determined to court failure no further. " Tear 'em " Roebuck was evidently chagrined and as annoyed as his clients, and he turned on them almost with a snarl. " You see, I can do no more ; the Government won't interfere," said he, and strutted away. The Government had left them to their fate ; but pressure was privately brought to bear on Lord John Manners, who was now Postmaster-General. The refusal of the Government to interfere on behalf of the oppressed and aggrieved postal employés after all the promises of the Tory party, and after all the patronage extended to them publicly, resulted in such a feeling of resentment and disappointment among all classes of the service, that Booth, the leader, had the utmost difficulty in holding his followers in check. There was, indeed, one abortive attempt at a strike among the Hull postmen, and the spark might have ignited the whole had Booth and his associates given encouragement to it. It wanted but a breath from the agitators at this moment to fan the whole into a blaze.

Booth during this time never lost heart ; he was as indefatigable as ever ; scarcely a day passed but what he interviewed somebody or was himself interviewed. He had carried the art of interviewing to such an extent that he several times personated the secretary of the postal movement, Hawkins, for the purpose of getting editors and pressmen to say a word or two in behalf of the baffled, but as yet not defeated, agitation. By personating his own secretary in getting himself interviewed he thus evaded the official rule which forbade any postal servant to communicate with the press, and which there is little doubt would have been mercilessly enforced against anyone in the service caught doing it too openly. But however little they had to expect from the permanent officials, they felt that with a Postmaster-General as representative of the party from which only recently they had received so much sympathy and patronage, active hostility would not be allowed to be carried too far. Moreover, they felt pretty safe in conjecturing that, come what may, what the law officers of the late administration had hesitated to carry to a completion would not in a hurry be resorted to under the new Government of the party which included so many tried and pledged friends of postal reform. True, the Conservative Government, which the postal vote had in some measure helped to bring back to power, had so far disappointed them in not at once taking up their case as they were led to believe it would. But they were aware that their grievances were still occupying the attention of a large number of the members on both sides of the House, and that a large amount of influence was being brought to bear on the Postmaster-General. From Lord John Manneis there was still something to be hoped for. And this hope was sustained by the plausible rumour that the Government's refusal to inquire into their grievances was only a diplomatic way of empowering the Postmaster-General to do all that might be found to be necessary towards ameliorating the conditions of the service over which he had been put to rule. Yet the cloven hoof peeped out in an unexpected manner, and sooner than was to be looked for.

Lord John Manners, so long as he was in opposition, had not declined to be counted among the Tory supporters of Booth and the postal agitation, he having replied in favourable terms to letters and circulars soliciting his support towards obtaining the asked-for inquiry. There is perhaps always some allowance to be made for one newly taking office, and inconsistency is to an extent allowable, if not to be looked for. But it came as a surprise and something of a shock to Booth especially to learn that the new Postmaster-General, resisting all overtures from those of his own party, was about to set his face uncompromisingly against their claims and against the representatives who might urge them. Certainly, on the face of it, it seemed a wonderfully gracious act in a Postmaster-General to consent to receive a deputation of the men for the purpose of hearing once more from their own lips the story of their grievances he was already so well acquainted with. An application for an interview had been sent forward, in itself perhaps a piece of audacity almost unheard of, and to the surprise of the men themselves it was intimated that the interview would be granted. It was granted, but only with the condition that Booth should not be present. By the time that this was announced Booth had got over his first surprise, and was quite prepared for the intended snub, but scarcely for the unjustifiable insult which followed. It had been previously arranged that he should lead the deputation, but it was now officially conveyed to him that the Postmaster-General, while willing to see a deputation of the letter-carriers and sorters, must refuse to receive Booth " on account of his official bad character." There was a feeling among the force that if the Postmaster-General would not see the leader the deputation ought not to go forward, but Booth put himself out of the question, and advised them to meet the head of the Department and to obtain what advantage was possible. It was therefore decided to do so ; but the undeserved insult, though inflicted on the man, was none the less felt to be aimed at the principle of combination, and their hopes were overshadowed with the suspicion that the interview was granted mainly for the purpose of better marking the agitators for future reference. The Postmaster-General's treatment of Booth was scarcely likely to reassure them or to maintain their confidence in his fairmindedness. Throughout the agitation Booth had been careful not to run foul of his superiors on official matters, and his official character had been good enough to please Lord John Manners and his party before the last General Election.

The deputation to the Postmaster-General was memorable if only from the fact that this was the very first occasion the public head of the Department had ever consented to receive representatives of the working staff. It looked like a concession, and as such would read well in the Tory press especially. But the men in their hearts were prepared for the disappointment which was to follow, and anticipated that it was the Postmaster-General himself who intended to get the most out of the interview.

A few weeks afterwards, about the beginning of August, a scheme was announced. But it proved to be nothing more than an inflated bubble which, when pricked, contained only a few paltry advantages for the letter-carriers. The advantages were small enough in all conscience, amounting to some small increase in pay and benefits as to stripes for good conduct.

But small as were the benefits, the letter-carriers so appreciated them that they decided to continue the agitation no further, and Booth, not without reluctance, resigned his position as the postmen's leader. The only return Booth got for all the labour and all the responsibility he had taken on himself was that he was left with a debt of £35—a no insignificant amount to one in his position. By the aid of one of his friends he was able to obtain a loan, and with a characteristic independence paid it off without troubling the men with his private affairs. It was not that his followers proved ungrateful ; they simply did not know the condition in which the agitation had stranded him ; and perhaps he was too proud to inform them. There was the usual effort to testimonialise him and those who had most assisted him ; but the thing was badly managed. An illuminated address was already prepared for Booth, and it was shown to him at his private house. There was also a purse of money subscribed, which would have proved a little fortune to him in his predicament, but there was some little sordid dispute among one or two who fancied themselves entitled to an equal share. This treatment so aroused the contempt of Booth that, seizing the illuminated address, which he regarded as more than conventionally insincere in the circumstances, he passionately tore it to fragments before them and flung it into their faces, ordering them to leave the house immediately. He refused to touch a penny-piece of the money subscribed ; but instead set himself steadily to work to pay off the debts he had incurred on account of his connection with the agitation. So far, if the Department wanted its revenge, it had it now.

Booth having freed himself from debt, shortly afterwards, owing to failing health, applied for and obtained the small pension of about eight shillings a week he was entitled to. And so departed one of the most persistent as well as one of the most courageously consistent agitators the Post Office or any other Government Department has ever been troubled with. Booth's career as an agitator had been a brief one, but it had been as brilliant as it was brief. And perhaps, after all, there was some truth in his claim that he had largely assisted to overturn two Governments and put in another.

CHAPTER IX

FORCED LABOUR—A GENERAL POST OFFICE RIOT—A POSTAL
POET—THE WANING OF THE MOVEMENT—THE PUBLICATION
OF A MEMORIAL—WHOLESALE DISMISSALS.

AT this time, and for long previous, there was no definite
eight-hour day officially recognised for the working staff at the
General Post Office. That was a privilege as yet definitely
enjoyed by few beside the clerical establishment. If there
was any official rule regulating and limiting the working
hours of the rank and file, that rule was vitiated by the
practice of the supervising officials. The men were subjected to nothing less than forced labour ; the hours which
should have been given up to sleep and leisure were
extorted from them ; and forced contributions of their
well-earned liberty were remorselessly levied upon them.
They were liable to be summoned back for duty at any
time during their intervals of rest. There was no assured
time for rest or proper sleep. They were compelled to
dispose of incoming foreign mails without remuneration
of any kind. As the Department had decided that such
mail matter must be disposed of without cost, at first
the men had to rotate for this purpose, and it generally
fell to their turn about once a month. In former days
this practice may not have constituted a great hardship ;
but when, owing to the increased and improved means of
transit across seas, foreign mails arrived several times a
week, it became a very real grievance. American mails
then arrived only about once a month, instead of daily
as at present ; but there were other mails to be taken account
of, and their arrival and treatment were often delayed for
disposal by this cheap method. If the practice had stopped

at the monthly summons, or an extra attendance for every man every week or so, the strong discontent arising from it might have been averted. But the principle of extorting from men already too poorly paid and harshly treated, this disgraceful poll-tax in time was still further extended after a while.

The occasion which principally provided the officials with an excuse for imposing on the force still further was the introduction of the halfpenny post ; and when this came to be recognised by the public as a boon, the men became the victims and the sufferers. The reduced rate for newspapers and circulars was soon taken advantage of by company promoters very largely. The notorious promoter, Baron Grant, who did everything on a colossal scale, sent in prospectuses, referring to the Emma Gold Mine, at the rate of half a million at a time, completely swamping the Newspaper Branch, where such correspondence was disposed of.

The authorities' only method of meeting the emergencies which so frequently arose was to get the extra work of the public (which already meant so much more profit to swell the revenue) done by forcing the over-burdened and under-paid men to do it for nothing in the time which should otherwise have been theirs. The method of forced labour, was not only thought proper but persisted in by the officials of an English Government department. Whatever excuses, if any, that might be made for rapacious East End sweaters, could not be made for the profit-minting monopoly of St. Martin's-le-Grand and those who guided its machinery.

The men protested again and again, but without avail. Refusal to comply with this form of tyranny or worse, imposed in the name of duty and discipline, would have meant rank insubordination, punishable by dismissal without character. Probably their protests never got beyond the branch superintendent to whom they complained ; but the authorities ought not to have been wholly blind to the men's treatment. If there was no Treasury grant of money to cover the cost of extra duty of this nature, as was pointed out, then the parsimony and meanness of the authorities were only to be excused by their utter laziness in not endeavouring to get such a demand met honestly and fairly.

The grievance speedily attained to the dimensions and importance of a grave scandal. Yet the authorities seemed determined that, kick and struggle against the pricks as the men might, they should submit to it. The men, grown weary of complaining against the injustice, and losing all faith in the fairness of those over them, were equally resolved that it should not continue much longer without one last vigorous protest from them. The climax of indignation was reached one morning in March, 1873, when the whole of the force were ordered, as usual, to stay behind their time. There were mails above and below in the Newspaper and Letter Branches, and tons of circulars waiting in reserve. The men rushed to their kitchens, and securing their articles of clothing, made for the principal exit leading to liberty and the Post Office yard. This they found closed and bolted against them and guarded by a posse of overseers, the official doorkeeper, and numerous amateur policemen—constables disguised as sorters. They were sternly ordered back to their duties ; but by this time, even if they would, they could not turn for those now pressing behind and thronging the lobby. The officials appeared on the scene and exhorted them not to disobey orders ; but the murmurs that arose convinced them that at last the mutiny had come. The men demanded the door to be opened and the removal of the constables. They took it as an added insult that such Siberian methods should be put into force against them, for whatever their humble position in the public service, yet still they bore the name of freeborn Englishmen. The officials, convinced they were acting within their right, refused, and repeatedly ordered them to fall back. For half an hour or more the men, nearly a thousand strong by this time, endured it ; the heat was oppressive in the closely packed crowd, and the stubborn obstinacy of the men guarding the door was making the crowd excited. There were cries of execration, and from the rear came a hurricane of balls of twine with sticks of sealing-wax. The officials retreated to safer quarters, leaving the men guarding the door to carry out their duty or die. The lobby, which was a narrow neck of space leading from the Letter Branch to the coveted doorway, was becoming like the Black Hole of Calcutta, and many men were on the point of fainting. The doorkeepers were pale but determined, and stood with their backs to the closed exit. The situation was as serious to them as to the mutineers themselves. With the men the injustice of the official instruction to stay at their duties without pay might be sufficient to palliate their disobedience to it, especially when there were nearly a thousand of them to answer for it. But with those at the door it was slightly different ; they had to do their duty, and they looked like men who were determined to sell their lives dearly if it came to it, though it is probable that if they could have trusted each other the bolt would have been quietly drawn. To those in the thick of the swaying, sweltering crowd of angry and excited men the heat was getting unbearable. Some one, or several at once, suggested rushing the doors ; but to break down the barrier seemed to spell mutiny of the worst kind, and numbers of the front ranks held back at the prospect of being afterwards named as ringleaders. The responsible officials retired to a distance and watched with the grim satisfaction of schoolmasters who were " keeping in " a refractory class of school-children. The realisation that they were being kept prisoners at the behest of one or two of their superiors was intensifying the impatience and the excitement of the sweltering crowd behind, and impatience soon grew to desperation. The air was repeatedly filled with groans and hisses, and the storm of groans was presently turned by some one facetiously striking up a bar of " Britons never, never shall be slaves ! " That was enough, for the men behind especially. They remembered they were Britons. A square of infantry with fixed bayonets could not have stopped them now. They were solidly packed several hundreds strong in one long stream, fed every moment by reinforcements as they gained courage to leave the sorting-tables. Fortunately some one by an adroit manœuvre had turned a line of heavy mail-trucks and trolleys, placed there either carelessly or purposely, or the result might have been disastrous to those in front. Menaces and shouts were directed towards the men who barred their way ; but neither threats nor appeals would move them, and it seemed they would be flattened against the door they were so zealously guarding, for those in front could no longer hold against the mighty pressure of the hundreds behind. The crowd heaved and rocked like a huge billow.

There were shouts and groans, and some were real, a tremendous scuffle, a sound like the cracking of ribs, a crash of woodwork, a shattering of glass accompanied with a louder yell ; the doors burst from their fastenings, and the hot, perspiring stream of angry men vomited itself into the open air and the daylight. Then the wild mob's several hundred feet scattered down the steps into the Post Office yard, and the men who had broken their red-tape bonds to assert the liberty of the person again burst into such a roar of triumph that a jaded horse on the cab-rank outside in Aldersgate Street took fright and bolted. The untoward commotion stopped the stream of traffic in St. Martin's-le-Grand, and crowds assembled outside the Post Office railings while the police hurried to the scene from every by-turning. The general traffic was disordered for half an hour, till the last remnant of the imprisoned men issued from the gates.

As the result of the scrimmage several men got scratches and bruises, and there were one or two bloody noses. It ought to have been as much a matter for congratulation for the authorities as for the men that nothing more disastrous occurred. But the officials chose not to see it in that light, and several who had been grabbed in the rush by the door-keepers were haled up like escaped convicts before the presiding superintendent and others of the smaller authorities to answer for the conduct of the whole. Six men were there and then suspended from duty without pay for an indefinite period, and with the prospect of dismissal before them.

It was only to be expected that the public would take an exaggerated view of the incident ; and the idea gained credence that a veritable riot had taken place inside the Post Office. Some, indeed, thought it meant a postal strike. The evening paper came out with an account of the " Riot at the General Post Office," which, it need hardly be said, was scarcely accurate.

The humour of the situation was skilfully hit off a day or two later by a parody on " The Light Brigade," by one Tom Glamorgan, already recognised as a postal poet. It was said that the verses were scribbled hurriedly on his shirt-cuff during moments snatched from the duty the same evening ; and being printed next day were sold for a penny a copy amongst the sorters and postmen and others, the small sum realised being sent to some charity. The actual verses perhaps would interest but few, but the printed paragraph introducing the lines epitomised the whole incident. The print formed one of a short series of " Postal Fly-sheets," and the paragraph in question read as follows :—

" INSUBORDINATION AT THE GENERAL POST OFFICE.

" On Monday morning, 31st March, 1873, a large quantity of ' Circulars,' the postage of which amounted to some hundreds of pounds, were required to be sorted and despatched to their various destinations. The men, assistants, and boys worked well till 9 a.m. (having been on duty since 4-30 a.m.), at which time the juniors struck work and congregated around the lobby door to depart ; several of the older officers were stationed there to prevent their exit, the ' Acting Superintendent ' on duty declaring they should not go till all the work was done. The assistants and boys replied to this by tremendous shouting, hooting, hissing, groaning, and pushing, declaring they would do no more that morning unless paid extra for it. At length some of the ringleaders, assisted by the crowd around, continued to push against the officers guarding the doors, striking at one of the ' overseers '— *breaking loose from all order, discipline, and control. . . ."*

The six sorters, innocent or guilty of the charge against them, were still suspended, but the resentment of the authorities did not stop here. One of the official doorkeepers was pounced on to account for his not successfully resisting the several hundred determined men who so forcibly objected to be made prisoners of. The doorkeeper was rather a small man, and built more on the lines of a jockey than of a gladiator. But it was useless to urge such a fact on the official mind bent on inflicting condign punishment. So the poor little man was pronounced guilty of failing to perform a feat which would have baffled Hercules. He was in consequence reduced to an inferior position, entailing greater responsibility ; and, failing to become competent in a duty which was entirely new to him, he was incontinently bundled out of the service on a starvation pension of six shillings a week. He did not long survive his defeat, but died a little while afterwards of sheer broken heart.

That the so-called riot at the General Post Office was only one of the straws which showed the way of the wind may be taken for granted. Whether it could have occurred in a better-regulated service is perhaps doubtful.

The scheme which with its small benefits had given so much satisfaction to the letter-carriers as to induce them, if not to remain satisfied, to abandon agitation for the present, had caused corresponding dissatisfaction to the letter-sorters. The only benefit derived from the Manners scheme, if it could be called such, was the increase of sixpence a year in the increment. The keenest disappointment prevailed, and a movement was already afoot to find expression for that disappointment in a memorial to the author, Lord John Manners. Yet, though the feelings of the men were scarcely concealed, it had been officially represented to the Postmaster-General and the Controller that the demands of the sorting force were now fully satisfied, and that the men themselves acknowledged it. This official misrepresentation was followed by an anonymous note being pinned on the notice-board in the retiring-room. It was to the effect : " Who thus misrepresents the spirit of the Inland Branch ? As mild a mannered man as ever scuttled ship or cut a throat." The note was detached and taken to the superintendent ; and one of the men, Glamorgan, who had already distinguished himself in the line of a satirical verse-maker, was suspended for some days on suspicion of being its author.

At the end of November, 1874, the dissatisfied sorters drew up a respectful and moderate memorial to the Postmaster-General, pointing out that " whilst grateful for the recent improvements made in . . . pay and prospects of promotion, they were yet unable to accept so small a revision as a satisfactory settlement of their claims to increased remuneration," and giving some very valid reasons for a reconsideration of their case. The petition was signed by 140 men as representative of the entire sorting force, and presented through their immediate superior. To the startling surprise of everyone, a copy of this memorial appeared in the *Times* and other morning papers the next day, and from that moment the most discerning could see that it was doomed to failure from the fact of being published in the press before the Postmaster-General had had time to consider it. For in those days, especially, such a thing was regarded as a most unforgivable breach of official etiquette, to say the least. Its publication at this juncture was therefore generally thought to be the last blow to all their hopes of further revision. But few dreamed what was to follow.

The text of that memorial is here reproduced, the better to mark the perverted sense of justice of the Postmaster-General who could read treason and conspiracy in an innocent appeal so temperately worded, and exact so cruel a penalty for so small an offence as that of prayerfully submitting that they still had grievances to remedy :

> " PETITION TO THE POSTMASTER-GENERAL from the Sorters of the Inland Branch, G.P.O., presented through their Superintendent on November 25th, 1874.

" *To the Right Honourable*
    LORD JOHN MANNERS, M.P.,
       Her Majesty's Postmaster-General.

" MY LORD,—We, the undersigned sorters attached to the Inland Branch, beg most respectfully to inform you that, whilst grateful for the recent improvements made in our pay and prospects of promotion, we are yet unable to accept it as a satisfactory settlement of our claims to increased remuneration ; we, therefore, beg to call your Lordship's attention to the following facts : Prior to 1867 the scale of pay for our class was as follows : Minimum of second-class, 23s., by an annual increment of 1s. to a maximum of 38s. ; minimum of first-class, 40s., by an annual increment of 1s. to a maximum of 50s. After the revision made in June, 1867, it stood thus : Minimum, 24s., by an annual increment of 1s. for six years, and then by 1s. 6d. to a maximum of 45s. In 1872 the minimum was increased to 26s., and in July of the present year the scale was again altered to the following :

Minimum 26s., with an annual increment of 1s. 6d. for six years, and then by 2s. to a maximum of 45s. Thus it will be seen that whilst the minimum and annual increment have been increased in amount, the maximum has been reduced 5s. per week. The only benefit derived from the last revision was an addition of 6d. to the annual increment. In former memorials we have asked that the increased increment of 2s. per week may begin at the minimum of the scale instead of after six years, as at present ; and also, that the maximum may be restored to the sum of 50s. per week, at which it originally stood, in accordance with the recommendation of the Commission of 1854, of which the present Chancellor of the Exchequer was a member. The scale would then have stood thus : Minimum, 26s., by an annual increment of 2s. to a maximum of 50s. We respectfully submit to your lordship that, having regard to our length of service (most of us have served over nine years), the increased value of labour, and the enhanced cost of commodities generally, the above would not be more than a reasonable remuneration for the important duties we perform. We therefore pray your Lordship to give this Memorial your favourable consideration, and earnestly hope you will see fit to grant our Prayer. We are, my Lord, your obedient servants."

[Here follow Names.]

The resentment of the Department showed itself almost immediately after the illicit publication of the memorial in the public press. The signatories were sent for by the Controller, and catechised as to what they knew about its appearance in print before it had actually reached the hand of the Postmaster-General. They were told it was a gross breach of official confidence, only a little less heinous than offering personal insult to the public head of the Department. They would be held responsible for sending it to the press for publication, and nothing now remained but to go home and pray for forgiveness and await developments. In vain the men protested their innocence, and pointed out that copies of the proposed memorial freely circulated among the men for their approval before it was submitted through the official channel ; indeed anyone but themselves might have forwarded

H

a copy to the *Times*. But it was to no purpose they sought to defend themselves on these grounds, and they were practically found guilty on the spot. That was one indictment only in regard to this unfortunate memorial. The second was that they had dared as the humblest servants of her Majesty's Postmaster-General to convey to him, by means of this aforesaid illicitly published memorial, that they could not accept as fully satisfying all their claims, the scheme which he had so beneficently prepared for them. What right had they to say they could not accept the scheme, or anything else which a Postmaster-General had so condescended to provide them with?

The poor menials withdrew from the light of the official cadi's presence, abashed and crestfallen. They predicted that something was about to happen to them, guilty wretches that they were; but they did not know what.

While the case was pending, a paragraph appeared in one of the papers to the effect that the indignation of the men in the General Post Office had now reached such a point that they had decided to petition for the removal of certain supervising officials who had rendered themselves brutally obnoxious to the men throughout. The ringleaders were again, as a natural consequence, suspected of this fresh paragraphic insult to the Department; but the men themselves were as indignant as might be the authorities themselves. They all solemnly protested to each other that this foolish blunder was not theirs. The appearance of such a thing at this moment could certainly effect no good purpose, and it seemed difficult to believe that any one of them, knowing that suspicion would most certainly fall on them, and discredit them still further, could have been guilty of such foolishness. Still, repudiate it as they might, they knew the shot would rebound on themselves. There were several among them who did not hesitate to think that both the memorial and the offensive paragraph had been sent to the press by some one of the creatures of the Department with a malignant ulterior motive.

If the Postmaster-General had been shot at with a popgun he was going to return it with a bomb; and the bomb, being ready, was primed for December 11. On the morning of that date it was thrown.

It took the form of a Postmaster-General's minute, and was sent the rounds of the Circulation Department by means of the general-order book. It started innocently enough, but the sting, like that of the scorpion, was in its tail. It was to the effect that the Postmaster-General had received the memorial from the sorters, but not until it had been improperly published in the newspapers. It proceeded to criticise the terms of the memorial, and to remind them that in the previous July the wages of the memorialists were readjusted by the Treasury, " after very full and careful consideration." A comparison between the sorters of 1854 and 1874 was then drawn to show that they were no worse off, and that the reduction in the maximum was more than compensated for by the creation of a new overseer's class. So far, so good, or bad, as they chose to think it ; but now comes the cruellest part of it. The Postmaster-General could not stay his hand here. In view of the recent settlement he felt it incumbent on him not only to oppose and check the spirit which the terms of the memorial and the course it had taken exhibited, but " to evince in some unmistakable manner " that he would " not yield to clamour what reasoned justice to the public would withhold."

Accordingly he desired that the memorialists be informed that if their present conditions of service were not suitable to them they were at liberty to seek for other employment. And further, he would understand it to be their intention to do so unless within three days they asked, in writing, for permission to remain. This permission, however, he should not give to those who, having signed the memorial, bore an " indifferent character," and were " not recommended by their superior officers for retention in the service." He understood that among those who signed the wicked memorial there were a number of younger men who had " no claims on the Department, either on the score of service or otherwise " ; and for daring to become dissatisfied already, their names were to be brought specially before him, in order that he might consider whether any, and if so, which of them, should be retained in the service as an act of grace. His lordship furthermore implied that the precious privilege accorded to the more poorly paid of being allowed to add to their miserable incomes by overtime, should relieve them of any cause for complaint in

regard to insufficient wages. His reference to their " liberty
to seek for other employment " was the bitterest mockery to
men who had given so many years to the public service, and
for the first time gave expression to that heartless theory of
the Department that the best cure for grievances was the
dismissal of those who dared to complain of them ; for that
practically was its meaning.

Such was the message of Lord John Manners to the men
who had been guilty of asking for a redress of their grievances
and a small increase of pay. Such was the manner in which
he requited the confidence reposed in him by his humble
subordinates, and such was the manner in which he set about
redeeming the fair promises of the party which had so sustained the agitation while they were in opposition. The
Postmaster-General's minute was almost as vile an instrument
as that with which the previous Government had contemplated
crushing combination and smothering the claims of the
aggrieved by prosecution, only that their heart failed them at
the last moment. It was virtually a demand for the heads of
the ringleaders. It provided a warranty for wholesale dismissal,
and placed a weapon in the hands of minor officials which,
apart from their inclination, they were fully authorised and
expected to use against a certain number.

They were told that they were to consider they had relinquished the service, but applications to be retained would be
considered, though there would be no guarantee. As was
only natural in the circumstances, the men, thinking of their
wives and families, and knowing that refusal to accept the
humiliation meant instant dismissal, complied, and wrote
their applications as directed. An overseer was sent round
to collect them into a bunch, and then it was the poor men
found themselves, as if drawn into an ambush, basely betrayed. Their last lingering confidence in the honour of the
aristocrat who made blue blood only the criterion of nobility
was rudely shattered. The whole thirty men who, as representing their fellows, had been induced to sign the memorial
were suspended from duty, with the prospect of dismissal, the
forced humiliation of their applications notwithstanding.

A fortnight before Christmas one hundred and forty men
of the sorting force were called up before the Controller for

admonishment. These included the thirty suspended men, who were taken last. They were all admonished in much the same terms in the name of the Postmaster-General, and to the majority it was intimated that the granting of their applications would depend on their future conduct. But five of the men, those regarded as more or less prominent in the recent agitation, were to be dismissed ; and the five condemned men were accordingly marched out of the office, with a bitter winter and the world before them.

Lord John Manners triumphed, and the smaller officials had their revenge. There was no doubt about that ; the men went back to their duties thoroughly cowed. It must have been a glorious hour for the Postmaster-General, and doubtless he felt that he had routed the enemies of society for ever. And so that the victory of the Postmaster-General should be fully complete, a subscription to provide the dismissed sorters with a Christmas dinner was stopped by order of the authorities. Cowed as the men were, an attempt was made to send round a subscription sheet, but the movers were warned of the consequences, and they were officially terrorised into doing nothing for the victims of Lord John Manners' discipline.

Several Parliamentary friends of the postal cause immediately set to work to induce the Postmaster-General to reverse his harsh decision. Particularly assiduous was Mr. A. J. Mundella, but he was doomed to get nothing but humiliation for his pains. Mr. Mundella used the whole weight of his personal influence with the Postmaster-General and the permanent authorities, only to find himself bandied about from one to the other till his sensitive nature became wounded and disgusted. The studied discourtesy shown him by the permanent officials especially he made a matter for some complaint inside the House, as he felt that more consideration than had been accorded him was due to his position and dignity as a public man.

These arbitrary dismissals destroyed the last vestige of confidence in the Tory party for some years to come among the letter-sorters. If the men had been dealt with merely for signing and sending forward a memorial, there was no justification for such harsh punishment. There would have been no justification for any kind of punishment beyond the refusal to accede to their request. But it was rendered too patent to everyone that it was seized on simply as a pretext for taking a revenge for the part they had played in the recent agitation. There was no discipline that demanded such a cowardly reprisal. It was worthy only of the narrow-minded aristocrat whose principal claim to distinction was his cherished little drop of blue blood, and whose contempt of the masses, of all who worked for their living, and all that was plebeian, was rendered shamefacedly notorious by his published lines. For Lord John Manners was the author of that silly and impudent pretence at an epigram—which shook the world with laughter, and covered the writer with derision and scorn—even from critics of his own party. His disgraceful lines, which ran—

" Let Arts and Commerce, Laws and Learning, die,
But leave us still our old Nobility ! "—

of which he was so distinguished an ornament—were as much an outrage on decency and the canons of poetry as his very first act as an administrator was arbitrary. Where he had failed as a poet, his party had generously given him a chance to succeed as an autocrat. And his one idea of auto-cracy, presumably, was to persecute the weak, as the only way to convince them he was powerful.

Lord John Manners was a poet, and a poetic revenge was to be wreaked on him by one of his victims. The generous impulse which had prompted the defeated men to subscribe for a Christmas dinner for those who had suffered for them, had been promptly strangled by the officials acting under the direction of the Postmaster-General. So it was attempted to raise a small sum for the distressed men by the sale outside the Post Office gates of the leaflet which appears on the following page.

Glamorgan's verse was as the last vehement cry of despairing freedom in the Post Office. The forces of discontent had been humbled and demoralised, if not wholly scattered ; and liberty, cowering in a corner, was to remain dumb for many a day to come.

THE LOCKED-OUT SORTERS OF THE GENERAL POST OFFICE.

To Lord John Manners, Her Majesty's Postmaster-General

What ails my lord to seek his doom,
Why hurl into the winter gloom
    His slaves of Want and Pain?
Art thou not of noble blood—
And noble only to be good ?—
    Then why insult thy name ?

Didst thou not write with poet's flame
To save our ancient nobles' name,
    Their rank and chivalry ;
Then why disgrace that ancient shrine
The only fount to *thee* divine,
    Why *damn* their memory ?

Democracy will laugh with scorn
And know a noble fool is born
    To curse his pedigree.
'Tis this oppression and this shame,
Deeds done beneath a *noble* name
    Will kill thy line for thee.

Art thou of human love possest,
With heart beneath thy silken vest,
    To claim thyself a man ?
Art thou a husband, father, say,
With *home* that none can take away,
    To bless thy earthly span ?

Bright jewels deck thy lady's head,
Thy children never wanted bread,
    Born into luxury.
Thy princely mansion so secure,
Thy hands nor *head* could ne'er procure
    This gift of *destiny*.

  .   .   .   .   .
The want and suffering that your hand
Has brought a helpless, martyr'd band,
    Will cry against your *deed ;*
The orphan's tears will *burn* your soul,
And curse you to the final goal,
    Where mercy you will plead !

                  THOMAS HENRY GLAMORGAN
LONDON, *January,* 1875.   (one of the men).

CHAPTER X

INTRODUCTION OF BOY LABOUR—CONDITIONS OF SERVICE—
DEATH OF COMBINATION AND ITS CONSEQUENCES—
POSTAL HELOTISM.

In the meantime, as if to show contemptuously that the
agitating sorters could be dispensed with at any time, or
their work done by child labour, the authorities, when the
halfpenny post started in 1870, introduced a number of lads
recruited mostly from boys leaving school. This was the
introduction of the boy-sorter system, and while it presently
assisted the Department to play off against the men who were
fighting for a better wage and other improvements, it efficiently
furthered that principle of economy which was the be-all
and end-all of those who governed. The Department was
henceforth to be run on commercial lines more than ever it
had in the past ; the more profit the great machine produced
the more it might. The introduction of the boy-sorter system
was yet another experiment in levelling down, and yet a
further depreciation of their work, for which twenty years
before the respectable salaries of clerks were paid. It was
justified in so far as it provided an outlet for the telegraph
messengers later on, whose only chance hitherto had been
to go as postmen ; but that economy was almost the sole
object with the authorities was proved from the miserable
wage that was offered these boys. Ostensibly, they were
brought in to do the rough routine work of assisting the
sorters, and of carrying bags and gathering in the correspondence for disposal. But in a very short while they were,
in addition to these menial tasks, put to the more arduous
and responsible duties of sorting, and work almost identical
with that of the ordinary sorters. For this these boys received
six shillings a week—errand-boys' wages. And the men who

had been through all the rough times of the service for ten, fifteen, and twenty years past were still agitating for better wages and better conditions of work. This, to an extent, was the answer of the authorities. The introduction of boy labour to displace men discontented with their conditions was the best card they had yet played, and one which they calculated to check the further operations of the sorters, at least. It was not long, however, before there were some signs of dissatisfaction among the poorly-paid youngsters themselves, besides which it was becoming difficult to obtain the required number, and it was soon necessary to raise their wages to nine shillings a week. The responsibilities of their work increased proportionately, and soon there was little appreciable difference between the work attached to them and that on which ordinary sorters in the Newspaper Branch had been engaged. The only sop that was thrown to the overworked and underpaid stampers and sorters of this branch of the service was their being allowed to present their sons as candidates for the vacancies ; though whether it was that they evinced too little sympathy with a scheme which might mean their own undoing, or that they were too disgusted themselves with the conditions of the service to think of bringing in their boys to share such prospects, is not certain, but few availed themselves of the opportunity. Not even the rise in wages to nine shillings a week for boys from fifteen to seventeen years of age, constantly surrounded with temptation to pilfer, and who were more or less saddled with work and responsibilities for which more wages had been paid only a short time previously, was any too generous for a profit-making public department. The boy sorters were emboldened to draw up a respectful petition urging a claim for a further improvement in pay. The petition was intercepted by a minor official, who smelt sulphur in it at once, and several of the poor boys were forthwith charged with leaguing themselves with the devil, or something as discreditable. It was enough for grown-up men with wives and families to ask for such things as higher wages and more considerate treatment, but when infants in the service followed such a bad example it was time to nip such juvenile ambitions in the bud. Possibly this little postal Bumble, dressed in brief authority, who thus undertook to protect the Department from the predatory designs of these youngsters, fancied that a higher wage might demoralise them, or tempt them to marry too early. A number of these poor little Oliver Twists were admitted to examination singly, and some were so frightened at the enormity of the offence of asking for more that they timidly confessed on the spot that their humble petition had actually been indited by a grown-up sorter named Jacobs. The self-important little official gasped with astonishment, and prepared to reach for his official club. The delinquent, Jacobs—" Gentleman Jacobs " was his sobriquet among the force—was peremptorily sent for, and an immediate written explanation demanded of him as to why he did, on a certain date, in direct contravention of printed Rule No. 01565, incite and encourage these junior officers of her Majesty's postal service to dissatisfaction in regard to their prospects and pay. Jacobs did as requested, justifying himself on three sheets of foolscap. It was not the incriminating " explanation " the official wanted. Jacobs flatly refused to state anything but the truth about the matter. If the over-zealous little official committed the folly of sending the case to the authorities, nothing came of it.

The trifling incident is mentioned only to show how subordinate officials with exaggerated notions of their duties may sometimes earn for the authorities even more criticism among the rank and file than they merit. The boy sorters afterwards were given twelve shillings a week, which was a little more in accordance with their value to the Department. The treatment of the boy sorters reflected but little credit on those who were responsible. Those who were not harried out of the service after enduring its hardships for six months or so frequently survived only to become premature wrecks, eventually disqualified by the Medical Branch. Lads fresh from the country entering with high expectations, and it might be said almost lured into the service under false pretences, often fell early victims to consumption through their having to provide for themselves on their meagre wage. In too many cases insufficient food, the vitiated atmosphere of the sorting-office, the unnatural hours of duty, the bullying and the nerve-strain put on them all told, and even left their traces on them in after years. It was not to be wondered at that so many of those who had been boy sorters were almost as soon as they reached early manhood claimed by the White Scourge—consumption.

It was not long before this principle of cheap labour was further extended, and the existing sorting force threatened to be swamped by young recruits fresh from the ranks of the telegraph messengers or from school. Doubtless it was partly owing to this as well as to the bitter experience of the cruel dismissals that the men of the sorting force continued to bear their grievances in silence. From that time forward there had been a period of stagnation ; the grumblings of discontent were reduced to a discreet whisper, and anything of the shape of agitation was now discredited. The sorters had not easily forgotten the sharp lesson that had been taught them, the risk they had undergone, and the ordeal through which they had passed. They knew they were now reduced by that defeat to the condition of serfs, that they were slowly being deprived of every right and privilege which goes to make the proud boast of an Englishman. It was either submitting to this or risking, almost with the certainty of further defeat, the bread and butter of their wives and little ones. The Department had scored ; but it had not entirely scotched the serpent of discontent. If the silence and inactivity of the men were thought to indicate contentment and a cheerful acceptance of the situation, the authorities were mistaken. Nowhere but in a Government department, either in England or Russia, could such a state of things exist. In no English workshop, where men had a trade in their hands and a kit of tools to call their own, would they have submitted for so long to the treatment meted out to them. For some considerable time after the dismissals, the remainder of the force were treated like would-be recalcitrants on whom it was necessary to keep a sharp eye, and on whom it was as necessary to inflict humiliation for their own good. Their convenience in the matter of sudden compulsory summonses for extra duty was entirely ignored, while the pay for such extra duty was unfair in the extreme. Commonly, at the behest of a minor official, they were compelled to stay beyond their legitimate time without any pay whatever. The growing intolerance of the smaller authorities towards the force gave encouragement to the minor superiors to exercise to the full their proclivity for bullying and brow-beating the men on the smallest pretext. And the boy sorters themselves met with the least consideration of all. Being the juniors they were made to bear a more than proportionate share of the hardships of their elders. Scores of them left after a few months of it ; and as many more had their dismissals procured by the merest whim of an overseer, or the caprice of a tyrannical inspector. The boy sorters had proved very handy to the Department, both as a foil to the possibility of further agitation among the men and as an economical experiment ; but they despised them ; or if they did not actually despise them they allowed others to, and were utterly indifferent to the manner of their treatment. The majority of these lads were of an age too tender to be withdrawn safely from the influence of the home circle ; yet many of them had only their bare wage of twelve shillings a week to enable them to lodge, clothe, feed, and keep themselves honest. They were of an age when the growing lad has all the appetites of the man, yet the authorities did not think it unfair to expect them to keep up a certain amount of respectability of appearance. The chance of supplementing their income was that of a compulsory summons in the middle of the night, or rather four o'clock in the morning, and tor work from this hour till nine o'clock, five hours in all, performed before their actual day's duty commenced, they were remunerated with one shilling, paid the following week. Whatever excuse was to be made for the East-End sweater, openly and professedly exploiting juvenile labour, there was none such to be made for a Government department like the Post Office.

So indifferent to the barest claims of humanity had the officials calling themselves the authorities now become that the men could barely call their souls their own. If they were allowed an ownership over their spiritual being, that was only to suit theoretical requirements, but in actual fact their personal liberty was more circumscribed than ever. They had always to remember that they were postal officials first, and men and husbands and fathers afterwards. Away from the office or otherwise they were to regard themselves as still on duty ; at least when off duty they were to hold themselves always in readiness to respond to a telegram summoning them

A HISTORY OF POSTAL AGITATION

to the office ; consequently they must never make appointments, except at their own risk. A man failing to respond to
the call of extra duty was not only set down as a shirker and
one unwilling to serve the Department in an emergency, but
he was very often punished and insulted into the bargain.
Superintendents and the " heads of departments " in those
days particularly, were allowed unchecked to give fullest vent
to their own personal predilections, their own particular likes
and dislikes, and if it was that they were not allowed a larger
discretion than in these days, it was mostly due to the fact
that the men had no means of resenting such barefaced
assertions of autocracy. While the men bore it without a
combined protest, a superintendent of a branch might, if he
chose, become a little despot, with the power to render
miserable the hundreds of men under his control. For as is
the master so are his stewards and bailiffs. The example set by
one higher official is eagerly imitated by his immediate
subordinates, and those over whom they have control are the
sufferers.

That the apathy of the force in respect to combination for
mutual interest was taken advantage of by their immediate
superiors was shown in many curious and significant ways.
Excuses for late attendance or for non-compliance with
regulation, which would be graciously accepted now, were
then often treated with open derision and contempt.   A
superintendent might either call a man with a ready excuse
a downright liar to his face, or he might, in his desire to be
strictly official, display such an utter want of feeling as to be
guilty of conduct almost bordering on brutality. It was the
vogue of one official of this period to regulate everything
strictly according to rule. He thought himself too loyal
a servant of the Department even to exercise that little
discretion vested in him by his superiors. Besides, he
thought it was saving himself a deal of trouble to do so, and
the muttered imprecations of the men or their hidden
scowls never entered into his calculations. He never deviated
a hair's-breadth from the rule laid down. If by an unhappy
mischance there had been a misprint in the rule-book or
instructions to postmasters and others ruling that a man found
absenting himself from the sorting-office for more than the

usual period should be " hanged " instead of only " suspended," he would have made no inquiry. He would have taken it for granted, and had the poor wretch hanged from the gallery forthwith in a coil of the red-tape so dear to his heart. He was not the only one of his tribe. It was not that the higher authorities either directly encouraged or were fully cognisant of this sort of conduct on their part ; if they did not know, they did not want to know ; these were trifles that did not concern them. Such things concerned them only when the men's murmurs rose to a pitch high enough to compel their attention. The men had ceased for so long to murmur openly that perhaps the authorities were not so much to blame for allowing petty tyranny on the part of the smaller to go unchecked.

While the men remained unorganised amongst themselves, the officials could see no wrong in putting fresh impositions on those under their control. The old device of forcing the men on extra duty, without pay or return of any kind, was more freely resorted to than ever. The eight hours' day remained virtually unrecognised, and those who had attended at four or half-past four in the early morning were more often than not imprisoned like galley-slaves at the sorting-tables an hour, sometimes two hours, beyond the time when they should have been free to go home to obtain rest, and prepare once more for the afternoon's duty.

The officials profited little by the experience of that occasion a year or so previous when the men, goaded beyond the limits of forbearance, took the law into their own hands and boldly broke through the imprisoning doors, and asserted their liberty as free men in a free country. These disgraceful rushes for liberty—disgraceful only on the part of the authorities, who sought to imprison them like convicts, forgetful that they were public servants in the service of the most freedom-loving country in the world—were several times repeated. And the men who dared to protest in this primitive fashion, which was now the only one left to them, were as frequently threatened and punished. The officials apparently thought that by singling out a few individuals here and there they would terrorise the rest into an acceptance of this unjust system of forced and compulsory labour without pay, and bolster up their own authority. Whatever extra duty that was paid for was on the lowest scale possible, and, coupled with that, was in most cases rendered compulsory between most inconvenient hours, so as to deprive the men of either rest or recreation. After completing the half of their day's work they would find themselves, perhaps on their arrival home, suddenly summoned back on duty right in the middle of the day, between 10 a.m. and 2 p.m. This, it will be seen, meant a serious loss of time to them, as they were on duty again at 4-30 p.m., and for all this they were rewarded with nothing better than payment equal to the " docker's tanner "—sixpence per hour.

There were two or three abortive attempts at rebellion against this cruel system, but protests were vain in convincing the authorities of its hardship or unfairness. The old official dictum that the permanence of their employment as Government servants amply compensated for every shortcoming, continually weighed with the authorities, and was as continually advanced against the claims of the men. Because the Department had vouchsafed to them something like permanence of employment, it took to itself the right of imposing any conditions the caprice of its officials might devise, and of abrogating their menials' privileges whenever they thought proper. Men who failed from whatever cause to respond promptly to these domiciliary summonses were severely reprimanded, and their conduct held in remembrance for use against them in the future. Moreover, in answer to the respectful complaint that sixpence an hour was a too unfair remuneration for those at the maximum of their class, it was pointed out that there was no Treasury grant sufficient to entitle them to more. But it is significant that on one occasion when the sorters at last showed a more determined front than usual by disregarding a peremptory summons of this nature, almost to a man excusing themselves on the ground that the pay was far too little, eightpence an hour was granted the following week ; and the men wondered all the more, as the smallest Treasury grant generally took more time than the proverbial mountain in labour.

CHAPTER XI

A PERIOD OF STAGNATION—THE BLIND POSTMASTER-GENERAL
AND A GLEAM OF LIGHT—A MEMORABLE VISIT—THE
FAWCETT SCHEME.

LORD JOHN MANNERS had descended from his pedestal of
office and returned to the comparative obscurity and inactivity
for which his attainments so well fitted him. Before leaving
the Post Office he had the satisfaction of knowing that, from
one point of view, he had done at least one thing well; he
had stifled discontent and reduced the common herd of postal
workers to their proper level of uncomplaining Government
serfs. Under his régime had grown and flourished naturally
a system of petty tyranny and sycophancy which rendered
open honest protest well-nigh impossible, which compelled
men to endure it or accept the alternative, resignation or
dismissal, and which made any attempt at combination as
impossible as in the prehistoric days before the Penny Post.
The condition, so far as the limitations on their liberty were
concerned, was every whit as bad as prevailed years before the
agitation. Nearly all the reforms which the late agitation had
started so hopefully to attain had been left undone. The
violent *coup* for which Lord John Manners was responsible
had taken the heart out of the men, and they had to take
the postal service as they found it or leave it for others to be
forced into their places from the stress of competition outside.
The hide-bound official tenet that the permanency of Government employment more than compensated for all shortcomings
was now being interpreted as if to mean that this quality of
" permanency " not only compensated for, but justified and
rendered necessary, the employment of petty persecution, the
deprivation of almost every claim to citizenship, and the cur-
tailment of most ordinary human rights. The utter contempt

of the officials for men's common rights and privileges as human beings, their churlish indifference to the common claims of manhood, have to some extent already been shown. Even the "permanency" of employment was commonly nullified on the smallest pretext, and seniority and long faithful service counted for little against the whim of a tyrannical supervisor. If it was creditable to the public service to have it manned by those who suffered from grievances and yet dared not complain of them ; if it was profitable to the Treasury to have the rank and file of the postal service remain underpaid and forced labour exacted from them ; if it was requisite that the woes of the men should be hidden alike from the public and from the higher permanent officials henceforth, most of the credit, most of the honour, was due to Lord John Manners. If it was well that all inquiry should be stifled and the men be kept in servile subjection by superiors whose common conception of their duties was that of Russian jailers ; if it was necessary in the course of proper discipline that men should be treated as though they had no soul to call their own, Lord John Manners, by the one act by which he achieved this success, deserved the gratitude of his country.

Thus it will be seen that nearly everything which the agitation had set out to do, all the reforms which it had promised, were left for a future generation. A long period of stagnation had set in, and but for the faint echo of agitation occasionally coming from the telegraphists, the Post Office, so far as uttered discontent was concerned, might have been wrapped in slumber.

Lord John Manners had departed for good, unwept, unhonoured, and unsung. His advent and departure had witnessed no change in the conditions of the service. Time in the Post Office dragged its slow weary length along till the year 1881 was reached. That year was to witness a glad surprise for the dejected sorting staff at least. If Lord John Manners was the one man who was to be bitterly remembered as having battened down the hatches on the galley-slaves, set a seal on their freedom of action, and put a premium on official exaction, Professor Henry Fawcett was the one who came at last to offer them a fuller share of air and liberty. Lord John Manners, belonging to the political party

I

which had encouraged their demands, and, in the persons of some of its most prominent men, almost, it might be said, aided and abetted the agitation, so far from carrying out the reforms which had been confidently expected of him, had discouraged their aspirations by means of a whip of scorpions. They had asked for bread, and he had given them something worse than a stone. Professor Henry Fawcett had scarcely been approached, certainly not by those who figured in the late agitation, yet remembering his promises of bygone years, and with a generous desire to meet the necessities of their case, he of his own free will, and almost spontaneously, offered reparation for the long disappointment they had sustained. Mr. Fawcett, though never taking a prominent part, or figuring too largely in the letter-carriers' and sorters' three years' agitation, yet had associated himself with it to an extent, often giving his wise counsel to Booth and the others, and always his sympathy and best wishes for bettering the conditions of the service. He showed that he was not likely to forget now.

Discontent among the telegraphists had reached a somewhat acute stage, and the new Postmaster-General busied himself for some time in arriving at the inner facts of their case. He rose from his study of the telegraphists' troubles with a conviction that something must be done to meet the justice of their demands. It was not clamour that weighed with him, but a genuine inclination to do the right thing so far as in him lay, and to put in order the household which his predecessors had more or less neglected. He had the fullest desire to mete out justice to the telegraphists, but there was the sister branch of the service to be considered likewise. That portion of the Augean stable was, if anything, in a worse condition, and he decided to ascertain for himself.

One evening, in his quiet simple manner, the blind Postmaster-General presented himself at the General Post Office unannounced and asked to be taken over the sorting department, and to have things explained to him. The scene was one of bustle and confusion ; and the dull roar and the clank of stamping machinery, and the movements of hundreds of men in a confined space, filled the overburdened air. He was conducted to a position on the gallery overlooking the busy, crowded Letter Branch, which to ordinary eyes resembled nothing so much as an overturned ant-hill. Mr. Fawcett's form and features were not familiar to the majority ; but presently the whisper went round that the tall, silent man seeming to stare down upon them through the big black spectacles which hid his closed eyes, was the Postmaster-General himself. For a few moments strict discipline was forgotten in curiosity, and few could really believe that one who could so intently follow the movements of the throbbing machinery below, as he did, could be wholly blind. They did not comprehend to the full the pathos of it ; they did not know that this was only a habit he had schooled himself into to hide his infirmity. Nor did they know that in him they looked on the first Postmaster-General who had come among them with an honest desire to prove their benefactor. It chanced—or it may have been that Mr. Fawcett himself preferred it—that a young junior sorter was deputed to take him over the building. The young man acting as guide succeeded in so interesting him by his manner of describing all that the blind eyes could not see, that at last Professor Fawcett asked him his position in the service, and further questioned him as to his pay and prospects. Presumably, from what he gathered on that occasion, he learnt much that set him thinking. A little while afterwards an official circular announced that the Postmaster-General would be willing to receive a statement of the men's claims to better pay and prospects.

The issue of such a circular was as unexpected as manna from heaven. It was some days before the letter-sorters could realise their good fortune in having a Daniel come to judgment at last after all their privations. Although the circular was a guarantee of good faith on the part of the Postmaster-General, the men still betrayed a certain amount of timidity in responding to so generous an invitation, until four or five of them, forming themselves into a provisional committee, called a meeting in one of the kitchens, and the basis of a plan was laid down. There were several such meetings with the sanction of the authorities, who could not decently withhold it ; there was much cackling before the egg was finally laid, as there usually is. But at last a petition to the Postmaster-

General was formulated and sent on its mission. The claims set forth were studiously modest, and comprised a request to rise to fifty shillings a week by yearly increments of two shillings instead of eighteenpence, and a yearly holiday extended to three weeks instead of only a fortnight, and an improved scale of pay for extra duty. This constituted the whole of the demand for the sorters.

Mr. Fawcett lost no time in doing what he considered the right thing, and in endeavouring to apply a remedy for all the discontent which had for so long prevailed. He went about constructing his remedial measure in a masterly manner and broad-minded spirit. It might have been expected that he, a professor of the " dismal science," would have sought for a ready means to evade the importunities of a discontented service. But not so ; he broadly recognised that discontent was a symptom, a symptom of a growing polypus beneath the surface, and he sought for a means to eradicate the cause. He apparently spared himself no pains to arrive at the true facts of the situation. The report which he made to the Lords of the Treasury signified much inquiry and many hours of labour. He wrote : " For several months past I have been collecting information from all sources, not only as to the alleged grievances of the staff, but as to the conditions of service and rates of pay of persons in private employment, whose duties seem most nearly to correspond to theirs."

Here in these few words is told a story of diligence, patient research, and laborious study—all the more wonderful for a sightless man—which it would take a complete volume to accord full justice to. The consideration of this alone should extenuate whatever few shortcomings might be found in his remedial measure, which came to be known as the " Fawcett Scheme." Such faults, such as they were, were but as the black specks on the white ermine, perhaps the more accentuating the real goodness of his intention.

In response to his solicitations, the Lords of the Treasury accepted his proposals for a revised scale of pay for tele-graphists and " sorting clerks," and on the 13th of June, 1881, the scheme was issued. It dealt with the principal complaints from the two branches of the service, the telegraphic and the postal ; and referred specifically to inadequacy of pay, arising from stagnation of promotion, the excessive amount of over-time, the small rate of pay allowed for it, and the severity of night duty ; the insufficiency of yearly holiday ; and a readjustment of pay for work performed on Christmas Day and Good Friday. The scheme apparently intended was to apply to telegraphists and sorters pretty equally, and altogether, if nothing more can be said of it, it was a bold attempt, and the bolder because it was the first attempt of the kind to bring order out of chaos, to unite in some manner the tangled and disconnected threads of a complex and perplexing problem. It was practically the first attempt to solve a problem teeming with petty jealousies and sectional discontents ; a patient attempt skilfully to untie the Gordian knot which Lord John Manners had only rudely hacked at with the knife of official despotism. It was an honest attempt to fulfil his obligations to a distressed and justly discontented service, with which years before taking office he had professed a sympathy. With him it was the accomplishment of a duty ; and it was as such that he laid his proposals before the Lords of the Treasury. It was a forward step in the right direction which ought to have been taken long before it was. Instead of attempting to suppress discontent in the same fashion as his predecessor, he gave to postal servants their first charter of liberty. It was not complete ; it was not made to fit the full demands of the case perhaps ; few first charters are ; but without it, further extensions of postal liberty would scarcely have been possible. If it was only a gleam of light in the darkness, and the beginning of a process of development, where only stagnation had prevailed, it was something ; and honour was due to its author for his rare courage.

By the Fawcett scheme the letter-sorters found their position materially improved. They who had dropped agitation, who had been reduced to a condition of timorous servility almost, who had scarcely dared to ask for what they were invited to take, found themselves nearly as well off as those who had fancied themselves entitled to far greater benefits. Everything that the sorters through years of vain agitation had sought to obtain it seemed was now to be granted. The claim to rise to fifty shillings a week, for the asking of which some time before five of their number had been dismissed, was now given them without demur. And what was more, the scheme was dated back to the preceding April, so that some immediate monetary benefit accrued to the majority. In addition to the increases in wages, there was to be payment for sacred holidays ; a revised system of payment for over-time, the recommendation being that extra duty be paid for strictly in proportion to the amount of weekly wages received ; while there were certain other minor advantages, including one which minimised the severity of night attendance. It is unnecessary here to give the whole measure in detail ; but such, broadly, were the advantages apparently vouchsafed to the sorting force, the defeat of whose legitimate aims by a former Postmaster-General and whose rejection had reduced them to a condition of hopeless apathy. The glad surprise, then, with which they especially received the Fawcett scheme may be still imagined.

Yet Mr. Fawcett's generous attempt to apply a panacea for postal discontent was to some extent doomed to fall short of the effect intended, and this from little fault of his own.

The just intention that animated Mr. Fawcett in his recom-mendations was shown by his actually offering, in one case at least, more than was demanded of him, and more than he was compelled to give in any instance. True, his liberality in this respect extended to only one section of the service—the London sorting force ; but the fact remains that he might easily have withheld all that he so freely gave. Had he been less liberal-minded, he might, with as much excuse and with as much success probably, have adopted the uncompromising attitude of every predecessor in office. Whatever compelling influence there might have been which resulted in the Fawcett scheme proceeded from the telegraphists' agitation of that period, though it is more natural to believe that Mr. Fawcett acted throughout independently, and was moved from purely just and liberal motives.

Unfortunately, however, it must be said, though there is excuse in abundance, that his good intention was hardly balanced by a due sense of proportion. That was the principal internal fault of the scheme. While it naturally satisfied the sorters for the time, it brought little more than disappoint-ment to the telegraphists, who expected so much more than was apportioned them. It left the postmen and the auxiliary postmen just where they were before in point of pay, their only share being a prospect of partaking of the minor advantages, such as payment for overtime and sacred days, which presumably were now to be enjoyed in common by all classes. A measure which, by its fault of disproportion, must inevitably engender the jealousy of the less favoured against their comrades in the service, could not be regarded as a final settlement. It was successful only to an extent as a temporary solution of an existing difficulty, but not as the ultimate settlement for all time of a troublesome problem. Probably its author would have claimed no more for it than this ; but even on these grounds it might have gone further. That this scheme, costing the country as it did £152,000 per annum, and affecting ten thousand servants, was not made to go further, so as to bring some measure of material benefit to the postmen and auxiliaries and others, was to be regretted. Doubtless, Mr. Fawcett felt that he had gone far enough in recommending benefits involving such a reduction on the yearly profits of the Post Office ; but a little closer consideration of the conditions of the letter-carrier class at that time might have averted the trouble among them which arose later on. There is this, however, to be said in extenuation of its shortcomings in respect to the letter-carriers. They either did not take Mr. Fawcett's invitation to state their grievances as seriously addressed to themselves, or, from some misunderstanding, their case was not put as fully and as convincingly as it might. The Postmaster-General therefore possibly felt justified in thinking that the letter-carriers were more or less satisfied with their position and prospects, and he was not induced to go out of his way on their behalf. With the letter-sorters the matter was rather different ; they had responded, even if none too vigorously, with the result, as has been shown, that the five shillings taken off their weekly wage some years before by Lord John Manners was now restored to them. That was the single advantage by which they scored over the letter-carriers. The strength and the justice of the Fawcett scheme lay principally in the fact that new privileges were to be enjoyed in common ; that at least every man in the Post Office could claim payment for Christmas Day and Good Friday ; and that payment for extra duty was adjusted in fair proportion to his salary. These were in themselves no inconsiderable advantages, which were worth being thankful for.

Such, at least, they would have been, only that the unfortunate fact remained that most of these advantages for some unexplained reason were for long withheld by the authorities who administered the scheme. The advantages and benefits intended for the sorting force were precisely and definitely laid down ; but the Department, either thinking that the force did not merit justice in such full doses, or from some mistaken conception as to the spirit and letter of Mr. Fawcett's measure, did not give them the full benefit of it there and then. Indeed, it even came to be contended that the Fawcett scheme was never meant to apply to the London postal staff. The men had been taught to be grateful for small mercies. They had been willing to open their mouth and shut their eyes, inspired by the new hope of getting something, just as they had prepared themselves never more to expect anything else than to live and die in the service, discontented and ill-treated to the last. The generous offer of an immediate small monetary benefit overwhelmed them. They were in the position of the pauper coming in for a windfall who is content so long as he gets only a portion, reserving till later his inquiries as to the peculations of others and the extent to which he has been robbed by the good kind guardians meanwhile. It is sufficient to say that very little of the advantages set forth in the scheme, which was said to cost so much, was interpreted to apply to them. In the matter of payment for extra duty even they found themselves no better off, while every other expectation that the scheme had raised slowly dwindled at last into a vague sense of disappointment and a loss of faith in the justice of the Post Office stewards. Resentment did not come until the actual discovery later on that they had been cheated out of Mr. Fawcett's good intention. It was not till the blind Postmaster-General was still and voiceless in the quietude of the grave that the suspicion took definite shape that some of his principal benefits had been so long withheld from them. It was that discovery and that conviction which furnished the real primary reason for the starting of a further great agitation in a few years' time. It is only necessary, however, to refer to this in passing ; that forms a portion of the narrative to be told presently. The scheme therefore failed in its effect through being applied only in a too niggardly fashion by those who administered it. It was made to fail mainly because of that ; but its failure was partly due to its own internal defects.

One fault of the Fawcett scheme—one which was not discovered until some long time afterwards, but which was destined to prove the source of further trouble—was its ambiguity in several of its terms as applied to the " sorting clerks " and " sorters." On the face of it the textual phrasing of the scheme was clear and precise enough, and there is no reason to doubt that both Mr. Fawcett and the Lords of the Treasury meant to be perfectly and honestly unambiguous. Yet owing, it may be supposed, to the lack of efficient organisation among those whom it most benefited, the full value of the measure was not so fully examined as it might have been. The sorters especially were only too glad to receive without criticism, and without looking such an unexpected gift-horse in the mouth, any remedy for their present grievances. And so the letter-sorting staff ate the lotus leaf of contentment, and for a long time were too busy with self-congratulation to have any suspicion of the doubt which was to arise by-and-by as to whether they were enjoying all that they were entitled to by the textual warrant and by the intention of their benefactor. The manner of its application and its interpretation by the officials was never questioned, therefore, until several years later, when the expansion of the service and the growing requirements of the force made it only too evident that the Fawcett scheme, conceived and inspired though it was in the most generous spirit, was impossible of adaptation to circumstances for all time.

That the London sorters were identical with the " sorting clerks " alluded to specifically in the scheme the sorters themselves had little doubt, while they had a vague impression that they were now given something nearly approaching to equality with the telegraphists. But they were not induced to inquire further, or to examine the terms of their bond more closely yet awhile. This was not the result of their apathy so much, however, as their want of knowledge about the scheme itself.

A notion prevailed that the printed scheme was something forbidden to the minor officials, and as unobtainable as the sibylline books. In fact, it was not till fully eight years later that it came to be discovered that it could be obtained in the ordinary way as a Parliamentary publication. It was reserved till 1889 definitely to inquire for themselves whether they had or had not received the full benefits secured to them under its provisions. And even then it seemed that their late benefactor was to be robbed of the credit and the honour that were due to him. In fact, as will be learnt, little less than an insult was to be offered to the memory of the dead statesman.

CHAPTER XII

BEGINNINGS OF THE TELEGRAPHISTS' MOVEMENT—AN EARLY
ATTEMPT AT A STRIKE—A COUP D'ÉTAT—" SCUDAMORE'S
FOLLY."

AT this point it is necessary to go back a number of years to
gather in a trailing strand that has yet to be spliced into the
body of the narrative. As has already been noted, the spirit
of discontent and agitation in the Post Office had strongly
manifested itself in various ways before the year 1870. For
nearly twenty-five years trouble in the postal ranks had shown
itself from time to time. And the taking over of the telegraphs
by the Government, and placing the old companies' staffs
under the wing of the Post Office, was to recruit new forces
for the army of discontent. If the men thus taken over had
had a little more consideration shown them from the outset,
perhaps much of the future trouble which from the first
moment was set brewing might have been arrested. But it
was not so, despite the promises held out to them, and it was
not long before they realised that they were to remain a
neglected body.

Before the transfer the telegraph business of the country
was divided amongst three principal companies, " The Electric," " The United Kingdom," " The British, Irish, and
Magnetic," and, for London only, " The Metropolitan District
Company." They had no connection with each other, but it
seems that the men in their employ indifferently rambled from
one to the other on the mere strength of having been formerly
employed anywhere as a telegraphist. The class of men for
the most part so employed was a very mixed one, and consisted largely of those who had " come down in the world,"
often men of birth and education, and those shipwrecked from
other vessels. They seemed to be an independent, Bohemian

lot, and somewhat nomadic in their habits, for not infrequently those dismissed or resigned from one company, with little difficulty took a seat in another of the three. The conditions were much about the same, and the salary equally poor, averaging about £1 a week. But though the salary was low, and the prospects ill defined and unsatisfactory, it was understood that there were other means of making money in a small way. There was apparently a looseness and a happy-go-lucky style of freedom obtaining among the telegraph companies of this period that enabled the operators to obtain for themselves certain privileges which ultimately became their rights. Their salary was low, but in course of time it was to some extent compensated for by the acquisition of perquisites and small emoluments. These often consisted of keeping the offices open after hours, and making their own charges, levying taxes for porterage on messages, taking allowances for string, paper, and other material. In some cases these privileges and emoluments accruing to the senior men were farmed out among the juniors to save time and trouble. A company's operator might occasionally constitute himself a temporary agent for his company in his spare time after ordinary hours of duty, charging sixpence extra on each message, and this the companies rather encouraged than otherwise. The men were on free and easy terms with most of the business men in their locality, and presents and Christmas-boxes of a substantial nature often came to them in the form of provisions, etc., in recognition of services rendered in emergency. There was generally a telegraph office at the more important railway stations throughout the kingdom, and the railway officials commonly extended privileges to the telegraph companies' operators. Railway fares were scarcely taken into account in the cost of living, and a telegraph operator attached to a telegraph office on any company's line experienced little difficulty in obtaining a free pass for almost any distance.

Such a precarious system of remuneration for their services was almost as unsatisfactory for them as it proved to be for the telegraph-using public ; and it is doubtful if such a state of things could have lasted much longer when the requirements of the service broadened and developed.

When it became known in 1868, through the passing of the

Telegraph Act in that year, that the companies and the men together were to be swept into the Post-Office, it was very naturally expected that there would be some improvement in their prospects, even if no immediate benefit were offered them. The men, therefore, in anticipation that their future under Government service would be somewhat improved, put themselves on their best behaviour, and stiffened themselves up a little more.

As was only to be expected among such an independent body of men, who, through all their career in the service of the old companies, had been allowed much liberty and discretion and those few privileges only possible in their employ, dissatisfaction soon followed on disappointment, when it was learnt that, after all, nothing was to be gained from the transfer. High hopes had been entertained by the telegraph clerks by the occurrence of one passage in the 1868 Act, to which great weight and importance had been attached. The clause read : " Such Officers and Clerks upon their appointment shall be deemed to be, to all intents and purposes, Officers and Clerks in the Permanent Civil Service of the Crown, and shall be entitled to the same but no other privileges."

Instead of which, while there was no improvement in salary, all the little privileges and chances of emoluments were of necessity withdrawn. They were subjected to a far more rigorous rule of discipline than they had in their free-born manner been accustomed to in their former employment. In the old companies many averaged £2 a week at least, though there was no fixed rate of salary ; but when the Government took them under its paternal care, there was no consideration made for what they had lost or left behind. The companies had been bought over lock, stock, and barrel, and the human machines, despised, but indispensable, were thrown in as chattels and makeweight. The estates had been bought, and with them the serfs living on the land ; and, being useful only to make the estates pay, they were, in the usual logic of the circumstances, least considered. The average wage was only 17s. or 18s. a week ; there were no meal relief for provincial men ; there was compulsory excessive overtime, in some cases for nothing, and in most cases next to nothing.

They saw that if they were to obtain better treatment and fairer prospects, as befitted their new character as Government servants, they would have to fight for it. This they commenced doing by means of petition. But these petitions were either ignored or refused, and not the slightest concession was made. The compulsion to bring up their starvation pittance to a normal wage by an excessive amount of overtime, poorly paid for—often no more than threepence an hour—with also excessive punishment by the imposition of extra duty, without pay, for the most trifling errors, soon proved that they had jumped out of the frying-pan into the fire. While the telegraph service was divided among a number of private companies, and while the telegraph clerks remained a limited class, they could play on the rivalry among the companies, and had things pretty much their own way when a grievance oppressed them. But under the new conditions of service they found that, on the score of their serving the Crown instead of a private concern, they were expected to accept conditions and treatment which would not have been tolerated for a month under the old system. The eight hours' day was reduced to a mere farce by the compulsion to earn anything approaching a decent livelihood only by means of miserably-paid overtime. They found that they were expected to pay dearly for the honour of serving a Government monopoly, and that, moreover, they were at the mercy of the Department because it was a monopoly. Their hopes and expectations, based on the explicitly-worded clause in the Telegraph Act of 1868, were almost from the first moment of their entrance through the portals of the Post Office dashed to the ground. They saw that the public and themselves had been hoodwinked by the specious promises held out to the old companies' servants. They therefore decided to put the public in full possession of the facts of their case ; and if they could not obtain redress from the Department which had so far betrayed their confidence, they would adopt other and more drastic means. The old companies' men were not so tame and submissive as perhaps the authorities had anticipated. They regarded the clause in the Telegraph Act as undoubtedly covering themselves, and at least, if it did not entitle them to being placed on an equality with the lower or second division of the Civil Service—upon which, they maintained, the framers of the Act intended them to be placed—they should be accorded better treatment in minor respects.

The scant hospitality the new comers had received at the hands of the authorities for months rankled deeply within them. They found that they had been delivered into the house of bondage ; and Mr. Frank Ives Scudamore, and the others of the authorities who wore their honours so thick upon them for effecting the transfer of the mighty business, were hard and inconsiderate taskmasters where their humbler servants were concerned. The disappointment increased with the realisation that the Department repudiated its promise and its obligations as contained in the Act, and the mutterings of discontent swelled in volume.

The first attempt at organisation for redress was made in 1871, the year following the transfer. If they came in like lambs, they preferred to go out, if they went out at all, like roaring lions. During the few months they had been in the employ of their new masters the thousands of company men had found a ready means of intercommunication and an exchange of news and ideas. Men became familiarised with each other from a distance all over the country, and the electric current of discontent ran freely along the wires from every large centre. In every large office throughout the kingdom there were eager spirits waiting for the opportunity to do something towards promoting the agitation and establishing a common line of action. They had the very instrument in their hands which most favoured their desire and their plans. The mine was laid ; it wanted but the electric spark of a united purpose to fire the train. Exactly how the mine was prepared and sprung perhaps will never be definitely known. It was communicated from several of the large towns that the aggrieved men were animated with a single purpose and desire ; each did their share in the way of convening meetings among the staff, in making collections for a general fund, and giving mutual help and encouragement. As is always the case, the leaders came forward as the occasion demanded it ; but it is somewhat difficult to assign the authorship of this first movement to any particular individual. The agitation was less the result of any personality or quality of leadership than it was the spontaneous response to a widely-spread sense of injustice. One curious result of the unanimity of feeling, and the spontaneity of its translation into action, was that almost every town in turn afterwards claimed to have taken the initiative, and to have produced the arch agitator who originated the movement. At this time of day the claim of Manchester is almost universally allowed. Manchester from the first moment uprose as a mountain of discontent ; it produced both men and money for the agitation, and became the seat of the memorable strike. But for long afterwards, before the fragments came to be pieced together into historic orderliness, and while the discussion which always succeeds the battle was proceeding among the late participants, it was contended that Bradford had an almost equal claim. There was one man at Bradford office, a counterman, a man of superior attainments, a gentleman by birth and education, who, realising the situation, conceived the possibility of a universal agitation among telegraphists, if not all postal servants who had wrongs to be righted and grievances to be redressed. He was not the only one who shared this dream at that time ; and possibly, had it come a couple of years later, when the postmen's agitation was in full swing, it might have been realised to an extent which would have proved even more embarrassing to the Government than it did. Ashden was the name of the Bradford man, whose ambition was equal to his discontent, and with a courage that outweighed both. He thought it necessary to complete the organisation without delay, and to this end at once threw himself into the fray, and tacitly assumed the leadership of the Bradford contingent. There was a series of the usual backstair meetings, and others more or less secret, but a meeting on a more pretentious scale was held outside the town at a place called Smithy's Bridge. This was an exclusive if not altogether private gathering, only a chosen dozen or so being present. It was in reality a conference of the powers, for it consisted principally of delegates from the centres of disaffection and the prominent agitators of those places, including Mulholland and Hacker of Manchester, and Norman of Liverpool. They met to decide on some common plan of action in response to the desire on every hand. It was shortly after the meeting at Bradford that the Telegraphists' Organisation was formally founded.

In the meantime, however, the same discontent begotten of irritation and disappointment at the manner of their modest claims being ignored, found a voice at Liverpool, Manchester, Edinburgh, Dublin, and various other places. The decision come to at Bradford was taken away to each of these centres, and there discussed and pondered over, and resulted in a small conference at Manchester being held in a room at the Railway Tavern, while a similar meeting was held at Liverpool at the Clock Inn, London Road. At each of these communions Ashden made his influence felt and helped to mould the plan of future action.

The meeting-place of these early secret deliberations—the historic Old Clock Inn, in the London Road, Liverpool— will always be remembered as a landmark in Civil Service Trades Unionism. The then landlord of the " Old Clock " was an active friend and sympathiser of the aggrieved Telegraphists, and during their secret conclaves on his premises found means to warn them whenever official spies were present or watching the house, while he also helped to provide alternative accommodation in emergencies.

In due course, on October 21, 1871, a Telegraphists' Association was formed, Manchester being the head centre ; and from the moment of its inauguration three Manchester men—T. W. Mulholland, Hollingworth, and Heald—were the acknowledged leaders. Needless to say, the newly-formed association found plenty of work to do from the very start.

Almost from that moment the leadership practically centered in T. W. Mulholland, the secretary, for his outstanding qualities both as a speaker and an organiser. He was specially fitted for the position. If he did not actually inaugurate the movement, he was certainly the most conspicuous of the prime movers. He favoured the militant or " forward " policy, the more daring line of action of inviting public notice and soliciting the aid of the Press and political support. And, further, if he was not the author of the aggressive and defensive strike policy itself, he was later given the credit of it by the authorities. It followed, therefore, that Mulholland was blamed for many things, and whatever

K

was on foot, or whatever turn events took relative to the
agitation, it was generally traced to Mulholland. Throughout,
he seems to have inspired everything, and infused his personality into it, and through all the events which led up to
the strike and which immediately followed it was the
doughty Mulholland that the authorities had in their eye
most of the time. Ashden of Bradford, Norman of Liverpool,
Heald and Hollingworth of Manchester, played their parts
with ability, and came in for a fair share of official attention,
but it was Mulholland who remained the central figure, and
the chief conspirator they were waiting to capture. And it was
T. W. Mulholland whose name was to become almost a
tradition in the service long after the coming storm had
passed.

T. W. Mulholland, the fair, inoffensive-looking young
man with the high, dome-like forehead, dark, deep-set eyes,
and gentle, studious expression, had entered the old " Magnetic
Company " as far back as 1854. Originally intended for a
journalist, he had entered the Telegraph Company only as a
temporary expedient, but, singularly, it was really the postal
agitation, through which he nearly got dismissed, that held
him in the service. His desire for postal reform became so
insistent that, it was said, he was offered the postmastership
of Jersey, then that of Kingston, Jamaica ; but he preferred
the stern delights of agitation, and sacrificed everything in
his efforts to improve the lot of his fellows. He was about
to get married when the trouble broke out, but the incidental
expenses of starting the agitation swallowed all his savings,
and left him nothing but his liberty to carry on the fight.

The authorities, seemingly anticipating that there would
presently be trouble among the men, had made some preparations for an emergency, and at the same time provided
themselves a means by which the old company men could be
discarded if they proved too importunate. In some of the
larger towns selected men were made " clerks in charge."
Those who undertook the rotation were for the most part the
old companies' transferred men and others who had been
engaged after the transfer, and who were beginning to smart
under the conviction that they had been enticed into the
service under false pretences. In their eagerness to put a foil

on the prevailing discontent the authorities took into the service any one who had the barest and most rudimentary knowledge of an instrument : the halt, the lame, and almost the blind being also accepted. Though often of little use, these newly-imported men in some cases succeeded in getting higher wages than the men who did the real work. Scores of old companies' men were getting but a pound a week or less, while ex-pupil-teachers and others were brought in from the streets and given twenty-five shillings. Such things could not but produce still further friction, and it looked as if the preference would be given to these men who were so unjustly set off against them. In fact, it soon proved so in some instances, and a number of the younger of the companies' men became so disgusted that some joined foreign cable telegraph companies, preferring to trust their future to private employers than to a Government department which could treat them so. Others went to America, and were still better received. A large number of the youngsters whose fathers or relations were already in the Post Office had been placed under tuition as learners before the transfer, and these and the others, ex-schoolmasters, etc., were induced to take little or no part in the drama.

It is significant that soon after the starting of the agitation, Mr. Scudamore, the Permanent Under-Secretary, promised a new scale of classification. This promise lulled the discontent for a while ; but the long-continued delay in bringing it out brought the feeling to an acute stage. The men did not let their mutterings go unheard.

The leaders of the Telegraphists' Association now became aware that all their communications to the various branches of the movement were, both letters and telegrams, being " Grahamed " or tapped, and it was more than believed that the authorities were exercising a rigorous censorship over the correspondence between members. To avoid this, messages to other towns were frequently forwarded by train, and eventually a secret code was arranged, the telegrams appertaining to the business of the movement being addressed to a private firm in Manchester. These telegrams referring to the arrangement of meetings and other business were handed in and paid for in the ordinary way over the counter, and, in the case of Manchester, all were addressed to Doncaster and Knowles, 75, Oxford Street, who, being in sympathy with the men, placed their address at their disposal. The code which was adopted was varied from time to time and as events progressed. The towns affected were referred to in these secret messages by various Christian names : " John " was London, " James " Manchester, " Charley " Birmingham, " Peter " Sheffield, " Tom " Liverpool, " Ben " Bristol, and so on through the whole list of towns. Numerals from one to nine were " tallow," " rape," " olive," " cotton," " linseed," " petroleum," " currants," " molasses," and " whisky." When the strike agitation was fully started the code was considerably amplified and rendered more complicated for safety.

Meantime the prevailing discontent and the threatening aspect of affairs did not escape the observation of the Press any more than of the authorities. A letter appeared in the London *Standard* directing attention to the movement in the provinces, and the imminence of a strike unless the authorities took action speedily. A day or two after, on the 7th December, 1871, officials from the Chief Office were sent down to Manchester to inquire into the condition of things. The result of this official inquiry was the immediate suspension of the leaders, Mulholland, Heald, Hacker, Hollingworth, and others forming the committee, while the same course was adopted at Liverpool and Bradford. The men were suspended for fomenting agitation and for forming an association in contravention of official regulation and the Law of Conspiracy. Similar Star-Chamber inquiries were also made at Liverpool the same day, with the result that one of the Liverpool committee, C. Nottingham, was suspended. It is difficult to understand why this man was singled out for suspension, as he was by no means the prime mover of the Liverpool movement ; Norman, Ryan (the treasurer), and others there being far more prominent. Nottingham was away ill at home when the officials desired him to be brought before them, and he was accordingly brought, ill as he was, in a cab to the office. After hearing his sentence of suspension, he was allowed to return home as best he might. When the Liverpool men realised what had taken place the excitement and indignation were great, and a meeting was called for the same evening. The meeting was held at a house in St. Anne Street. They had no sooner met, however, than they were made aware that the house was being watched by official detectives, who were stationed to take the names of those attending. The warning was passed to those on their way to the meeting ; while those who had already assembled were passed out by another door. Another rendezvous was found a little later at the Great Eastern Hotel, and here the eager crowd of outlawed telegraphists met to discuss the serious situation. Here it was decided, as the result of their deliberations, to present an ultimatum to the postmaster to the effect that if the suspended men were not reinstated by noon, and a definite time fixed for the proper classification of the staff, they would turn out on strike. To solemnise the decision come to, a borrowed Bible was produced, and the men present swore upon it that they would be true to each other, and not desert the cause. Telegrams were forthwith despatched that night informing other towns what Liverpool had decided on. These telegrams were, however, as it was suspected, intercepted. The ultimatum was next day, December 8th, presented to the postmaster, and they waited. Twelve o'clock struck, and simultaneously a gong, the sounding of which was the prearranged signal for decisive action, began to ring. Immediately everyone rose from his place in the instrument-room. But before they could leave in a body, the postmaster appeared on the scene, and standing in the doorway, made a speech in terms of entreaty and warning and proceeded to read an official paper. By this time the feeling had got out of bounds ; the tide had risen and was not to be pushed back with a mop. The postmaster had to stand aside, and the operators swept past him, then into the street ; and the strike began. If there was one office in particular that showed the example it was Liverpool ; Manchester, Bradford, Edinburgh, Glasgow, Dublin, and Cork, where similar scenes had occurred, following suit immediately afterwards.

The same evening a meeting was held at the Clock Inn, when a telegram was read from Mr. Scudamore to the Liverpool postmaster stating that the Manchester strikers had gone in to their duties. In his anxiety and excess of zeal during this troublous time the Under-Secretary was not above practising deception on the men, believing probably that the end justified the means. It was to get the recalcitrants back to work that this telegram was sent from headquarters. But the ruse was detected by the presence in Liverpool of a Manchester delegate, who was able on the spot to contradict it at once and reassure the Liverpool men that his town was firm. The suspension of the leaders was the signal for a general strike, and brought to a culminating point all the resentment and dissatisfaction which had been rankling within the breasts of the men for a twelvemonth past. In an instant the disquieting news was flashed from Manchester and Liverpool to every outpost in the kingdom. The beacons flamed up everywhere in a single hour. With one accord the men not only of Liverpool, but of Bradford, Edinburgh, Glasgow, Dublin, and Cork struck, and refused to resume their duties until the suspended men at Manchester were reinstated. As showing the spirit that animated them, one of the Manchester officials of the association, who was on sick leave through an accident, immediately on learning the step that had been taken, sent a message to his chief to the effect that he also was to be regarded as out on strike.

The secret censorship exercised over all telegrams suspected of emanating from the affected men considerably handicapped them in their action. Still, by the use of their prearranged code—whole sentences being signified by such names and words as " Turkish," " Canadian," " Trunks," " Bonds," " Arabia," etc.—they were fairly well able to communicate with Manchester and other places. Conflicting rumours, which it was not always easy to contradict or verify on the spot, were set afloat as to the movements. But what had been a strike at Manchester and elsewhere became a little later a lock-out at various other offices in the provinces. The assistance and sympathy shown by the telegraphists of other towns betrayed a feeling of general unrest, and there were other symptoms as unmistakable which decided the authorities to deal summarily with the whole. They decided on a *coup*, hoping that one bold stroke would terrorise the men into obedience and smash their organisation.

At noon next day it was noticed at various offices that the

messages received bore the signatures of strange senders at the other end of the wires. The fact occasioned no little comment, and the telegraphists of Bradford, Hull, and elsewhere, and in all the offices which of late had made themselves prominent in agitation, were not long in arriving at the correct conclusion. The storm had come, and they had got to face it, as they relied on their comrades in other distant towns also to face it. The same method of procedure happened everywhere, and in every affected office alike. A man was mysteriously sent away from his instrument and did not return, then another, and another. Meanwhile, those remaining at the instruments were endeavouring to obtain some information from the other end, but to all their inquiries there was dead silence, and they realised that their interrogations had only met with the fate of being silently recorded against them many miles away. Then some one in the room would break the tension of silence, and they would troop out in a body, knowing as if by instinct that the same was being faithfully enacted elsewhere. Then in most cases as they trooped out from the instrument-room they would be confronted with several burly town policemen, who would half direct, half hustle them into another room, where they were virtually made prisoners awaiting the pleasure of the local postmaster. In some cases the postmaster would carry out his official instruction neatly and politely. If it were so, all went well ; but in several instances the blundering over-zeal of an unpopular martinet nearly precipitated a riot. There is reason to think that the official instruction from London was to the effect that it should be effected as quietly and as discreetly as possible, and with few exceptions the delicate task of the postmasters was so carried out. Then while the telegraphists were waiting the arrival of the postmaster and other officials from whom they were to learn what was expected of them, a number of strangers newly arrived from London took their vacant places in the instrument-room. That being done, the door would be opened and the work of inquisition began. Generally, the local postmaster would be accompanied by the officials, and in some cases by the influential public men of the town, the mayor or the vicar. They were admonished for their behaviour in leaving their instruments in the manner they had, even though it had been so confidently expected that they would act so, and they were offered the opportunity of going back to their work, but on conditions which they as a body could not accept.

In one case, at Bradford, they were preached to for half an hour by a colonial bishop, the vicar of the town, Bishop Ryan, on the duties of obedience to their pastors and masters, and the desirability of remaining good and dutiful in that position in which it had pleased God for some wise purpose to place them. The good bishop, however, did not forget, in the course of his little homily, to turn to the officials forming a cordon round the postmaster, and remind them that it was his opinion that the men were being disgracefully treated. The postmaster addressed them, and others addressed them. But the men having taken the step they had, and feeling certain that exactly the same step was being taken in all other towns, would not return to work that day. The men were then released. Later, however, they were again called up, and directly questioned as to whether they each belonged to their association ; if so, would they sign an agreement to relinquish their society, and promise never again to agitate ? As was only to be anticipated, every self-respecting man refused. They were then, in some cases by policemen already stationed, unceremoniously bundled into the street as dismissed from Post Office employ.

In each of the towns where this took place there was generally much sympathy shown for the locked-out or, rather, dismissed men. At Liverpool there was a public meeting outside the William Brown Library. A strike fund was organised, and some of the leading cotton and stockbrokers of the Exchange contributed to the fund, no less than £70, by passing round the hat.

On the following Monday a prominent representative of trades unionism in Liverpool waited on the committee and offered to pay all expenses if they would raise an action at law against Mr. Frank Ives Scudamore for having suspended the leaders of their movement, as the trade unionists of Liverpool were of the opinion that such suspensions were illegal. A sum of £1,000 was freely mentioned, and it was stated that they were anxious to see the matter tested. This offer to defray the expenses of the prosecution was the result of a discussion on the question that arose at the Trades Union Congress at Nottingham. It was definitely proposed to prosecute Mr. Scudamore not only for illegally suspending members of a trades union, but for illegally suppressing their telegrams, and also wilfully delaying Press messages. The Trades Union Congress would assist financially.

On the day before the strike a telegram was forwarded from Manchester to the *Daily News*, intended for insertion as a press item, from one of the staff in relation to the suspension of the leaders there. The stoppage of this telegram by the authorities aroused the strongest indignation of the *Daily News*, and next day it commented in no measured terms on the " arbitrary and unjustifiable conduct of the London authorities." It was described as an attempt to establish a Russian censorship over news. Delays of telegraphic communications were frequent within this brief period, and to conciliate the public on the point the Post Office Secretary was afterwards publicly admonished with a wink by the Postmaster-General.

The press of the kingdom vigorously protested against the action of the Post Office Secretary, whose excuse was that he was compelled to do so in order to prevent what he termed the mutiny from spreading. This, however, did not stop the complaints in the House of Commons ; and at last the Postmaster-General, Mr. Monsell, stated that Mr. Scudamore had to be officially censured for his action. This was considered the first gain of the despised telegraph employé in the House of Commons.

On the same day that this offer was made, it was announced that the postmaster had been informed by one of their representatives that if all the men who had struck were allowed to return without prejudice the strike would terminate. But the postmaster, in reply, stated that no terms from the disaffected clerks themselves would be accepted ; and none would be allowed to resume unless they signed an officially-prepared form, expressing regret for insubordination, and begging to be allowed to resume duty on the terms of Mr. Scudamore's notice. At a meeting of the Liverpool men, held at the Clock the same evening, this announcement from the

Liverpool postmaster was received with hisses and dissent.

The day following a circular was issued to the strikers, signed by Mr. Scudamore, which was to the effect that they were to be recorded as being dismissed.

The Department, in deciding on taking this simultaneous step at a certain hour on one day, had made what preparations were possible at so short a notice ; but, as was only to be expected, the public service suffered accordingly for many days to come. Men with a knowledge of telegraphy were not so easy to obtain, as those who knew their work were appraised by the remaining companies at a somewhat higher value than the Government chose to put upon them. Consequently the men who were engaged to fill the places of those dismissed constituted a various and motley crowd for the most part, and in some cases actually had to learn their work as they went along. The natural result of so many immature tele-graphists being put to the work was a complete wrecking of telegraphic communication for days afterwards. The men, who were recruited from London principally, were, however, little to blame, either for the breakdown in the service or for the part they were made to play. For the most part they were complete strangers to each other ; men picked up from almost every walk in life ; many of them had known privation, and were glad of a berth under any conditions. It was, therefore, not greatly surprising that they knew as little of *esprit de corps* as they knew of telegraphy when first engaged.

What had really happened in London when the Postmaster-General and his advisers decided on a preconcerted signal to the postmasters of the provincial towns, was this : The class of psuedo-telegraphists already described, having been engaged some weeks before and put through a painful course of self-tuition, were at the end of that time regarded as having matriculated sufficiently for the purpose for which they were principally wanted. Then they were each in turn asked if they would care to be transferred to some provincial town, Liverpool, Manchester, or wherever it might be. All objections and demurs, if any, were immediately met by the offer to pay all expenses. One at a time, they were called into a room at the Chief Office in Telegraph Street, and told to prepare at a few hours' notice to be sent where their services were most required. The question of railway fares, and wives and children, and removal of home belongings was peremptorily brushed aside. They had only to name an approximate amount as covering all expenses, and, to their pleased astonishment, that sum was placed before them. The Controller's clerk was a few feet away presiding over an open box of gold, and on each of these poor seedy fellows being asked to name his amount, it was given him with no more trouble than obtaining his signature. It is not to be wondered at that the men were so easily tempted. If they were guilty of what in trade-union parlance is known as " blacklegging," then their offence was a venial one, inasmuch as they were not in a position to realise to the full what was being enacted.

The telegraphists' strike would probably have proved a greater success, from their own point of view, but for this temptation. And it was this reflection that occasioned the somewhat strained feeling between London and the provinces for some years following the incident.

The strike collapsed owing to the difficulties in rendering their organisation complete before such a drastic step was taken, and their unpreparedness to meet the prompt and decisive action of the Department. The contemplated attitude of the telegraphists was known to the authorities long before it was definitely taken up by the men ; their every move was anticipated. It was, therefore, and considering all things, not to be wondered at that they found themselves outmanœuvred at the finish. That the Department should have so completely squelched the movement in the manner it did was a matter for congratulation from a public point of view. But it must not be forgotten that all the legitimate appeals made by the telegraphists had produced no result but bitterness and disappointment ; while the very means adopted by the authorities to avert such a contingency went far to precipitate it. If the men's line of action was unconstitutional, the provocation was great.

It is only fair to say that the Department on this occasion extended a little clemency even in the hour of its victory. It was sufficient for it to have proved its power and authority, and—especially taking into consideration how useful, after all, were the services of such men at that time of day—it was amenable to reason, and allowed itself to be influenced on behalf of the dismissed and locked-out men. Six or seven of the more prominent agitators had been dismissed outright, while the locked-out men were kept out a considerable time before they were allowed to resume duty. These were all, with one or two exceptions, brought back one at a time through the influence of public men. Mulholland and three other Manchester men were not given the chance to return until six weeks afterwards. During the time of his suspension it was made pretty plain to him that he might return whenever he chose, on certain conditions ; but Mulholland resisted both blandishments and threats, and stuck to his guns unflinchingly during all the severe examinations through which he passed. The official desire was to obtain the books, documents, and papers in Mulholland's possession, which related to the business and the working of the agitation. That desire of Mr. Scudamore was communicated to him through the Manchester officials.

After the strike attempt failed for lack of funds, Mulholland, it seemed, was marked down for dismissal. And during his six weeks' suspension he was subjected to every temptation by the local officials to betray his trust by handing over the books and documents in his possession relating to the formation of the Association. As this would have meant implicating his associates and revealing the part played by certain other provincial ring-leaders, he resolutely refused.

The Department's desire to obtain this evidence was great, but Mulholland's attitude was to remain consistent during the period of his suspension from duty.

The only reply sent in by the sturdy agitator was that the entire matter of his recent interview with the postmaster having been truthfully communicated by him to the rest of the suspended men, there was nothing to submit for Mr. Scudamore's consideration but the grievances of the telegraph operators, which led to the formation of an association. While his fate was trembling in the balance, he still maintained, in the most respectful terms, however, that this combination of telegraphists meant nothing more than an endeavour to obtain, not only their fair and equitable demands, but the performance of promises given by Mr. Scudamore himself. Further, Mulholland vigorously maintained that only the absence of an association at the time of the transfer was responsible for their being neglected for so long by the State department. During the whole time that these overtures were being made by the Manchester officials desirous of obtaining possession of the papers which would implicate others, Mulholland never for a moment lost his self-respect, or was tempted to forget what was due to himself as an honest man. On his refusal to deliver up the coveted documents, the official whose duty it had been to negotiate the bargain of betrayal attempted to deny that he had " either insisted on it or made a condition of it." Immediately following on this came a request for an explanation in writing as to why he should not be dismissed the service. The " explanation " was furnished promptly enough. But whether the official mind was ashamed to carry the matter so far, or the authorities felt bound to respect the honourable consistency of the man, Mulholland was not dismissed after all, at the end of six weeks' suspension being quietly allowed to resume his place. The rest of the Manchester staff meanwhile, misled by the false and contradictory reports that the clerks in other towns were wavering or willingly returning to duty, gradually themselves resumed work.

If Ashden of Bradford was the man who conceived the federation movement on a big scale, Mulholland it was who, in the eyes of the authorities, was the " rebel chief " and the " head and front of offending " in the first strike among the telegraphists. Norman of Liverpool was an outstanding figure at the time, and did much to earn the loyal remembrance of his colleagues and his class, but Mulholland of Manchester, as the head of the central branch of the Telegraphists' Association, bore the brunt of the inquisition which followed. The ordeal through which he then passed, and the firm but respectful attitude maintained, showed the manner of man he was and the stuff of which he was made.

The attempt at " direct action " with which Mulholland identified himself, and for which he was in a measure responsible, may have been ill-judged, as the issue showed, but his gifts, qualities, and zeal for the cause he believed in, were worthy to have adorned a more successful movement. Forlorn hopes, though afterwards condemned for their rashness, often bring to light qualities of leadership which in other circumstances might have made fine generals.

Mulholland's reputation was long to survive the collapse of the strike, however, and the future years were to see him still the honoured chairman of the Manchester Branch of the P.T.C.A., and still the sturdy agitator to the end of his days. Under a mild, genial, and unassuming manner, as they had learnt, he had the qualities of the born fighter. From that time onward he was never to lose his hold on the affections of the whole body of telegraphists, and thousands who had never seen him or heard the sound of " Old Mul's " voice, acknowledged him as the leader and father of the movement. He was, indeed, to become almost an idol in the service. T. W. Mulholland lived to be honoured by his confreres, and respected even by those who had been his official opponents, and passed away while still in harness in 1894, leaving a name that will long be remembered as that of a fine pioneer and a fearless advocate.

But to get back to the strike period. While most of the men who comprised the committees in the various towns were still under suspension, a grand concert was organised at Liverpool on their behalf, and to help to defray the expenses that had been incurred. The concert took place at the Concert Hall, Lord Nelson Street, on December 22nd, 1871. It was highly successful ; Mr. Osmond Tearle, the well-known actor, who in his earlier days had been a Liverpool telegraph clerk in the old " Magnetic Company," rendering great assistance with his recitations of " Eugene Aram " and other pieces. A special prologue was spoken on this occasion, in which the following lines occurred :—

> " But hold, enough about the little wire
> Which carries all the tidings we require.
> 'Tis of the workers we would speak to-night,
> Who, but for asking what was just and right,
> Are turned adrift to face the world anew ;
> And first they seek their sympathy from you.
> Withhold it not in this their hour of need ;
> And may to-night's proceedings quickly lead
> To well-paid work, where energy and skill
> May meet with justice, kindness, and goodwill."

The suspended men on whose behalf the concert was held were Messrs. Norman, Ryan, Robinson, Nottingham, and others.

Within a fortnight after the collapse of the strike the whole of the suspended men at Liverpool were reinstated. The men of other affected towns were similarly recalled to duty, or induced to return by promises that the grievances of telegraphists generally should be immediately seen into. Thus terminated the brief but exciting strike period of 1871.

Ashden of Bradford, regarded as one of the principal ringleaders, being allowed to return, was after a while dismissed for " generally unsatisfactory conduct." Few of those who had participated in the recent unfortunate attempt at a strike were allowed to remain at their own offices, for fear their influence might survive, and it was thought a very necessary precaution to transport them to other distant places. By this means they were well distributed about the country, as it was thought that a man finding himself among strangers would be less prone to give effect to his proclivity for agitation.

Judged on the surface, the strike was a complete failure ; but its actual effect was a lesson both to the men and the authorities. It rudely awakened the Department to the fact that some improvement was imperatively necessary ; and at the same time it paved the way for a protective organisation on an improved and permanent basis.

There can be little doubt that these few days of excitement and agitation must have been very trying to one in the position of Mr. Frank Ives Scudamore. Though perhaps he had to take some share of the blame for making possible the strike, it must be said he acted with some tact, firmness, and moderation in the handling of an extremely delicate as well as difficult problem which had thus suddenly confronted the Department. But he might have averted it in the beginning by a little of the good judgment and moderation displayed towards the end. His warning circular issued to the strikers the day after they broke out of bounds, was almost as much an appeal as a command to the erring ones to return to the fold. He seems to have been a man of a somewhat gentle nature whom circumstances eventually hardened into an indifferent diplomatist.

Then there was a breathing time for some months, and the men cautiously refrained from discussing and advertising their grievances too freely, but they were sustained by the hope, based on semi-official information, that some sort of remedial measure was being prepared by the Department.

In August, 1872, the hope was realised. A scheme of classification was introduced, and its reception was hailed with increased satisfaction when it was found that it dated back nearly a year, and covered the strike period. Under this scheme some few clerks received an immediate rise in wages, and considerable sums in back pay. That in itself was a most palatable sauce, and helped the digestion of the scheme very considerably for some. Whatever the intention of its authors, it proved to be not so fair as it appeared on the surface ; and its application to practical uses proved its worthlessness in meeting all the demands of the telegraphists. With the monetary improvements, so far as the maximum was concerned, there was perhaps least to grumble at ; but it left entirely untouched the other grievances which pressed so sorely upon them.

Perhaps the name of "Scudamore's Folly," by which it afterwards came to be distinguished, most aptly described it. The dissatisfaction which it so soon produced placed it almost beyond doubt that it was full of leakages. The higher rates of pay were regarded as so far beyond the immediate reach of the majority that the solatium of back money bestowed on the fortunate few was soon forgotten ; it was found that the promised promotion speedily came to a standstill ; and there obtained, generally, the same annoying and irritating conditions as prevailed before the strike. The evils which the Scudamore scheme was set to cure were by its operation rather accentuated than mitigated. The telegraph staff, which then numbered 5,233, were divided into numerous classes with absurdly low wages, and increments which were microscopic. The ultimate prospect of a decent living wage was so dim and distant that it was scarcely worth taking into account. By the scales of pay indicated in the scheme, a telegraphist had to creep up from a minimum of eight or ten shillings a week by annual increments of a shilling till he reached the halting-ground of twenty-one shillings a week. By the time he

reached this guinea a week he was a full-grown man, ready in
the natural course of things to become the head of a family in
the full performance of his duties as a father and a citizen.
Many of them then, needless to say, had so far tempted
misfortune. And having arrived at the guinea a week, the
lowness of their wage rendered them the ready slaves of the
Department at sixpence an hour for overtime. A period of
sixteen years was allowed by the scheme for a man to reach
the Elysium of the second class, which rose from £70 to £90
a year. For the sum of a guinea a week gratuitous Sunday
labour was imposed, and for eighteen years was rigidly exacted
because it was in the bond. When at last public opinion
compelled the resumption of payment for Sunday work, the
Department with unconscious irony granted it as a " concession," and afterwards pointed to it as a reason for continuing an inadequate scale of wages.

At the introduction of the scheme the London force consisted of 688 men and 1,038 women. To seven-tenths of the
male staff it gave an average wage of 23s. 5d. a week, and
to the remaining three-tenths, 55s. 4d., or 32s. a week more
than the others. The reason for such a striking difference on
so trifling a wage-scale was not made public. The female
section met with similar Shylock-like generosity. Eighty-one
per cent. got between 16s. and 17s. weekly, and the rest 31s.
The actual scale in the Central Telegraph Office was :—

Senior Class	.	.	£140 to £160 by £5 per annum.
First Class .	.	.	£100 to £130	,,	,,
Second Class	.	.	£70 to £90	,,	,,
Third Class .	.	.	£45 to £65	,,	,,

What has always been derisively referred to as " Scudamore's Folly " condemned the London telegraphist to a life
of poverty ; but it condemned his fellow in the provinces
to something worse. The provincial male force numbered
3,507, and out of this number the generous author of the
scheme placed 213 male officers on fixed wages of 7s., 8s., and
10s. a week ; while to 151 young men it gave 12s. a week,
rising by annual increments of 6d. to 15s.—a state of things
closely analogous to the disgraceful boy-sorter system in
vogue on the postal side at the same period. The rest of the
provincial male officers were divided into small groups, but

L

it is sufficient to say that the greatest money-making department of the State had the effrontery to fix the average mean
pay of 3,012, or 88.4 per cent. of the whole staff, at less than a
guinea a week. Only 405 received the weekly wage of 50s.

By the great majority the " Scudamore Folly " was received
with resentment ; and it was not long before it produced a
plentiful crop of petitions, protests, and appeals, which,
however, were received politely only to be pigeon-holed.

A Select Committee of the House of Commons sat in 1876
to inquire into the whole working of the telegraphs, and in
their report to the House strongly recommended the desirability of training the operators in the scientific and technical
knowledge of the complex and delicate apparatus by which
they had to perform their official duties. This was expected
to procure some further official acknowledgment of the value
and importance of telegraph work. But the importance and
significance of this recommendation do not appear to have
struck the official mind till June, 1880, when the Secretary
notified that in future promotion would to a considerable
extent be dependent on the acquisition of this technical knowledge. The invitation was responded to very largely in the
hope that some benefit would accrue ; but all the time, energy,
and confidence were wasted completely.

Men had still to perform overtime at inadequate rates of
pay to supplement their incomes, and they were still
inordinately punished for comparatively trivial errors and
shortcomings. Altogether, the service, in spite of this
Scudamore scheme, became so unpopular and so unbearable
for a number that, according to a special Parliamentary return,
no fewer than 2,341 out of 6,000 telegraph clerks left during a
period of eight and a half years, a large number joining the
cable companies, where they received better treatment and
more encouragement. Certainly there must have been something radically wrong to account for this extraordinary
exodus, and for the fact that public servants were driven
wholesale to seek refuge with private employers.

Dissatisfaction became so rife that after about eight years,
namely, in November, 1880, a fresh movement was set afoot.
This time it was at Liverpool that the phœnix was to rise from
its ashes.

CHAPTER XIII

ELECTRICAL influences had been in the air for some years
since the Manchester outburst, but a feeling partly of timidity,
partly of apathy, had prevented section joining with section
until some time after the Scudamore scheme. Nothing seemingly was done by the Department to attempt to check the
wholesale exodus from the service. One consequence of this
" great retreat," as it was called, was that those who remained
to supply their places were worked the harder. Nominally
the hours were eight, but fourteen, fifteen, and even seventeen
hours were commonly worked in a single day when the
exigencies of the service demanded it.

The Scudamore scheme of classification, which should have
stood self-condemned by this time even from a departmental
point of view, was nevertheless tenaciously clung to by the
officials as a parent clings to its child. Yet opposed as they
were to all modification towards bettering the condition of the
telegraphists, it was at length driven home to the authorities
that something was needed to allay the daily growing discontent caused mainly by this detested scheme. But only a slight
modification was made, and that with timidity and reluctance,
The Scudamore system had egregiously failed of its purpose.
but its authors were yet slow to see it. Not even the patent
fact that it was false economy and a waste of public profits to
spend large sums in training telegraph operators who, one out
of every three, ultimately took their knowledge and experience
elsewhere, was sufficient to convince them. The improvement
that they were at last compelled to make consisted of a

sixpence increase in the year—an eighteenpence increment instead of a shilling—and one or two barriers to promotion were removed. But tinkering and botching of this kind were of no avail in mitigating the real hardships and injustices for which " Scudamore's Folly " was responsible.

When it was seen that the Department were bent on doing nothing further, the most cautious became indifferent to consequences, and their loyalty to the public service was put to the severest strain. Men who before had held back, with no stomach for agitation in any shape or form, now began to feel that it was their duty to take up arms in the common cause ; the most conservative felt that what they were risking was scarcely worth preserving.

The dissatisfaction became so general and so acute towards the beginning of 1880 that it was evident it could no longer be kept within bounds.

That the Post Office had persistently ignored what was averred to be a direct instruction of the Legislature as signified in the particular clause of the Telegraph Act of 1868 was the mainspring of the agitation of this period. On that clause the hopes of the telegraph service were centred, and the renewed agitation which was now to commence was mainly to be directed towards the attainment of this object and the fulfil- ment of this clause. Great uneasiness had existed among telegraph clerks for some time with regard to their position and future prospects ; but it was not till the beginning of December, 1880, that their grievances found open expression ; and only then in isolated petitions from various offices, which failed to secure attention. The third-class clerks of Birming- ham had endeavoured, by means of correspondence in the *Civil Service Gazette* and communication with other towns, to establish an understanding as to a plan of future action among telegraph clerks throughout the country. These efforts were, however, only partly successful, few towns responding to the call to co-operate.

The seed had so far fallen on stony ground, but not so at Liverpool. An article from the *Civil Service Gazette* being received there from Birmingham on 26th November, the question of co-operation was placed before the staff for con- sideration. A meeting was held the following evening, and after a lengthy discussion it was unanimously decided to enter upon vigorous action and rally to the assistance of Birmingham. A committee and officers were appointed, and a correspondence at once opened with other large towns to ascertain what steps had already been taken towards united action. These inquiries this time elicited a ready and hearty response, which far exceeded the most sanguine expectation, and it was safe to conjecture that a plan of campaign was now really possible.

The movement, if such it might be called, had up to that moment been purely a third-class one, and it was now established on a broader and more comprehensive basis. The *Civil Service Gazette* was more than ever used for ventilating their grievances. But confusion ensued from the many and multifarious schemes proposed ; and this only forced home the conviction, which had been slowly growing, that the ranks should be brought into proper line, that a few should assume a recognised command, and that they should have a workable base at one of the large town offices, from whence proposals might be put forward for general adoption. Liverpool, being in the first line of importance and convenient as a centre, in conformity with a generally expressed desire, therefore consented to take up the position of premier and pioneer. After mature deliberation on all available suggestions cognate to the work before them, Liverpool issued a circular to every office in the kingdom, and branches were instituted everywhere. Fresh offices flocked to the new standard every day, and the movement developed with astonishing rapidity. The metropolitan offices added new columns of support to the rapidly increasing structure ; London and the provinces were at last welded into one.

Their progress had, however, been not altogether unchecked, for in some quarters the authorities, looking askance on the strongly advancing tide, in a futile manner tried to resist it by bringing pressure to bear on particular prominent men. But the feeling had gained ground too rapidly ; the fire was alight, and had taken hold of the entire service by this time, and as fast as the official foot sought to stamp it out in one quarter it reappeared in another. At Sheffield and Cardiff there was some little trouble, and a few were made the sufferers for their progressive efforts ; but the telegraphists everywhere else proved equal to all the coercion that was brought to bear on them.

By this time they were not wanting for public friends, and many members of Parliament, who had expressed their surprise at the low wages and poor prospects held out to telegraphists, some thirty or forty of them, had voluntarily offered to do what was possible for them in the House of Commons when the time came. Prominent among those members of Parliament who had guaranteed their support were Mr. Monk—who years before had obtained for postal servants the enjoyment of the franchise,—Mr. Macliver, Sir Henry Drummond Wolff, Mr. Joseph Cowen, Mr. Jacob Bright, Lord Sandown, Lord Charles Hamilton, and Mr. (afterwards Sir) Stafford Northcote ; while Mr. John Bright and Mr. Joseph Chamberlain had also expressed sympathy and were interesting themselves on behalf of their Birmingham constituents. Added to this phalanx of Parliamentary support, the press had warmly taken up the telegraphists' cause ; and there was scarcely a paper of importance that had not from time to time made some reference to the agitation, and commented on the moderation and reasonableness of the claims put forward by the men. There was also a petition from the members of the London Stock Exchange on behalf of the men to the Postmaster-General, which bore 2000 signatures.

Professor Henry Fawcett himself, who had now become Postmaster-General, had led them to believe, in a speech at Manchester in January, that they might expect the fullest justice at his hands, and had promised to consider carefully their petitions. But one and all felt that it was necessary to strengthen the hands of the Postmaster-General, however liberal his intentions might be. They knew, and their public friends knew, that there was a power behind the throne which would have to be reckoned with.

The flowing tide of discontent, swollen by numberless tributaries from all over the United Kingdom, emptied itself into Liverpool on the 15th and 16th January, 1881. On those two days the first conference of telegraph clerks was held, and from then was to date the progress of the real telegraph movement.

The success, so far, of the telegraphists' agitation, and its being brought so rapidly to this important stage, was due for the most part to one man, Norman, now a telegraphist of Bristol, transferred from Liverpool in 1871.

Norman was a distinct personality, and from the first moment in 1871, when discontent became rife, he had been an influence. He, in conjunction with Ashden, Mulholland, Ryan, and others, it was who brought about the earlier agitation. Originally himself a Liverpudlian, he had been made to suffer for the part he took on that occasion by being transported to Bristol. In Liverpool he was on his native heath once more, and he was destined to take the lead for some time henceforth. He had had no difficulty with a few others, Kellamay, Brighton, and Alvine, in setting fire to Bristol. He could not be classed as an eloquent speaker, yet he nearly always convinced ; his well-measured tones always carried their point. His organising capacity was that of a general. He was a character eminently trusted, and easily begot a feeling of security among his followers. At Bristol there had been some doubts among the juniors that if this agitation were entered on the " pre-transfer " men might try only for a satisfactory settlement of their own case to the detriment of the juniors, and some little friction seemed likely ; but Norman simply gave one word of assurance, and all had such faith in him that perfect unanimity was restored.

This conference at Liverpool, which he had been so instrumental in bringing about, was to shape their future, and Norman was to point the way. A common programme was planned : a permanent Telegraphists' Association was decided on, and the work of formulating a national petition was put into the hands of the Liverpool committee. A permanent association was agreed on as the outcome of this first conference of telegraph clerks ; but it is a little curious to note that even Norman, whose original proposal it was, displayed some hesitation in the open adoption of the trade-union principle. It might be called an association for mutual benefit, or anything they chose, said Norman, " but whatever shape it might take, it must be as broad as possible, so that the Department could not say, ' You have a trades union.' " Even Heald of Manchester, one of the strike agitators, and a man who had suffered for his temerity on that occasion, took the view that to form a trade union of telegraphists would be to forfeit the support of the public, whose interests were so closely allied to those of the Department. In this year of 1881, when trade unionism recognised as such reared its head among every class of labour and was not ashamed, they as Government servants did not deem it wise to inscribe so much as its name on their banner. Bound as they were, almost, to accept it in spirit and essence, such was their conception of the public's requirements in the matter, and such their inclination to make concession to this old-fashioned sentiment indulged in by so many of their Parliamentary supporters, that they felt it would be imprudent to distinguish their movement by any label likely to offend such a prejudice. They were progressive enough in principle. They had men among them who had suffered in the cause of progress, and who were willing to do so again ; but they were not yet prepared to go the length of the postal agitators of a past decade, who had openly proclaimed themselves by joining with the London Trades Council. There were some among them who, indeed, had doubts about the legality of Government servants doing so in any case. So far as any such doubt was entertained, it was possibly a survival of that feeling which had caused the telegraphists of 1871 to refuse the offer of a sum of £1,000 for the prosecution of Mr. Frank Ives Scudamore for suspending men for forming an association.

Again, it had to be remembered that they were claiming to be classed as Lower Division clerks of the Civil Service as embraced by the terms of the Playfair scheme, and, as they conceived it, confirmed by an Order in Council in 1876. The arguments in support of this claim seemed most valid, and they had the authority of eminent counsel in support of their ambitious, though, after all, reasonable claim. It was, therefore, very natural, perhaps, that while they endorsed and accepted the principle, they should hesitate to weaken their case by avowedly adopting its ritual and its garb. Whether they were fully justified in so thinking is another matter, and it is the fact that has to be recorded.

It was not that Norman and those associated with him had not sufficient sympathy with the principle or the necessary courage to proclaim the fact. It was only that they were not as yet certain of their followers, who were made up of men of every shade of opinion, or of the advisability of calling a spade a spade. Yet they were to have their trade union just the same ; and from the first moment of its being launched some few months later, in December, 1881, the whole organisation was to be run on trades-union lines. But up to the present they had done no more than agree as to the necessity of a permanent society ; its actual formation must wait a little longer.

The one immediate outcome of the first Liverpool conference was the drawing up of a united petition, setting forth for the first time, concisely and clearly, their various claims. There were five principal grievances enumerated, together with the reasons for their removal. The first grievance complained of was the inadequate salary, and the hindrance to promotion given by classification. The second was as to the irregular as well as inadequate mode of payment for overtime ; the third complained of was that there was no special payment made for Sunday, Good Friday, or Christmas Day duties ; and it was therefore asked that these holidays be paid for as overtime. The fourth complained of was the insufficient annual leave of absence ; and the fifth complained of the insufficient subsistence allowance to clerks employed away from home on special or relief duties. This petition was signed by every office of importance in the kingdom, Liverpool, Manchester, Glasgow, and Birmingham taking the lead in the number of signatures ; and it was then presented in the beginning of February. With far greater expedition than they had hoped for, the Postmaster-General, Mr. Fawcett, intimated his willingness to discuss the points with a deputation of telegraphists. Accordingly, on the 15th March, 1881, a deputation of telegraph clerks, including their leading man, Norman, was received by Mr. Fawcett. It was on this occasion that the real strength of Norman was well displayed. The accredited orator of the telegraphists' movement, Michael O'Toole, was present ; but it does no injustice to him to say that Norman's closely-reasoned statement, made up principally of facts and figures which were incontrovertible, must have been more convincing to Mr. Fawcett than were O'Toole's more brilliant pyrotechnics. Instead of being allowed to state their grievances unreservedly, however, they found that the supporters and advisers of the Postmaster-General would allow them only to answer questions. Even the brilliant O'Toole was told that he was " not answering questions, but making a speech."

The interview, from which so much had been expected, was therefore not deemed satisfactory. The deputation found that they had to impress and convince not only Mr. Fawcett, but the permanent officials, who were numerously represented, and who considerably hampered freedom of discussion by their insisting that certain questions only be answered. The men desired to plead their own case in their own fashion, as they had been invited to, but it was seen that Mr. Fawcett's honourable desire was being quietly and firmly overruled, so that the interview terminated without many of the very necessary explanatory statements being introduced as was intended.

The disaffection grew apace, and a consciousness of their strength and the justice of their demands rendered them self-reliant. The agitation was renewed with increased activity. Mr. Macliver and other M.P.s rallied to their support. Numerous meetings were held all over the country, while the sympathy of the press and the public gave a character and an importance to their movement that could not much longer be ignored by the Government. The service was swept from end to end by a hurricane of discontent that had had no parallel even in the postmen's agitation of a few years before. The telegraphists were angered, and anger was becoming defiance. It was becoming a question as to how much longer they could be kept within bounds.

Mr. Fawcett, true to his democratic instinct, felt the greatest reluctance in imposing restrictions on the right of free public meeting among postal servants. His attention had been drawn, by both the officials and in the House of Commons, to reports of public meetings of postal and telegraph employés, and he expressed himself cognisant of these proceedings, at the same time intimating that it was not his intention to interfere or to visit any official punishment on those who had taken a prominent part. Undoubtedly some of the platform utterances of this period were rather extreme, and the distinguished Postmaster-General was not kept in ignorance of the fact. His forbearance was that of a strong and courageous man, and he probably felt that the best reply he could give to all the far-fetched assertions of the impatient army under his control was presently to offer them the scheme which he was then so busily preparing.

But meeting followed meeting and protest followed protest, till the blind, badgered Postmaster-General felt that he was at last face to face with the stern reality of a threatened strike. Then for the first time he uttered a cry of resentment. They ought to have learnt by this time that the delay was not due to any neglect of his ; they ought to have known by this time that he who had allowed the utmost freedom both in petitioning and public meeting, who lost no opportunity of finding out for himself what was wrong, was in reality an enemy of the official fetishism of which they most complained. In a Post Office Circular issued March 30, 1881, he strongly animadverted on the extreme course they were pursuing, and the manner in which the facts of the recent interview had been distorted by several members of the deputation. He maintained that he had never made any intimation that he would receive them alone without the presence of the permanent officials ; that it would have been contrary to all practice in the public service had the principal officers of the Department not been present ; and, as he had stated elsewhere, the object of the interview was simply to furnish him with such additional information as he might desire to receive. He expressed his strong disapprobation of their impatience and their method of showing it, but at the same time he conveyed a promise that nothing would prevent him from " doing full justice to the case of the telegraphists generally."

The very severe rebuke contained in Mr. Fawcett's circular to the postal telegraphists was by many among them felt to be in nowise undeserved, and being administered publicly did not tend to assist the movement at the time, alienating as it did some amount of public sympathy. The honesty of purpose of the Postmaster-General was generally recognised, and his rebuke, coupled with an unequivocal promise to do them justice within reasonable time, somewhat restrained the more ardent among the agitators. The reflection that this blind philosopher and statesman was grappling with an immense difficulty and a complicated problem, affecting thousands of others besides telegraphists, demanding time, patience, insight, and judgment, at last sobered their impatience. For the most part they came to acknowledge they had been too impetuous, though a number regarded the reproof as unmerited.

Mr. Fawcett kept his promise honourably, and on June 18, 1881, his scheme for improved pay and revised classification, covering both the telegraph and postal sides of the service, was issued. It was then seen how stupendous must have been his task. While a threatening and angry crowd without were demanding immediate redress, he was now patiently and busily preparing proposals for their contentment, and now battling with the Treasury on their behalf, and to get those proposals accepted. He had accomplished a great task, and in the circumstances the telegraphists felt that deep gratitude was due to him. As he had been the very first to deal with the postal side of the question from a truly statesmanlike point of view, so he had been the first to approach the telegraphist difficulty in the same manner. The application of the Fawcett scheme to the telegraphists brought them immediate and material benefits, and gave them a status and a better-defined position as Government servants. The defects of the late Scudamore scheme were greatly diminished, but, needless to say, the improved scale of pay was even better appreciated than the improved prospects of promotion, while a more equitable rate of payment for overtime, and a reduction of night attendance to seven hours, payment for Christmas Day and Good Friday, constituted the more acceptable features of Mr. Fawcett's measure for the telegraphists.

FAWCETT SCHEME, 1881 (TELEGRAPHISTS).
PROVINCES.

MALES.	FEMALES.
Second Class.	*Second Class.*
12/-, 14/-, 16/-, by 1/6 to 30/-, 33/-, 36/-, or 38/-, according to class of office.	12/-, 14/-, 16/-, by 1/6 to 23/-, 24/-, 25/-, or 26/-, according to class of office.
First Class.	*First Class.*
40/-, by 2/- to 50/-.	27/-, by 1/6 to 32/-.

LONDON.

MALES.	FEMALES.
Second Class.	*Second Class.*
12 /-, 14 /-, 16 /-, £45, by £5 to £100.	10 /-, 12 /-, 14 /-, by 1 /- to 17 /- ; then by 1 /6 to 27 /-.
First Class.	*First Class.*
£110, by £6 to £140.	28 /-, by 1 /6 to 34 /-.
Senior Class.	
£150, by £8 to £190.	

The concessions brought to them by the Fawcett scheme were evidently the result of much hard work and strong endeavour on Mr. Fawcett's part. Everyone felt that he had been animated by an honest desire to meet them fairly, and for such endeavours and such desire on his part they expressed their gratitude and thanks. At the same time it was universally felt that he had to a great extent been balked in his intention to accord them full justice. They were sincerely grateful to him for his manly and honest treatment of their demands ; but they knew that Mr. Fawcett's hands were tied, that his liberty of action was circumscribed, and that what he had obtained for them had been strenuously contended for and grudgingly conceded. In high quarters the scheme was regarded as a generous one, and it is perhaps doubtful whether the recommendations of Mr. Fawcett, if made by a lesser man and other than a Professor of Political Economy, would have been entertained and accepted. So that, in so far as it fell short of meeting their demands, they blamed Mr. Fawcett less than an unkind fate and the permanent officialdom in league with a suspicious and parsimonious Treasury.

As it was, however, they might have been prepared to accept the few flies in the ointment but for their discerning a disposition on the part of the authorities to whittle down at every opportunity the most acceptable and valued concessions contained in the scheme. Next to the improved wage-scales, perhaps one of the most highly-prized boons it gave them was that of reducing the night duty from eight to seven hours. But it had scarcely been conceded ere it was filched back from them with the declaration that " night " only meant from 10 P.M. to 5 A.M. The ungenerous spirit in which the benefits of the Fawcett scheme were applied to the telegraphists taught them to examine into their bargain a little more closely. The result was they found many things wanting, and the absence of which convinced them that they were justified in continuing the agitation. It was acknowledged that Mr. Fawcett intended to place them on an equality with the postal staff in the matter of preferment, but it was contended that it was not done. It was pointed out that there was an apparent similarity of wages, but that it was more apparent than real. While it was admitted that Mr. Fawcett's evident intention was to confer lasting benefits on both branches of the service, events would show that his retention of the discredited system of classification meant leaving to his successors a legacy of strife between them and their subordinates. Failing as the Fawcett scheme did to eradicate entirely the malignant growth of classification introduced by Mr. Scudamore, this scheme could not be accepted as a permanent remedy. By its operation, it was maintained, their rightful increments towards the maximum would be artificially arrested by class barriers. The effect would be to bar them from attaining a reasonable wage within a reasonable time, and they declared that they required a present living wage rather than the far-off prospect of reaching £400 a year at the moment of being forced through old age to retire from the service. Such a " prospect " was nothing more than a cruel *ignis fatuus* while this delusive system of classification was sustained.

One curious result of the Fawcett scheme was that the telegraphists declared that they were not placed on an equality with the postal side, as was intended by the spirit and letter of it, while the postal agitators a little later adopted similar arguments to prove that they had not been placed on an equality with the telegraphists, as was also intended.

Dissatisfaction with their position in the service, despite the late scheme, gradually became acute once more among the telegraphists. On July 17, 1881, one month from the issuing of Mr. Fawcett's intended remedy and stop-gap for further agitation, a conference held at Liverpool resolved that a permanent organisation covering the whole of the United Kingdom was an absolute necessity to prevent further encroachments upon them and to preserve what little they had already gained. December 3, 1881, saw the Postal Telegraph Clerks' Association launched into existence. Immediately, from all over the country, support was forthcoming, the greater part of the provincial offices rallying round the standard set up at Liverpool.

Mr. Fawcett, as may be imagined, was not pleased at the manner in which his well-intended scheme was received by the telegraphists, but he met all criticism and all opposition with that unflinching courage of the philosopher which was his chiefest trait. An utterance made by him at this period, when speaking at Hackney, November 2, 1881, affords an interesting glimpse into his mind on this question. On that occasion he said, " All experience shows that the sense of wrong remains long after a grievance has been redressed and an injustice remedied."

Whether or not the grievances had been redressed and the injustices remedied, as he honestly intended they should be so far as lay in his power, certainly the original sense of wrong was to remain long afterwards. This surviving sense of wrong, Mr. Fawcett probably hoped, would gradually die out as his remedy applied its healing balm. But it was to survive longer than he anticipated, and to be fostered till it developed into almost a passionate outburst which, in a few years to come, another equally great and strong man, Mr. Raikes, had eventually to calm and check temporarily by yet another measure of relief.

CHAPTER XIV

SEVEN YEARS OF STAGNATION—THE POST OFFICE AND GUTTER
JOURNALISM—REVIVAL OF POSTAL JOURNALISM—A CHRISTMAS
STRIKE AVERTED—FIRST GLIMPSE OF A NOTABLE AGITATOR—
THE PETITION THAT " HELD THE FIELD."

As there was a long period of inactivity and stagnation between
the period of the cruel dismissals in 1874 and the introduction
of the Fawcett scheme, so among the letter-sorters there
followed another such period after 1881. This time the period
of stagnation lasted nearly seven years. During that seven
years or more the service had relapsed into much about the
same condition as prevailed before Mr. Fawcett took office.
But for the slightly better rate of pay, the increase on the
maximum and an increased holiday for the senior men only,
the state of things was little better, if any, than twenty years
previous. The men had no organisation to safeguard their
interests, and consequently were more or less at the mercy of
minor officials, who very often did not scruple to take advantage of their helpless condition. That the indoor staffs on the
postal side of the service should have drifted into this, that
their very lack of combination should have courted the
over-zealous attentions of the minor authorities, is not to be
wondered at. Still less is it to be wondered at that their
interests were neglected ; that privileges were lost sight of
where they were not openly filched from them ; and that
sporadic and individual attempts to obtain redress remained
unnoticed and went unheard.

The monotony of this period was occasionally broken only
by the appearance of some criticism of Post Office administration, or of the petty tyranny of the lower officials, appearing
in one or two papers which pretended to have espoused the
cause of the men. Two of these papers circulated principally

in the gutter. One was the notorious *Town Talk*, which from time to time printed several ably-written articles on Post Office treatment of its employés. Had they appeared elsewhere than in its too-spicy pages, they might have commanded more attention and carried more conviction of their sincerity. Another was an appropriately-named print called the *Rag*, sold at a halfpenny, and with which for the brief period of its existence there was associated a lately-resigned sorter, who, from a knowledge of his own cruel experiences in the General Post Office, either wrote or inspired the bitter and vulgar paragraphs which, with pointed personality, were aimed for the most part at the minor supervisors, who were represented as acting the part of bullies and petty tyrants towards their helpless underlings. The *Rag* and *Town Talk*, however, came to an untimely end, and, so far as their peculiar advocacy of the postal cause went, perhaps it was as well. The Post Office employés were in such an oppressed state that they were ready to welcome any criticism almost that was supposed to be aimed at their taskmasters. But though such criticisms were read with some amount of interest by many, they gratified very few, while with many they disgusted more than they interested.

There was also started soon afterwards another belonging to this class of ephemeral journalism, but of somewhat better tone and character, an East-End local organ called *Toby*, which, during 1886, dealt week after week with Post Office abuses. *Toby* was supposed to have some additional claim on the patronage of postal servants by its being edited by a man who had once been behind the scenes in the Post Office. It enlivened its more or less pointed criticisms with rough caricatures of certain of the so-called petty tyrants who were supposed to gloat on human misery ; but the simulated and insincere malice of the caricatures was, fortunately for the intended originals, almost completely lost in the quality of the art. *Toby* for a time flourished in the gutters of St. Martin's-le-Grand, and sold in the streets about the City, but it was principally while the caricatures lasted to afford the amusement and excitement of guessing competitions among the sorters and letter-carriers of the General Post Office. When the caricatures gave out, and there were no more guesses as

M

to who was meant as the latest victim of the new Hogarth's pencil, the star of *Toby* waned in St. Martin's-le-Grand.

Advocacy of this nature, such as it was, did no more than cause annoyance and irritation to those who found a ready means to visit reprisals on the men whom they might suspect of being the secret instigators of such insults, while among the men it only satisfied an idle curiosity. Yet the men undoubtedly would have welcomed some proper medium to ventilate their growing grievances. The *Postman*, which had been started as the organ of a previous agitation, was long since defunct, and a copy of the *Beehive* was now almost a relic of ancient history. It was in response to this growing necessity for discontent to once more find utterance that a new postal organ started. It was called the *Postal and Telegraph Service Gazette*, and was contributed to by both sides of the service. It was admirably edited, and from the pens of the ablest writers among the telegraphists and the postal force some stirring articles occasionally appeared. It afterwards became the *Postal Service Gazette*. These new ventures in postal journalism provided a healthy outlet for the pent-up discontent of years. The articles were generally ably written and forcible, but there was not too much personality allowed in the letters from correspondents with a grievance. These organs helped in no inconsiderable measure to shape the course of future events, and, while promoting a spirit of freedom among postal servants, gave it a healthy and manly tone.

Still, even with the help of these organs, there was not yet a properly-organised movement either among the letter-sorters or the letter-carriers. Their recovery from the unmerited onslaught of Lord John Manners, and the effacement of the memory of it, was slow.

But, as is inevitably the case in the same set of circumstances, the harvest was sowing : there was a repetition of the same grumblings, and all the elements of discontent were once more developing. Gradually the old impositions as regards compulsory extra duty were being introduced ; the men's time counted for little or nothing, and their convenience as little. The Fawcett scheme had laid it down expressly that Christmas Day and Good Friday should be paid for as extra duty, but the whole recommendation, if not rendered altogether nugatory, was applied in a very unsatisfactory manner.

Christmas morning, 1886, was nearly witnessing one of those disgraceful rushes for the doors which had taken place on several occasions some years previously. The sorting force had been on duty all through the preceding night, and a long time before many, indeed, had been working the round of the clock. The men were dead beat, and they had been promised their liberty at nine o'clock. Perhaps there would have been nothing very unreasonable in the request that they should work a few hours longer, had it not been that they had to be back again on duty in the afternoon. But they had experienced this kind of treatment too many times before ; and when the clock struck the welcome hour of nine they left the sorting-tables and made to leave the office. Christmas extra duty at this time was looked on with aversion by the most of them, for, as an actual fact, the money they earned on that occasion, they knew, would not be paid them for three or four months to come. Every branch in the office, especially the Inland Letter Branch, was choked with work from floor to ceiling. The men were eager to get home to snatch a few hours' rest. Once more they found all the exits closed and bolted against them ; and they stood about in sullen groups considering what was best to be done. Mr. Jeffery, the then Controller, who had a reputation for great kindliness and consideration, came on the scene and appealed to the men to clear up the duty. He asked them why they refused to work when the Department was willing to pay them so well. There was no response for a few moments, when a youngster named Groves up and spoke to the great man, and told him that it was because they had to wait so long for the money ; and pointed out that the Christmas extra-duty money the previous year was not paid till the middle of the following summer ; he offered an assurance that if the money were quickly paid the men would doubtless be willing to stop. The Controller, it appeared, had not been aware of this senselessly-unfair cause of delay.

He readily gave his promise that if the correspondence were all cleared up before the morning was over, he would see that the money should be paid as speedily as possible, and that a special staff of men would be employed to get the account out. There was a cheer, and every one started work. The extra-duty money was paid within a fortnight, and was afterwards paid as quickly.

It was such petty annoyances and such instances of neglect as these, so long continued, that at last began to awaken the men to a fuller sense of their grievances, and which once more fostered the desire for combination amongst them. In addition to this, too, the idea was gaining ground that they were being systematically cheated out of benefits which the Fawcett scheme entitled them to. Now that he was dead, Mr. Fawcett was more than ever regarded as the postal Moses, and they looked for a clearer interpretation of the tablets of the law which he had left behind to help to build his monument.

The new desire for combination at first only asserted itself in a somewhat feeble manner when it became known that a Royal Commission on Civil Establishments would be likely to look in at the doors of the Post Office. It was then for the first time after so long that a few of the more venturesome banded themselves together for the purpose of collecting and tabulating suitable evidence on postal grievances generally, and for working up the interest of the men affected. Of this little committee J. H. Williams was chairman, and W. E. Clery was secretary. These two sorters, the latter especially, were destined to play a more important part in agitation later on.

The Commission on Civil Establishments had been moved for and obtained by Lord Randolph Churchill, and it was confidently expected that it would take evidence from the Post Office employés. An invitation had appeared in a Post Office Circular of December, 1886, for postal servants to prepare evidence, if any, to lay before the Royal Commission. Consequently, there were several meetings held, and representatives of almost every branch of the service on the postal side were present at these meetings, comprising sorters, letter-carriers, porters, bagmen, and even clerks and members of the major establishment, who were as anxious to make their case heard. A stupendous amount of evidence was thus got together and properly prepared. But though an enormous amount of labour was thus expended on the accumulated grievances of so many years, it was all love's labour lost, and never got beyond this stage. They sustained another disappointment, added to so many others, and learnt that the promised Royal Commission was not intended to come their way, but had concluded its labours. There was nothing left but for the postal committee to disband likewise, which they did with feelings of disappointment which went to feed still further the smouldering discontent among the men. They felt they had been deliberately fooled by the Department in being thus invited to prepare evidence which was to be wasted. Yet it was far from wasted, for the lesson had a real educational value, and one which was to bear fruit a little later on. The little experience, though fraught with disappointment, had none the less taught them the better to prepare their weapons for a future occasion.

At this time, if anything there was more real discontent among the juniors of the sorting staff than among the seniors. The greatest dissatisfaction prevailed among them mainly owing to the lack of promotion, for the sorting force being divided into two classes, first and second, the juniors had to remain at a certain barrier until a vacancy occurred in the class above them. They virtually had little but the hope of waiting for dead men's shoes. This system of promotion was becoming utterly discredited, owing to the fact that while the juniors' class was practically unlimited in number, that of the seniors was limited, and by no means in fair proportion. The average of deaths and pensions among their elders afforded a prospect only to the merest section of their number. It was maintained by them that the only fair remedy was the substitution of promotion by service, and not by death or pension. Five years, it was urged, was a fair period of service to entitle them to promotion to the class above them, and a movement was soon on foot to submit their proposal to the Postmaster-General. They were the young bloods of the service, and new blood had brought new courage and new vigour. Their case, carefully prepared, had been awaiting the arrival of the expected Royal Commission which never came. They, in consequence, resolved—or rather the youth who led them did, the same W. E. Clery who had acted as secretary of the late abortive Royal Commission movement—to effect what they could in amelioration of their position by using the readiest means to hand. Mr. Raikes was now Postmaster-General, and from all that had reached them of his justice and impartiality, they were inspired with a desire to go forward. It was thought that from every point of view this resolve was a wise one, as should another Royal Commission after all be ready to accept their evidence, and it was learnt that they had failed to petition the Postmaster-General, it might be urged that the hardship of a lack of promotion was one specially manufactured to suit the occasion, since nothing had before been heard of it. So there was a preliminary meeting of the juniors held in the largest refreshment-room of the General Post Office, and a bigger meeting was held in the same place a few days later, when a draft of the proposed petition was read and discussed. In the following month, September, 1887, the second-class men's petition was forwarded. This petition, to the Postmaster-General direct, was memorable if only from the fact that it was the first petition worth speaking of, the outcome of a general meeting, which had been forwarded to the public head of the Department since the day when Lord John Manners dismissed five and punished over a hundred of others for practically the same thing. The petition forwarded on the present occasion expressed in no unmistakable language that the men were unqualifiedly dissatisfied with the system of promotion by vacancy made by pension or death in the ranks of their seniors, and pointed out that, young men as the petitioners were, most of them would be superannuated before their turn for promotion came. It was conveyed to the Postmaster-General for the first time by means of this memorial that the provisions of the Fawcett scheme had not been given full effect. Now, one of the most marked features of the 1881 scheme was that the remuneration of postal employés should be " based upon the intelligible principle of paying for work solely according to its quality." It was urged, therefore, by these juniors, who so commonly were put to perform higher-class duties for their scanty wage, that their responsibilities should be recognised on the principle laid down by Mr. Fawcett. The petition concluded with a respectful request that, if the Postmaster-General required a further explanation on any particular point, he would receive a deputation of their body. There were two months of silence and waiting. Then in January, 1888, permission was obtained to hold another meeting in the refreshment-room, the meeting being called by the youth Clery, to consider what further steps should be taken to obtain an answer.

Clery had by this time practically assumed the leadership of the young men's movement, and though but a mere stripling, displayed from the first, in a very marked degree, qualities of leadership far beyond his years. He was a tall, pale-faced youth, with a rapidity and a fluency of utterance, tipped with a musical brogue, that at once betrayed his Hibernian nationality ; a decisiveness of thought and action, united to a method of close reasoning, that at once charmed, convinced, and astonished. He was just the spirit and the calibre to set down in the midst of a few hundred young fellows sore about their unredressed grievances, and he obtained their confidence without asking for it.

It was resolved at this meeting that a deputation should wait upon the Permanent Secretary, Sir Arthur Blackwood ; but in answer to their request for an interview it was curtly intimated to them that their memorial had been duly considered by the Postmaster-General, that he could not comply with their request, nor did he see any good in granting the interview asked for. By some means Clery got the answer so as to keep it to himself till the last moment, but by it he was decided to call another general meeting that same evening. There were such whisperings and a pretence at mystery on Clery's part that expectation was roused to the highest pitch, and a few minutes after eight o'clock the meeting-room was crammed almost to suffocation. Not since the days of the movement twelve or fourteen years before had such enthusiasm prevailed among a meeting assembled within the precincts of the General Post Office. The silence of fourteen years was broken, and, like the cheers of a beleaguered garrison who see the relief expedition within sight, the shouts of the crowded meeting testified to the new hope that had been aroused by the announcement that their petition " held the field." The convener and chairman of the meeting, Clery, had in his discursive and picturesque fashion gone over every single point of the petition which had been forwarded, and at last, after a rhetorical pause, he announced that he had received a reply which justified him making the declaration that the "petition held the field." This phrase became memorable to some extent from that moment because of the electrical effect and the enormous enthusiasm it momentarily produced. But it amounted to nothing more than a subtle trick of rhetoric on the part of the speaker, the success of which was not wholly effaced even by the subsequent disappointment when they learnt that the Postmaster-General had met their demands with an unequivocal refusal on every point. Their petition held the field only in so far as that not a single reason had been advanced against it. The feeling of mingled anger and disappointment which had taken possession of the meeting immediately after Clery's announcement was quickly turned to one of determination to press their claims still further despite the official rebuff. Another petition was forthwith prepared, asking for a reconsideration of the various points, but this met with no better fate.

The guns of the second-class movement was thus silenced, and as a sectional agitation the movement itself soon afterwards fell through. But it was not to die in the ordinary sense that sectional movements usually do die. It simply transferred its energies and its resources into a wider field. The conviction had been growing among all grades of the sorting force that they all had grievances in common, and the one that demanded their united action was the manner in which certain benefits of the Fawcett scheme had been persistently withheld. It was therefore decided to combine forces and unite in common action, the juniors and the seniors alike in one camp. This wider fraternal feeling between the first and the second class of sorters was principally brought about by the discovery by Williams—a sorter who had diligently been investigating the matter—of a copy of the full and original text of the much-disputed scheme itself. It seemed to have escaped observation that the text of this document had been printed in the public press at the time of its introduction, and that it had also been printed as a Parliamentary paper, which might have been procured in the ordinary way with very little trouble had they only thought of it. It is, however, a somewhat curious fact to be remembered that for some reason or other it was thought printed Parliamentary and official papers relating to the Post Office were unobtainable, and that postal officials, to get a glimpse of them at all, must do so secretly and surreptitiously. There was a feeling that one might only purchase them by proxy, while they waited out of sight with fear and trembling lest their criminal intention should be suspected by some prowling Post Office spy dogging their footsteps. This was the kind of feeling which indeed had governed most of the actions of postal servants for the previous ten years or so, and doubtless this timid reluctance to be seen reading or seeking to obtain printed official documents by the light of day was a survival and a result of the long serfdom to which they had been reduced.

Yet like most dangers, this was more shadowy than real, and there was no reason why a man should not, if he were so minded, have ordered this particular Parliamentary paper through his newsagent, or gone boldly to the counter of the Government printers and, putting down his few pence, demanded to be served with a copy. Furthermore, there was perhaps as little reason why a postal servant should not be seen openly reading such a document within the precincts of the Post Office itself. He might have cheaply gained a character for boldness had he but known it. But Williams, who first set himself to bring the mysterious document to light, though he shared the original belief about the exclusiveness of this particular class of literature, was made of different stuff, and entered on his quest like one equipped for an expedition into unknown regions. Probably he was disappointed that he met with so few difficulties. The simple purpose was invested with a dramatic interest from the start.

Williams, though he was not weak enough to lose the opportunity for surrounding his exploit with the necessary amount of mystery to enable him to pose as the one man on earth to whom the gods had been kind in vouchsafing him the ownership of the sacred screed, yet, nevertheless, if the truth has to be told, came into its possession in the most ordinary prosaic fashion. But the moral courage of him who was thus determined to brave the unknown terrors of publishers' rebuffs and awkward official inquiries was none the less real, nor was the document itself when so cheaply obtained any the less valuable.

Williams was undoubtedly a man of grit, of indomitable perseverance, combining the qualities of an attorney with the cold-blooded zeal and high-minded courage of a Puritan of old. The suggestion of the Puritan in his manner was accentuated by a tantalising slowness of utterance even in the moments of highest expectancy, and when his audience felt and knew he had something rich to offer them.

Williams, the original discoverer, and the chosen few whom he took into his confidence, hugged their precious document close for a considerable time, withdrawing themselves now and again to little out-of-the-way and unguessed-at meeting-places to distil from it the honey drops which they judiciously every now and again sprinkled among the thirsty multitude of their followers.

It was the knowledge of this discovery and that new leaders had been born to them that tended to erase the class differences between the senior and the junior men, uniting them once and for all in a common purpose and under one standard. This was brought to a culmination on April 18, 1889, when, for the first time since the memorable meeting called by Booth, the earlier agitator, a huge gathering of postal servants of every grade and class met in one of the disused rooms of the Parcel Depot of St. Martin's-le-Grand. There had been other meetings within the building, but not till now had every class and every branch been represented on the platform and among those in front. The occasion was note-worthy as being the first after so many years on which the classes had met to unite on a common basis, and as therefore being representative of the entire postal staff of the Chief Office. The previous meeting in the refreshment bar had whetted the appetite of the younger men, and a new courage permeated all ranks ; for they discerned the dawn of a new era. The two principal leaders and expounders of their discontent were already become as apostles of right and truth. It was Clery for the younger, the more ambitious and the more spirited among the sorting force ; it was Williams for the elder, the plodding, the painstaking, the cautious. It was Clery for the dashing, audacious manœuvre ; it was Williams for the certain, slow, and sure.

Williams was voted into the chair by acclamation, and from

that moment wore the epaulettes of an officer and a recognised leader. The Fawcett scheme of 1881 was henceforth to be accepted as their banner, their charter, and their palladium ; and with that in their midst they determined to march to victory, and wherever their leaders should direct. Williams, in his careful, painstaking, lawyer-like manner, expounded the scheme they had met to discuss, and showed to their entire satisfaction that the recommendations of the late Mr. Fawcett had not been applied to them ; and that certain things mentioned in the bond having so long been withheld from them, it was their duty to themselves and those coming after them in the service to see that they got all that they were thereby entitled to. There was the tremendous enthusiasm usual with those newly awakened to a sense of their long-suffering, and the realisation of things they were yet entitled to have and to hold. There was much determination expressed, but as yet no plan to proceed upon. It was a great meeting, a splendid cohesion of kindred particles too long held asunder, but as yet there was no proposition before them. Then it was that young Clery stepped into the breach, and proposed the heroic method of ignoring the postal officials by addressing a protest to Parliament or flying right away to the Lords of the Treasury. After their experience with the Postmaster-General, Mr. Raikes, petitions and protests addressed to him were regarded as having no more effect than paper-pellets. If ever a Postmaster-General came in for a rough handling in his own household, Mr. Raikes did on this occasion. The meeting eventually decided on petitioning the Controller of the London postal service for the full benefits of the Fawcett scheme, and pledged itself to forward a similar petition to the Lords of the Treasury in the event of meeting with unfavourable replies from the Controller and Postmaster-General. Probably no one candidly believed that such a petition would have any more effect than former paper-pellets of similar nature ; but it was very necessary as a preliminary stage in the opening of the campaign. A committee, selected from eager candidates, was formed therefore to draw up the terms of a joint petition. The proposal had been much too modest for Clery, who vigorously recommended taking higher ground, and dealing with Parliament direct ; but he was now induced to consent to become one of the number henceforth to be known as the Fawcett Scheme Committee. The sorting force as a body had thrown in its lot together ; there was to be no more class distinction, the whole contained the lesser ; there were to be no more petty rivalries, no more internecine, branch, or sectional differences —not until next time. They were confident they had touched solid ground at last.

CHAPTER XV

WORK OF THE FAWCETT SCHEME COMMITTEE—A NOTABLE
PAMPHLET—MR. RAIKES AND THE " AGITATOR "—A NEW POSTAL
ORGAN—THE FAWCETT SCHEME AND THE " LUMINOUS
COMMITTEE."

THE seed had germinated ; the plant had taken root even in
such seemingly stony and barren soil, and was destined within
a short while, despite chill winds and frost-bite, to become
flourishing and fruitful.

The newly constituted Fawcett Scheme Committee set
about in real earnest in preparing the further petition which
should suitably represent the united claims of the two classes.
As the representatives of the first and second classes of sorters,
they called attention to the fact that several important
provisions of the scheme of reorganisation, recommended by
the late Mr. Fawcett when Postmaster-General, and sanctioned
by the Treasury in 1881, had not been carried into effect ; and
on behalf of the sorters, they wished to take such steps as might
be in their power to have those provisions effectuated. The
improvements of position which had been sanctioned by the
Treasury, and which, they submitted, they had been entitled
to since April 1, 1881, were comprised in the sanctioned
recommendation of Mr. Fawcett to redress the grievances
coming under the first two of the five points to which, in his
letter to the Treasury, he reduced the whole of the representations and petitions which had been addressed to him
by the various classes of the postal and telegraph services,
viz :—

" 1. Inadequacy of pay arising to some extent from
stagnation in promotion.

" 2. The excessive amount of overtime, the small rate of
pay allowed for it, and the severity of the night duty. The

inadequacy of pay referred to in the first point was redressed by a new classification and scale of wages, which was to be uniform for the postal staff of the Sorting Branch and for the telegraphists (*vide* Treasury reply), and which was ' based upon the intelligible principle of paying for work solely according to its quality ' (*vide* Mr. Fawcett's report to the Treasury)."

The grievances embodied in the second point were redressed by the recommendation in paragraphs 5 and 6 of Mr. Fawcett's report, viz. :—

" 5. That the period of ordinary night attendance, both for telegraphists and sorting clerks, be reduced from eight to seven hours ; already recognised at several offices as the proper amount of night attendance for the postal staff.

" 6. That payment as for overtime work at provincial offices, whether of telegraphists or sorting clerks, be, in the case of male officers, at the rate of one-fiftieth part of a week's pay per hour, and in the case of female officers (who, as a rule, are not called upon to do more than 48 hours' work per week) at the rate of one-forty-eighth part of a week's pay. That when the overtime at any given office on a single occasion exceeds three hours, the rate of pay for such excess shall be one-quarter higher than the ordinary rate. As a rule the 16 hours which form an officer's work for two days shall be so divided as to avoid giving him more than 11 hours' work on either day ; when an occasional exception is necessary, all excess beyond 11 hours in any one day shall be paid for as overtime, although the two days' work in the aggregate may not exceed 16 hours."

The petition proceeded to point out that :—

" None of these provisions have been carried into effect. The scale of wages under which we are paid should, as stated in the Treasury reply, be uniform with that of the Central Telegraph Office, which is detailed in Schedule B in the copy of the papers ordered to be printed by the Honourable the House of Commons. Nor is work paid for according to its quality, as sorters of the second class are regularly required to perform duties of the highest quality, and consequently appertaining to the first class. On this point we hold that a hard and fast limitation of the classes within certain prescribed numbers is opposed to Mr. Fawcett's recommendation, and therefore not in accordance with the letter or spirit of this reorganisation scheme sanctioned by the Lords of the Treasury; for it is clearly explained, that the paying for such work solely according to its quality is to be effected by regulating the ' number of places ' in the class carrying any particular scale, ' strictly in accordance with the aggregate number ' of duties appertaining to that class.   The number of places in the class carrying the first-class scale should, consequently, be limited solely by the number of first-class duties.

" The recommendation to reduce the night duty to seven hours has not been carried out, as in the N.P.B. and I.B. a duty exists extending from 5 P.M. to 12.30 A.M., and in the E.C.D.O. there is in existence a duty extending from 4 P.M. until 12 midnight.   We are aware that a portion of these duties comes within the hours of the ordinary evening attendance, but in the case of a midnight duty of seven hours (say, from 12 midnight to 7 A.M.), a certain portion also comes within the hours of the equally ordinary morning attendance, and we therefore contend that the duties we have mentioned come within the reference of the scheme of midnight duties, and should not, therefore, exceed seven hours.

" We need not point out that overtime is not paid for in accordance with the recommendation of the scheme.   That we are entitled to payment at this rate is certain, for although the paragraph reads, ' for ordinary overtime work at provincial offices,' it is expressly stated in another paragraph of the report that the sorting force in London cannot be excluded from any improvement of position which may be conceded to the telegraphists and provincial sorting clerks.

" These are the provisions which have been expressly sanctioned by the Treasury for our benefit, and which we have been elected to endeavour to have carried into effect ; but we may also mention the reference in Mr. Fawcett's report to point 3 respecting holidays, viz. :—' I am now considering a scheme the effect of which I hope may be to give one month's leave in the course of the year to many who now have only three weeks, and three weeks to many who now have only a fortnight, respecting which we have been instructed to inquire, if the order of the Postmaster-General in the Post

Office Circular of 30th November, 1886, is the effectuation of Mr. Fawcett's contemplated scheme, and, if so, to ascertain if the fortnight's leave of absence enjoyed by the second class should not be extended as in the case of the first class to three weeks. We are also instructed to inquire what foundation exists for the prevalent impression, that the payment as for overtime work given for all work done on Christmas Day and Good Friday should be at the rate of pay for overtime work on Sundays, and not on week days.

"We think it the most courteous and respectful method we could adopt to bring these facts under your notice, and before taking any further steps to ask you for any information on these points which may be within your knowledge, and for guidance as to the methods we should pursue, which, while fulfilling the trust reposed in us by our brother officers, would meet with your commendation. In conclusion, we beg to press on your consideration the fact that this is a representation emanating from the entire sorting staff of the Circulation Department, who feel sure that some of the most important provisions granted to them by the Lords of the Treasury have been withheld from them since 1881, and that you will therefore be kind enough to regard this letter as a matter or urgency, and favour us with an immediate intimation of its having reached you, and a reply at your earliest convenience."

[Signed by the Committee.]

This petition from the united classes of the London sorting force broadly covered the whole of the ground on which they based their claims to the Fawcett scheme, and the various other petitions presented to Mr. Raikes were modelled upon it. As was almost inevitable under the circumstances, and as was almost expected by the promoters themselves, another unfavourable reply to their petition was received from the Controller. It was therefore soon afterwards determined to seek for permission, this time from the Postmaster-General himself, to hold another general meeting inside the official building.

In the meantime, however, Clery, the enthusiastic and resourceful young leader of the new movement, had written and published a pamphlet, "An Exposition of the Fawcett Scheme," which gained a ready sale among the interested and expectant men. The exposition was a clever piece of literary dissection, and a clear analysis of the much-debated question of Mr. Fawcett's intended meaning. With rare legal acumen, the text and spirit of the 1881 scheme were compared and examined, and considered at some length. The conclusion was, of course, favourable to the contention that the sorting force were still being robbed of their rightful privileges.

The audacity of openly and undisguisedly rushing into print in the face of what were supposed to be most hard and fast regulations against it, caused in the minds of many no little anxiety as to the safety of the author. There were even some protests from the committee, and at least one resignation. But the men as fully appreciated the necessity of some explanatory information on the subject as did the writer, and almost every one possessed himself of a copy, if only to try to discern through the chink in the door of the treasure-chamber what proportion of the promised treasure should be his, and to speculate as to his chances of getting it in the sweet by-and-by. The pamphlet undoubtedly did good, and had no inconsiderable educational value, while it strengthened the conviction that their cause was a just one, and their course a safe one. The recent general meeting at which it was thought that every one had arrived at a perfect understanding had left much to be desired in the way of information, and the majority came away from that meeting with as varied and divergent opinions as if a text of Scripture had been under discussion. It was indeed only to be expected. It is a peculiar quality of the human mind that the more a given printed text is discussed and debated the less definite is the understanding upon it. There is scarcely a paragraph in the daily newspaper as to the literal and actual meaning of which a heated discussion, and possibly sectarian differences, could not centre upon. There had been all sorts of rumours bandied about and opinions expressed about this wonderful scheme, till at last, while every one agreed to believe that it was next to divinely inspired and that the spirit of the dead lawgiver still hovered about it, very distinct differences prevailed as to the meaning and bearing of particular paragraphs. Every

N

man had his own pet paragraph, and wore it about his person in his waistcoat pocket or elsewhere, as a Mohammedan wears texts of the Koran, for ready reference and the confusion of one of opposite view. It was to meet this state of things that Clery very sensibly conceived the idea of supplying a long-felt want at threepence per copy.

The publication of this pamphlet was for the most part thought the most daring thing that Clery had ever attempted, especially as it was so unblushingly offered for sale within the Post Office itself, and under the very noses of the authorities. None knew what would become of the man who could fly in the face of one of the most cherished traditions of officialism ; for it had never yet been doubted that the same rules which governed the action of " communicating with the public press " covered such a case as this, and was sufficient to proclaim the author an outlaw. But the writer himself, so far from acting in ignorance of existing rules on the subject, in this very pamphlet challenged the authority of the Postmaster-General in this matter of personal liberty, and in one movement swept the musty cobwebs of tradition aside. In this pamphlet it was incidentally pointed out for the first time that there was absolutely no prohibition against an officer of the Post Office being, if he chose, actually connected with the public press while performing his official duties. The whole matter had been immersed in obscurity ; not one person in five thousand could have quoted the rule which was supposed to overshadow their actions in this respect. But herein for the first time it was shown that the minute issued by the Treasury so recently as 1875, and adopted by the Postmaster-General as a rule of the postal service—and which had been regarded as a menace because not understood—was directed against " Unauthorised Communications to the Public Press of Information derived from Official Sources." It was scarcely likely that the rule would be so strained in the present instance ; and if it were Clery was prepared to fight it.

Certain it is that Clery in no way enhanced his character in the service by taking up such an exposed position. His character officially, indeed, had been represented as scarcely anything to be proud of ; he met with scant leniency at the hands of those over him, and it was rumoured that his days would not be long in the land, that is, of the postal service. It is said that during this troublous period he was " suspended" no less than thirteen times.   Then, to the surprise of every one, the supervising officials especially, young Clery, the agitator, was suddenly informed that Mr. Raikes, the Postmaster-General, had expressed a desire to see him.   Such a proceeding on the part of any former Postmaster-General was wholly unheard of ; and if it was regarded as *infra dig.* for the gilded figurehead of a great public department voluntarily and un-asked to grant an interview to an underling so low down on the rungs of the service, the subordinate himself was to gain a little more credit and respect from that moment.   The youth was doing the ordinary work of the juniors at the time, and his duty had to be provided for by the superintendent of his branch, to enable him to gratify the Postmaster-General's extraordinary request for an interview with this agitating subordinate, whose notoriety had reached the august ears.   He had but to step across St. Martin's-le-Grand to find himself in the presence of Mr. Cecil Raikes, and that gentleman he found all smiles instead of all frowns, as he had been led to anticipate, and a welcoming nod reassured him that at least the Postmaster-General was not about to order him to be bow-strung on the spot.

 "I have sent for you, Mr. Clery," said the Postmaster-General, eyeing the stripling, whose height was by no means dwarfed by Mr. Raikes's own six feet three or four inches, " principally because I wanted to satisfy my curiosity.   You have such an exceptionally bad official character that it made me curious to see what you are like."   This private interview lasted an hour or more ; and many points were discussed between them ; and from that interview it is probable that Mr. Raikes learnt more of the actual grievances of the staff than he might have learnt in a month through the ordinary channels, and wading through memorials and petitions.   It was the very first time in the annals of the Post Office that a Postmaster-General had invited an agitator into his presence ; but it is more than probable that Mr. Raikes had some knowledge of the man before he met him.   He must have learnt something of his antecedents, his connections, and his character before-hand ; and when he met the youthful agitator face to face, it is

likely in a man of Mr. Raikes's disposition that he felt some
sort of a sympathy with the ambitious and energetic youth
whose literary aspirations were to an extent a reflex of those
of his own earlier days. For Mr. Raikes himself had been an
industrious literary hand, a leader-writer for the *Standard*, a
poet, and a playwright. But over and above all that it is only
reasonable to think that Mr. Raikes's principal motive was to
gather first-hand and in an informal way, from an accredited
authority, the leading agitator himself, what really were the
grievances of the postal side of the service.   In selecting
Clery he selected a ready and a logical exponent of the case.
If Clery was not flattered, he certainly went away with a
better understanding of Mr. ·Raikes than before.   His and
others' estimate of the Postmaster-General had been based on
a misconception of him ; his utterances in regard to him,
though always as respectful as the official regulations
demanded, betrayed the impression that Mr. Raikes was one
of whom they had to expect scant consideration.

Meanwhile, the Fawcett Scheme Committee were not idle,
and proceeded with the work of organising the men on a more
definite basis ; voluntary subscriptions per man being collected
systematically, and the principles of trades unionism quietly
disseminated.   Clery and his immediate following were now
agreed that the time had arrived when the sorting force should
set an example to other postal servants who were not yet
organised by combining on trade-union lines.   The project
was privately discussed in all its bearings ; meetings were held
in every available nook and corner, at Clery's residence and
elsewhere, till at last a definite resolution was decided on, to
be moved at the next general meeting. A requisition was
sent to the Postmaster-General for the use of one of the
branches in which to hold it, and this was accompanied with
the polite request that one or two newspaper reporters might
be allowed to be present.

It was a rather cool request under the circumstances, and
very naturally, perhaps, Mr. Raikes at first demurred.   But
eventually the little matter was negotiated ; the use of the
Foreign Newspaper Branch was given them, and reporters
were allowed to be present to take notes of the proceedings.
This was a distinct concession, which was thought to be as

much due to Mr. Raikes's desire to be generous as to the
pertinacity of the men's representatives. Perhaps the significance of this little concession may be better understood when
it is remembered that the resolution which Clery and his
supporters had decided to submit at that general meeting
within the Post Office building was to the effect, " That the
time had arrived for the sorting force to combine on trade-
union principles."

In moving this, reliance was doubtless placed on the fact
that previously Mr. Raikes in the House of Commons had
proclaimed his belief that civil servants had a right to combine
for mutual benefit. At this time, before it became fashionable
for Tory ministers to express such tolerant views in regard to
the claims of labour and the recognition of trade-union
doctrines, such a declaration was perhaps a little remarkable.

The meeting was accordingly held on December 11, 1889,
practically under the smiling patronage of the Postmaster-
General, whose action and whose judgment were to afford food
for criticism. It was the greatest gathering that had ever
assembled within the General Post Office, far exceeding even
the one of ten or eleven years before, which had been called
by Booth the postman. The Foreign Branch, which was not
used after eight o'clock ordinarily, was on this occasion
packed almost to suffocation with considerably over two
thousand men of all grades. The wildfire of enthusiasm
permeated the meeting from the first moment till the last.
Men from every district office and from every branch squeezed
themselves into the place, and climbed even into the girders
of the roof, and the very weight of the enormous mass of
humanity almost constituted a grave danger, of which, however, they were not at the time cognisant. Subsequently,
when Mr. Raikes went over the building and visited the scene
of that memorable meeting, he observed, " What ! over two
thousand men here ! It is a wonder the floor stood the strain."

Overcrowded and enthusiastic as was the meeting, nothing
more serious occurred than some damage to a few sorting-
tables and the unanimous passing, amidst the wildest excitement, of the all-important resolution. Williams was in the
chair, and in his measured, cold, metallic fashion, as a lecturer
of the Hunterian Society might, with scalpel in hand, deliver

a clinical lecture on nerve tissues and their ramifications, he once more pulled the Fawcett scheme thread from thread.

The sorters were by this time pretty well acquainted with the *pros* and *cons* of the Fawcett scheme in its application to themselves. The proposition, therefore, that they now petition the Postmaster-General in connection with the unfulfilled conditions of the Fawcett scheme required but little argument to convince them of the desirability of doing so speedily. The second, and perhaps the more important resolution of the two, that they now combine on trade-union lines for purposes of mutual benefit, they were equally agreed on. Both resolutions were carried unanimously, and it was also resolved that the Fawcett Scheme Committee should be forthwith dissolved, and that its members should become the provisional executive of the new organisation, to be called the "London Sorting Clerks' Association." The immediate outcome of this great meeting was that a monster petition, embodying the points of former petitions, was signed by the whole of the London sorting force.

The Postmaster-General almost immediately this time consented to receive a deputation of the aggrieved men at an early date. The well-worn facts were once more refurbished, and the necessary preparations were made to recite before him the thrice-told tale. The deputation almost expected to find themselves confronted by an austere, frowning official, ready to trip them up and to limit them both in points and minutes. But to their agreeable surprise the ogre they had come to storm in his castle turned out to be a gentleman who treated them with studied courtesy, who immediately put them at their ease, telling them to feel quite at home and to sit down with him, so that they might reason together and settle the matter in dispute amicably and without prejudice. The various points were urged at length by each speaker, Mr. Raikes meanwhile listening patiently and taking voluminous notes. At the conclusion he turned to Clery, who was in the deputation, and pleasantly remarked, "Now perhaps Mr. Clery will sum up." Nothing loth, Clery did promptly and briefly. He said the sorters had not got the missing portion of the Fawcett scheme, and they should never be contented or happy till they got it, and he suggested that it should be referred to a small committee of public men, who might satisfactorily solve the difficult problem and interpret the scheme to everyone's satisfaction. Mr. Raikes smiled and responded, " That is a very luminous suggestion, Mr. Clery, and I will talk it over with the Secretary. In the meantime, although from your point of view your contention appears a very just one, I must say I do not read this scheme as you do." " Then," said Clery, " it resolves itself into a literary exercise." There was some merriment expressed, and joined in by Mr. Raikes. The Postmaster-General further assured them that he deeply sympathised with them in their disappointment that he did not read the scheme as they did ; but it appeared to him nevertheless that there was a substantial equality between them and the telegraphists, who were supposed to be so much better off. Entering more fully on the ground of his difference with them, he pleaded that Mr. Fawcett's intentions could not be assumed by them, inasmuch as the language in which they were couched was of such an ambiguous character. Second, that the interpretation which the permanent authorities put upon the more important passages was directly opposite to that which the deputation claimed to be their true meaning. Third, that at the time the Fawcett scheme was formulated the authorities and Mr. Fawcett understood each other, and that the arrangements at present in existence were exactly what the late Mr. Fawcett desired to see.

The deputation withdrew naturally disappointed in their quest, but none the less impressed with the surprising difference between their first picture of him and the man personally.

Following on this deputation yet another meeting within the precincts of the General Post Office building was asked for and official permission obtained ; and on January 16, 1890, the combined sorting force met, again two thousand strong. The temper and enthusiasm of this monster gathering were if anything more pronounced than the last, curiosity running high as to the result of the recent meeting between their leaders and the Postmaster-General. J. H. Williams and W. E. Clery were the moving spirits of the platform, and the men looked to them as the heralds of good tidings. It was resolved that the sorting force express their regret that while the Postmaster-General seemed to consider their view a justifiable one and sympathised with them in their disappointment, he was not prepared immediately to carry into effect that which had been for so long withheld from them. He was also reminded of the "luminous suggestion" of a "three-cornered committee" of public men. It was decided to request that official permission be granted for holding a further meeting in a more convenient place, so that public men could be invited. Further, it was definitely decided to form an organisation on trades-union lines.

The want of an official organ for the interchange of ideas among the members and for the advocacy of accepted principles among the letter-sorting staff was at this time beginning to be strongly felt. Clery, seeing the necessity which the new movement had created, now determined to supply the deficiency. At his own risk he started a small journal, the *Post*. The first number appeared February 8, 1890, and was an unpretentious, pamphlet-like little print of eight pages, sold at a penny weekly. Clery himself was not only editor, but almost the sole contributor, as few dared to join in the risk of "writing for the press," and the fact is to be commented on only because of the surprising amount of work and responsibility he saddled himself with at this period. Besides performing his ordinary eight hours' duty at the General Post Office, and his association as an officer with the Fawcett Scheme Committee, and the efficient discharge of all the detail work which such an office entailed, he was an industrious contributor to the public press, a prolific writer of fiction, and a playwright of some little repute. Under a *nom de plume* which afterwards became well known, he found an entrance into the pages of the *Gentleman's Magazine*, and found himself, among other things, special dramatic correspondent of the *Morning Advertiser*—no mean attainments, it will be confessed, remembering his years and the hampering conditions under which he worked. The *Post* appeared, but it was predicted by many that its life would be short, as, if it did not die of ill-nutrition on the part of its patrons, the Postmaster-General would undoubtedly strangle it with red tape. But Mr. Raikes, though he could not have been wholly oblivious to the daring innovation in postal journalism, did not in any way attempt to burke it, and for a considerable period it was allowed to be sold and circulated within the precincts of the Post Office. Clery himself was prepared to defend his action if called on to do so, and stoutly maintained that before the authorities could legitimately question his right to act as the editor of a Service paper, they would have to institute a new regulation.

Preparations by this time had been set afoot for the great occasion towards which all the events of the preceding few years had been slowly but surely trending, the formation of a real postal trades union. There was no attempt at disguising the object and the nature of it ; and somewhat to the surprise of the older and more cautious among them, there was no opposition from the authorities. Indeed, the then Controller, Mr. R. O. Tombs, who, it may be mentioned, in his callow youth had himself been an agitator among his own class, seemed only too glad to remove every unnecessary official obstacle. He offered the use of the old disused prison-chapel at the parcel depot at Mount Pleasant for their forthcoming inaugural meeting, and even deputed Clery and Nevill to go there and complete arrangements. But finding it to be scarcely suitable for the purpose, a new difficulty arose. Then it was proposed that the postal authorities hire the Memorial Hall, Farringdon Street, and for the time being turn it into an official annexe, so as to meet the existing rule that meetings might not be held outside Government buildings. This proposal was actually seriously considered. It was then decided by Mr. Raikes to relax the rule. By showing confidence in the men in this matter, he thought they might be relied on not to abuse the liberty so far accorded them. While still retaining the right to send an official reporter, none was present, though it was generally understood that the proceedings were under the espionage of known spies. It was originally intended to call the new organisation by the name of the " London Sorting Clerks' Association," but the title " sorting clerk " being one of the minor points in dispute—it is still in dispute—some official exception was taken to its being used in this connection. It was then decided to rechristen it the " Fawcett Association," partly because it was a development of the Fawcett Scheme Committee, and partly out of respect to the memory of Professor Henry Fawcett, the benefactor, whose full benefits they were endeavouring to obtain after now eight years.

The new postal trades union of letter-sorters, the Fawcett Association, was inaugurated February 10, 1890, at the Memorial Hall, Farringdon Street. There had been many meetings of postal officials before, indeed much of the history of postal agitation had been made up of meetings either open or illicit ; but this was memorable, as it marked an epoch and proclaimed a new departure. It was the first meeting held in public by postal servants since 1866 which had not been proscribed and officially banned. During a previous agitation, that of 1872-74, there had been enormous mass meetings at Cannon Street Hotel and at Exeter Hall, and many public men of weight and influence supported their platforms ; nevertheless each of those meetings was held in open defiance of the existing rule, and in spite of the official warnings against them. But now Mr. Raikes had shown his confidence in them by removing the restriction so far as they were concerned. Henceforth they would be free to meet when and where they liked, the only slender link of connection between them and the Post Office being the presence of the official reporter. And this right to send an official reporter to the public meetings of postal servants was by some regarded as not wholly objectionable, as it had the compensating advantage of providing a ready communication between the departmental chief and themselves. Mr. Raikes had been the first Postmaster-General who had condescended to receive a deputation of lower subordinates for the purpose of discussing points of difference between them and the Department. He had also been the first to set aside an old-established rule, and to allow postal servants a fuller liberty to meet in places of their own selection, where they might engage in discussion amidst more congenial surroundings than the Post Office could offer. Their deliberations were henceforth not to be so cramped and confined as they had hitherto, but brought into the freer light of publicity. It was a concession much to be appreciated, and one which set a valuable precedent.

The indefatigable Williams presided ; and once more, with lawyer-like precision, he stated the case for the fulfilment of the Fawcett scheme ; the numerous speakers who followed, including Clery, drove home the necessity of forming this association, not only for securing immediate benefits, but for safeguarding the privileges already possessed. The result of this inaugural meeting was that a membership of over a thousand was immediately enrolled, and within a short time the number was more than doubled.

Scarcely to be compared numerically with the former postal trades union, embracing the letter-carriers and letter-sorters, which was led by Booth, the Fawcett Association was yet to succeed as a movement where the other had failed. The enormous movement of 1872-74, covering so wide a field as it did, and numbering its branches in almost every town throughout the kingdom, with great resources financially and morally, and counting among its sponsors and supporters dozens of the most notable men of the day, after living through a brief and stormy period, had achieved little. The withdrawal of the personal influence of Booth, the organising and the dominating spirit, caused it to shrink and crumble away in decay and disaster. It had spent thousands of pounds one way and another, in expensive mass meetings at Exeter Hall and elsewhere, with their bands of music and colours flying, and public men parading their platforms in pomp ; but the agitation had produced little beyond a sensation. The postal servants for whom the movement was begun were left practically just where they were in the beginning. It was an agitation which, while it ran its brief course, filled both the public eye and ear ; it bedecked itself with trappings and tinsel ; it was magnificent in a way, but directly Booth left it, it was no longer war. He undoubtedly it was who mainly inspired and inflated it ; and his withdrawal in a moment of pique, following indisposition, left it without a responsible leader, and the fight became a rout. With victory almost within sight, the principal leader withdrew and others followed, and the rank and file of the movement, left to their own resources, abandoned the siege and unaccountably beat a hasty retreat, as if a panic had seized them. The very looseness and wavering in their ranks was an invitation and an encouragement to the official patricians who garrisoned the till now beleaguered citadel of privilege, and directly this was seen the cavalry issued forth and smote them. The Assyrian came down like a wolf on the fold; and the undisciplined and leaderless organisation had to return captive along the paths of submissiveness and obedience. Hope for the redress of their grievances was abandoned for years to come.

This, then, was the first real opportunity since the collapse of the previous agitation that had been afforded the men of the sorting force to reassert their liberty to organise. But for the tact and moderation of the Postmaster-General, Mr. Raikes, or had he been less sympathetic towards them, that opportunity might have been still further delayed. That the opportunity would have been sought for or forced ultimately there can be no doubt. The younger men were not to be expected to be intimidated by the warnings issued fifteen or sixteen years before. That was ancient history written on a slate. On top of the grievances left unredressed by Booth's agitation, others had accumulated ; and none but those contented with being born into serfdom could much longer have tolerated or accepted such conditions. But it was due to Mr. Raikes not only that the moment for starting a new movement was brought nearer, but that that movement was made to run along the constitutional and legitimate lines it did. Mr. Raikes, unconsciously perhaps, pointed the road they should take, and by following that direction they found the road travelled to success. However he may have been averse to the introduction of organised trades unionism in the Post Office, Mr. Raikes took the sensible view that open and deliberate opposition to the sorters' agitation at that time of day and in the circumstances would not only give a fillip to it, but probably force it into a less commendable shape. Mr. Raikes was a man of the world, who knew human nature and human impulses as they showed in the aggregate. He had his duty to himself, to the Department, and the public to consider, and in this instance the just motive of the man was not inconsistent with that of the tactician. It had been conveyed to him that there was a general storm brewing among the telegraphists and the letter-carriers, as well as the sorters, and he was not blind to the necessity, from a Departmental point of view, of keeping each organisation distinct and confined to its own ground of operations. He probably knew by this time that the sorters were sufficiently determined to run an organisation of some kind ; and failing to prevent it, even if he would, he decided to show some tolerance as the best means of arresting or suppressing what might otherwise become a turbulent spirit among them. It was under these auspices and these conditions that the sorters' association was inaugurated.

From this moment a better feeling of security and a consciousness of strength took possession of what had hitherto been but a loosely united crowd, and, disciplined and organised as they now were, they felt that some material benefit must be the outcome of their efforts. The Postmaster-General evidently recognised that it was necessary to make some concession to the spirit of demand everywhere manifesting itself throughout the postal service, and shortly afterwards appointed a small Committee of Inquiry to deal particularly with the interpretation of the Fawcett scheme. The " luminous suggestion " of the young leader Clery became translated into the " Luminous Committee." This committee, formed to assist the Postmaster-General in determining the correct interpretation of the much-discussed document, consisted of Sir Francis Sandford, Sir Rupert Kettle, Q.C., Mr. William Woodall, M.P. for Hanley, and Mr. F. J. Dryhurst, a personal friend of the late Mr. Fawcett, as secretary. A deputation of the staff were invited to attend the sittings, and Messrs. Williams, Clery, Kemp, Groves, Leader, and Macartney, as representing the men, attended and stated their case. The Fawcett scheme, which had for so long remained a bone of contention over the grave of the dead benefactor, was, it seemed, at last to be removed beyond cavil or dispute.

It was on this occasion that a high compliment, intentional or unintentional, was paid to the young secretary of the Fawcett Association, W. E. Clery, the author of the " Exposition of the Fawcett Scheme." The deputation had no sooner taken their seats than the late Mr. Joyce, one of the leading officials of the General Post-Office, handed to each a copy of the pamphlet, though where and how they had been obtained was something of a mystery. Not only the deputation, but every member of the committee were provided with a copy, and the incident occasioned no little surprise.

The points were discussed and the evidence given, and the

representatives of the men entertained high hopes of the matter being speedily settled in their favour. " Waiting to hear the verdict " became a watchword and a commonplace saying among the men for several weeks, and few seriously doubted what that verdict would be. On March 25, 1890, the report of the committee was issued, and it was then found, greatly to the surprise and disappointment of all, that the decision was against them on every single point. There was a feeling that they had been betrayed ; but this speedily gave way to a new hope that Mr. Raikes, after all, intended to compensate them for the disappointment sustained ; for, in the meantime, the Postmaster-General had offered a still further compromise to the general spirit of discontent by instituting a Departmental Committee of Inquiry to inquire fully into the quality of postal duties. The new hope that had inspired them became clouded with much uncertainty during the next few weeks ; but a general meeting of the men decided to await the result a reasonable time before taking further action.

The verdict of the Luminous Committee was taken strong exception to by the general body of the force as being inconclusive and unconvincing. The official verdict, so far as the Fawcett scheme was concerned, had gone against them certainly, but they had lost nothing but the verdict. They lost neither courage in themselves nor hope for the future. They had pursued an ideal that had eluded their grasp, but it had enticed them into pastures they might never have explored. It had taught them how to organise ; it had taught them self-reliance, and had given them a better appreciation of their own value as public servants. Their pursuit of the Fawcett scheme ideal, while it had given them some acquaintance with the difficulties to be faced, had taught them how to surmount those difficulties. It had inspired them with a new and a stronger ambition to better the conditions of postal life ; and it had been the means of discovering to themselves that in their two leaders, Clery and Williams, they had two officers of more than ordinary ability, to whom they could confidently look for ultimate victory. They had lost the verdict, but this much they had gained, and more. If nothing more substantial had been gained from the Postmaster-General, they had at least secured his respect and even his goodwill, and that respect they reciprocated. At first unwilling to consider their claims, Mr. Raikes had come to realise that they were in deadly earnest, and were not easy to refuse. And they had reason to think that from this realisation had sprung the conviction that, after all, they had grievances which, at any cost, would have to be remedied.

The impression had gained ground among the leaders of the sorters' agitation that though the verdict had gone against them Mr. Raikes was disposed to do all that was within his power to improve the position and prospects of the sorting force, on similar lines to those laid down in the Fawcett scheme itself. The Postmaster-General was asked to receive a further deputation from the men, and fourteen points were submitted for his consideration, these fourteen points covering all the ground of their previous demands. Mr. Raikes consented to receive the deputation to discuss with him all the points submitted with the exception of two, which were, the reorganisation of the medical department, and the request to have some voice in the formation of any revision before it was finally applied. The points the Postmaster-General was asked to discuss with the deputation were :—

" 1. Uniform scales and privileges for the chief office of the Sorting Branch with the Central Telegraph Office ; and holidays in accordance with the Post Office Circular of 30th November, 1886.

" 2. That the number of officers on each class be regulated strictly in accordance with the number of duties rightly appertaining to that class, due provision being made for lack of promotion by the establishment of a class of seniors as in the Central Telegraph Office ; and that allowances be abolished in favour of higher scales where duties of a higher quality are performed, except in cases of risk or *temporary* performance of superior duties, when the minimum of the higher scale should be paid.

" 3. That the minimum rate of pay for any appointed officer of the sorting force be 24s. per week ; and that the first class be restored to the metropolitan district offices, the scale of pay to be that of the district telegraphists.

" 4. That officers of the sorting force may have the right

of promotion to superior appointments, especially to those dealing directly with the control of the work.

" 5. That in order to generally abolish ' split ' attendances, and reduce the extreme pressure under which the duties are performed, a sufficient increase of the permanent staff be at once granted.

" 6. The abolition (1) of indirect punishment, such as the capricious ordering of midday attendance, etc. (not officially recorded as punishment) ; and also (2) of confidential reports, except in suspected criminal cases ; and (3) that the notification in the Post Office Circular of punishment awarded to any officer be discontinued.

" 7. That compulsory extra duty be abolished.

" 8. That inquiry be made into the pay, duties, and position of the sorting staff attached to the Savings Bank Department, with a view of readjusting their position in the Service, no such inquiry having been made for the past seventeen years.

" 9. That the term ' sorting clerk ' be in all cases substituted for that of ' sorter.'

" 10. That the official duty be seven hours per diem, such to be continuous ; but where a ' spilt ' duty or night attendance is necessary, six hours.

" 11. That full pay be granted during absence on sick leave.

" 12. That Sunday rates be paid for all work performed on Christmas Day and Good Friday ; all other public holidays to be paid for at the ordinary extra-duty rates.

" 13. That the Medical Department as at present constituted be abolished, a medical officer being retained solely for the examination of candidates for employment and superannuation claimants through physical incapacity.

" 14. That in order to render satisfactory to those concerned any future revision we urge the necessity of our being consulted before it assumes its final form."

Early in the June following Mr. Raikes received a deputation of six, including the indispensable Williams and Clery, and the points were amicably discussed between them, a shorthand writer being present. The Postmaster-General gave every attention, and treated them as usual with consideration. And his kindliness of nature displayed itself on this occasion when spontaneously he made one very valuable concession on the spot. He had been reminded that members of the postal staffs had not yet enjoyed the privilege extended to telegraphists, that of being transferred to country and seaside offices when in ill health. " I should like *that* done," said he, turning to the Controller. And this privilege was to be enjoyed from that moment for years to come. The business of the deputation having concluded, the Postmaster-General complimented them for having urged their case with great reason and moderation, and promised he would give every consideration to the matters laid before him ; and that they might expect an answer at as early a date as possible. Besides the concession of temporary transfer to seaside offices in cases of ill health, which they had gained at the interview, Mr. Raikes had already a few days before granted full pay in sickness, and this was now made to extend to the whole of the London postal service. After this they had to curb their impatience for four months, for other happenings of more serious moment were directing Mr. Raikes' attention elsewhere.

O

CHAPTER XVI

A REAWAKENING OF THE LETTER-CARRIERS—PETITIONS—
DEGRADATION AND DISMISSAL OF THE LEADER—FORMATION
OF THE POSTMEN'S UNION—MR. JOHN BURNS—AN OUTSIDE
LEADER SELECTED—THE INTERVENTION OF W. E. CLERY—
THE BATTLE OF MOUNT PLEASANT—THE POSTMEN'S STRIKE.

FOR some years after the decline of the agitation of 1872-74
the letter-carriers were practically quiescent. There was a
prolonged hiatus, not of contentment exactly, but of unvoiced
discontent, a restless slumber, with but an occasional turning
and a muttering in their sleep. It was not till 1887 that the
letter-carriers again woke to the full realisation that they were
being overburdened with an accumulation of old and new
grievances, and that the time had come to prepare for another
effort. There was the usual recrudescence of grumblings and
a groping in the semi-darkness, the usual repetition of
unrecorded back-stair and back-room meetings, some misunderstanding as to exactly what they wanted, and which
way they should turn to get their grievances redressed. They
had the disadvantage of being split up into a number of
sections and classes, and there was the danger from the outset
of their being disunited by internal jealousies.

It is the man that makes the movement as much as the
movement makes the man. There were several ready
champions of the general cause, but when they came to take
stock of the claims of each it was found there was only one
man who could be followed with confidence. This was a
young fellow named Dredge, known familiarly to most of
the London letter-carriers as Tom Dredge. He was a good
speaker, with a hearty, bluff manner, and he gave the idea
of a fighter who could carry his point and would not flinch.
Dredge set about organising the letter-carriers at his own

office at the North-Western District Office, and gradually
extended the sphere of his operations to the other districts.
In this he was ably assisted by two or three fellow-postmen
acting as delegates from their various centres.   The first
meeting of any importance, and the one which mainly decided
their future action, was held at Tolmer's Square Institute,
Drummond Street, N.W., on July 23, 1887. Dredge was
the central figure and the principal speaker ; and from
that night the agitation extended to the whole of the
London district postmen, and embraced a considerable
number of the suburban men.   The first item on the
programme of the new agitation, of course, was the
preparation of a petition setting forth their claims.   These
were to include limitation of working day to eight hours,
necessity of increased pay, extra duty to be paid for
according to wages ; the granting of boots for all postmen,
and lighter clothing for summer wear ; equality for all
postmen in London ; the resumption of the title of " letter-
carrier " in lieu of " postman " ; earlier maximum pay ;
a minimum of 18s. a week for all second-class postmen ;
the abolition of the collection and delivery of parcels by
London postmen ; and several other good things, including
a better pension scheme.

The petition was presented, but nothing satisfactory came
of it. There were more meetings, growing in indignation,
and Tom Dredge became a power everywhere among the
letter-carriers or, as they were now called, postmen. They
secured the support of Mr. H. L. W. Lawson, M.P., and he
presided over a meeting at Tolmer's Square Institute, more
than a thousand men of all grades being present. Besides
this public countenance to the efforts of the letter-carriers,
his influence on their behalf was exerted in the House of
Commons on several occasions. One result of Mr. Lawson's
efforts in this direction was the obtaining of a departmental
committee to examine the question of uniform, concerning
which so many complaints were made. In many ways did the
member for St. Pancras assist the letter-carriers in furtherance
of their aims. The public holiday agitation, which dislocated
the telegraph staff at the time, drew forth the interest of Mr.
Lawson, and many were the communications between him

and the Postmaster-General. But the holiday was not granted, nor was extra pay allowed.

Through him the letter-carriers presented a petition to Mr. Raikes, praying for a consideration of their case ; and the Postmaster-General intimated that he would do all he possibly could, consistently with the interests of the public, to meet the wishes of the men. But just when it was thought that their sails had caught the fair breeze of public approval, and it was felt their barque was nearing a safe harbour, their vessel suddenly grounded on a rock. Tom Dredge, the secretary of the organisation of district and suburban letter-carriers, was pounced on for a dereliction of official duty, and punished with reduction in the ranks. The circumstances of the case seem to have been rather harsh, but being away on sick-leave at the time, it was not till his return to duty that he felt the full force of the official rebuff. The local postmaster informed Dredge that the Secretary had advised Dredge's reduction, because he had taken a prominent part in the postmen's agitation for increase of pay, etc. The Postmaster-General endorsed the recommendation that he be reduced to the second class of postmen, and instructed that he be warned that if he continued in the same way he would be dismissed. The specific charge brought against Dredge was that of writing to the press on official matters, and for purposes of promoting an agitation, in contravention of rule.

Mr. Raikes was charged with inconsistency and unnecessarily interfering with the right of combination among the postal servants ; but the Postmaster-General defended his action, and maintained that he had dealt leniently in the circumstances. The reduction had been accompanied with a caution to abstain from such questionable methods of agitation for the future ; but a few months later the secretary of the postmen's organisation tempted fate still further, and the end came. A printed notice had been issued and signed by Dredge calling a mass meeting at the Memorial Hall, without the proper sanction of the Postmaster-General having been obtained, and in contravention of Rule 42 of the regulations. This meeting the Postmaster-General prohibited, but a few days afterwards, Dredge called a general meeting for the purpose of discussing matters of departmental control, including the action of the Postmaster-General. He was called on to explain why, after being emphatically cautioned, he had persistently endeavoured to stir up agitation. His explanation notwithstanding, Dredge was dismissed.

The Postmaster-General's treatment of this particular case, and his attitude towards the postmen's agitation at this period, may seem strangely in contrast with the indulgence shown towards the letter-sorters. But it has to be remembered that with the latter body there was never any attempt to force the right of public meeting before the rule was relaxed ; and besides, they experienced little indulgence at Mr. Raikes's hands till some time after the period of Dredge's dismissal. It was not till a year after that Mr. Raikes began to mellow in his demeanour towards the sorters' agitation.

His mellowing somewhat towards the growing spirit of trades unionism in the Post Office may perhaps be ascribed to expediency as much as to conviction of its justification. For about this period of 1890 a tidal wave of discontent, it seemed, affected almost every class of public and Government servants, and threatened to sweep them off their feet. The spirit of restlessness and discontent not only affected the police, the telegraphists, the sorters, and the postmen, but it even made itself felt to some extent in the army. Mr. Raikes had to realise that he was facing a very delicate and difficult problem, and though he did not take kindly to his lesson at first, he squared his shoulders and faced it manfully and tactfully when he saw the cloud about to burst. It was his duty to play his own game from the Departmental side of the board, and his move consisted in keeping the discontented bodies apart at any hazards, and this by his tact and good judgment he succeeded in doing. He was sorry that he was compelled to dismiss Dredge, and perhaps foresaw the consequences. There was immediately a strong feeling manifested among the postmen ; for Dredge was popular ; and though the blow caused them to retire for a moment to get their wind, they came up in stronger fighting trim than ever. It was this dismissal really that led up to the formation of the ill-starred but, for a time, formidable Postmen's Union. Dredge's dismissal was interpreted into a direct attack on the postmen's right of combination, and the Chief Office men, who hitherto had been rather lukewarm towards the agitation led by him, now as a matter of principle formed square with the districts. It was decided to form a General Postmen's Union, but it was ill managed through misunderstanding from the start.

In the early part of 1890 the discontent born of a long period of neglect and refusal to consider their moderate demands reached an acute and critical stage. The necessity for some sort of an organisation of postmen was beginning to be recognised among them, and it was then decided to start the Postmen's Union. A request privately made by the postmen themselves to several prominent labour leaders was the means of bringing it into existence. The Postmen's Union, doomed to have an exciting career ending in disaster and failure, was hatched under the wing of the well-meaning but in this case misguided Labour Union leadership.

Some few of the more discerning, however, were looking for a leader elsewhere. John Burns, the labour leader in the great Dock Strike, had achieved fame in the memorable and bitter struggle over the " Dockers' Tanner," and had emerged from the fight with great personal credit. As a consequence, the hero of the hour was for some time afterwards inundated with invitations and appeals to organise all sorts of bodies of workers. John Burns, always the champion of the under dog, had some time before interested himself in the poorer Government workers—the Woolwich Arsenal men, Macnamara's Contract Mail Drivers, and the Postal auxiliaries. The London postmen, partly organised but lacking a real leader, now remembered John Burns' assistance to their humbler fellow postal workers, and a number privately sought his advice. He attended several committee meetings, and promoted discussion as to what steps should be taken, while pointing out the pitfalls to be avoided. A forward policy was decided on, but no thought of a strike had yet entered into their deliberations.

The Postmen's Union at first looked like becoming a power for good, but rivalry soon crept in, and presently two distinct rival factions were in evidence. The seeds of reciprocal distrust were mysteriously sown. This could only have been overcome by the general acceptance of the strong leadership of a man who knew his own mind, with a will to

enforce discipline in the ranks, and who knew all the requirements of the situation. Mr. John Burns, with the laurels of
the Dock Strike fresh upon him, had already formally offered
his services to form and conduct the Postmen's Union, but
while he was prepared to stand by them as " guide, philosopher,
and friend," he could not under any circumstances become a
paid official. Had this offer been accepted just when it was
made, it is most probable that John Burns' good sense, tact,
and experience would have been used towards averting one of
the most lamentable catastrophes that ever sullied the pages
of Labour's history. If it was necessary to form the Postmen's
Union, it was just as necessary to place the leadership in
strong, capable hands, not too heavily weighted with other
interests. It was not to be, however, and the opportunity
of securing John Burns as leader was lost. And it was lost
only because it was feared that John Burns would want to
exercise a too autocratic sway. The postmen did not mind
marching in military formation, but they couldn't brook
being " disciplined " by an outsider. Yet better perhaps had
it been so, for as will be seen, they went from one extreme to
the other, and, it seemed, preferred to follow their own
impulses, undecided for some time who should be chosen as
actual leader.

The postmen eventually, however, selected another
outside the Service, one whose health probably at the time
rather ill-fitted him for so strenuous a task and so big a
responsibility, who, moreover, as General Secretary of the
Labour Union, must have had his hands pretty full in giving
assistance to various other bodies of workers. It was in these
circumstances that Mr. J. L. Mahon, with the best of intentions
and a ready desire to help an almost unorganised body of
men struggling for their rights, allowed himself to be persuaded
to accept the position of Secretary of the Postmen's Union.

The representations made to the Labour Union were to
the effect that postmen as a body and all postal employés
were in a helpless and disorganised condition ; that they
dared not take the initiative for fear of instant dismissal.
These representations were accepted, and a meeting was
speedily called on a Sunday, the meeting-place being Clerkenwell Green. This meeting was called by means of a manifesto

published in the Saturday's *Star*. There the Postmen's Union was publicly inaugurated, its principal sponsors being Messrs. Mahon, Chambers, and Henderson. All postal employés were invited to join the organisation. The executive, consisting of Mr. Mahon and the other gentlemen mentioned, announced that their only desire was to establish the new postal association on a proper basis, and that when this consummation was effected they would be willing to leave the postmen to manage their own affairs.

The restrictions as regarded public meetings had already been considerably relaxed by Mr. Raikes, and from being strictly prohibited were now allowed under certain conditions. The conditions imposed by Mr. Raikes were :—

" That notice be given to the local Post Office authority that such a meeting was to be held, and where it was proposed to hold it. That the meeting be confined to Post Office servants only who are directly interested in the matters to be discussed. That an official shorthand writer be present if required by the authorities."

It was under the operation of this new rule that the letter-sorters' organisation was publicly inaugurated at the Memorial Hall on February 10, 1890. But the leader of the Postmen's Union detected in the second condition imposed by the regulation a direct blow at the right of combination, and an attempt to deprive the postmen of their accepted leadership. It was to test this as much as to form the Postmen's Union that this meeting was called on Clerkenwell Green in June, 1890. Mr. Mahon had been one of the sub-organisers of the late dock strike, and on assuming authority over the Postmen's Union he endeavoured to make himself the accepted mouthpiece of the men's demands. But whatever qualities of leadership Mr. Mahon may have possessed, the frail figure in the blue serge suit that day looked too poor in health for so formidable a task as lay before him. He was a delicate, thin-featured, pale-faced man, with a slight red beard, and light blue eyes. The postmen, however, wanted an outside leader, and if Mahon was to prove their Moses of postal labour they were to make the most of him and obediently follow. Nevertheless, the members seemed possessed by a fear that they were doing something wrong and might only conduct their affairs in secret, precautions being taken to prevent the identity of members becoming freely known. Both officers and members were known only by numbers, and adhesive stamps were used to indicate the subscriptions paid ; these stamps being supplied to members to affix them to their cards when they felt free from espionage. There was but one exception to this extraordinary secrecy, and that was in the case of Clery, the secretary of the Fawcett Association, who had become a member from sympathy with their objects. He stoutly declined to be known by a number, and advised the Postmen's Union that they were perfectly within their right in combining openly and without this element of secrecy. He went further, and wrote a pamphlet on the subject of postal combination, which was published by J. McCartney, a member of the Fawcett Association, and issued from the offices of the Postmen's Union.

The postmen now seemed so determined on following the dictates of the Labour Union, and so enamoured of an outside leader, that for the time Dredge, their quondam secretary, seemed forgotten. The manifesto which had heralded the birth of the Postmen's Union invited them practically to come and have their grievances redressed by men not in the Service, who could not be dismissed for speaking up for them. But the dismissed Dredge could have done all this as fearlessly and as ably as any of the Union leaders had he been invited to —and better for the postmen and better for him had the leadership been at this stage placed in his hands entirely.

The Postmen's Union had not been called into existence very long before there was a split in the executive, and the postmen were treated to the demoralising spectacle of a double-headed leadership—a Girondist and a Mountain party in miniature. There was a manifesto printed in the *Evening News and Post*, and signed by Messrs. T. Dredge, Fred Henderson, and W. Chambers, in which they announced that they had dissociated themselves from the rest of the executive. W. E. Clery of the Fawcett Association endeavoured to bring about a *rapprochement* between the parties, and Mr. Morrison Davidson, the author, was asked to act as arbitrator, to which he agreed. The proposal, however, was not carried out, those remaining on the executive not agreeing to the suggestion.

Messrs. Henderson, Chambers, and Dredge were regarded as having seceded from the movement by the publication of the manifesto ; but this did not put the matter straight, as, to a very large section of the postmen, Dredge, Henderson, and Chambers were still the leaders of the movement. The books and the funds of the Union were, however, still in the hands of Messrs. Mahon and Donald, but the others kept discreet silence about the split in the camp, while quietly and industriously receiving subscriptions and enrolling members. Messrs. Chambers and Henderson set about organising a meeting in Marylebone, to which postmen were invited to hear a true explanation of the situation and the nature of the difference between them and their late colleagues. The meeting was held under the presidency of Mr. Champion, and Mr. John Burns and Mr. Conybeare, M.P., were present. The latter gentleman was at this time treasurer of the Union.

Mr. John Burns did not mince matters with anybody, but once more treated all alike to a helping of strong straight talk and wholesome advice which, if only remembered and followed, would have saved them many bitter regrets. It was on this occasion, after the business of the meeting, that John Burns now definitely allowed it to be known that he would accept a position on their executive, but that they would have to approach him. There was serious consideration on the part of some, and a further excited meeting, at which Mr. Mahon was present ; but it was found that neither party could claim the full confidence of the postmen, and so it was decided to submit the matter of the disputed leadership to a commission of inquiry having power to demand all books and correspondence, and to report on the condition of the Union, and the trustworthiness of the executive in power. A general meeting was to be called to hear this report as soon as ready. The commission of inquiry consisted of three, and Clery, of the letter-sorters' agitation, was elected chairman. There was a deal of recrimination between the parties before the decision of the commission was made known. It was recommended that the Postmen's Union executive should sever its connection with the Labour Union, but that the executive should consist of nine gentlemen not in the Service, and an equal number of postmen. The gentlemen who were to serve

on the executive were to include Mr. Mahon as secretary ;
Mr. Conybeare, M.P., as treasurer ; Mr. A. K. Donald ; Mr.
Bennet Burleigh, the war correspondent and journalist ; Mr.
John Burns, and Mr. H. H. Champion. But Mr. Mahon and
Mr. Donald objected to Mr. Burns and Mr. Champion being
on the executive. W. E. Clery and his fellow-commissioners
were in favour of these two gentlemen, and only agreed not
to press their election out of consideration to the wishes of
Messrs. Mahon, Donald, and Binning, who had certainly done
a deal of rough work in connection with the Union's formation.
Clery and the rest of the commission had reason afterwards
to regret that they had not persisted in their first decision.

The Postmen's Union was accordingly taken out of the
hands of the Labour Union, and its control was taken over by
a distinct executive. Mr. Burns and Mr. Champion withdrew
their offer of services, and allowed Mr. Mahon to take the
helm of the clumsy and ill-fitted vessel that required much
clever steering. Those who originally came into the movement only as friendly helpers developed into leaders and
masters of the new organisation. Mr. Mahon now assumed
control, and the fact that he was allowed to do so can only
be accounted for on the supposition that the other members
of the executive, Mr. Bennet Burleigh and Mr. Conybeare
and the rest, were paying more attention to their own private
business. W. E. Clery meanwhile had used the whole weight
of his influence to induce the postmen's executive to switch
the organisation on to more constitutional lines of action, but
the very attempt at counselling moderation seemed only to
have begotten suspicion regarding the honesty of his intentions.
Mr. Mahon and a few about him were apparently under the
impression that the letter-sorters and the indoor staffs were
in duty bound to make common cause with them, and if only
their co-operation could be secured the walls of St. Martin's-
le-Grand were certain to fall. Had the indoor staffs of the
postal side of the Service been induced to join hands, there
can be no doubt that such a federation would have proved
very troublesome to the authorities. But Clery, who was
by this time virtual leader of the sorters' organisation,
seeing that the postmen under their outside leader were determined on pursuing a heroic course and adopting a policy of

defiance, steadily set his face against any combination of his class with the Postmen's Union. Mr. Mahon and many of the postmen themselves thought it would greatly assist them if the indoor classes could be induced to join them, and it was sought to set aside the authority of Clery with his own class by making overtures direct to the sorters. This was done by a printed manifesto, but Clery thought so little of its effect that he contemptuously reprinted it with a few lines of comment in his own organ, the *Post*, of June 7, 1890. Yet in spite of this free advertisement there was no response to the appeal of the general secretary of the Postmen's Union, and, so far as was known, not a single sorter joined. The manifesto was a creditable literary production, for Mr. Mahon could write as well as speak, but the only thing he could boast of having done in a period of eight months was to have formed " a rapidly growing union with a weekly contribution." From this declaration it was further gathered that the principal reason for its existing at all was to assert " the right of public meeting and demonstration," in defiance of an official regulation now so modified as to be no longer regarded as harsh. This was the main point of difference between the postmen's policy and that of the sorters. The sorters had won the right of public meeting fairly, squarely, and constitutionally, and Mr. Raikes was pleased to acknowledge it ; the postmen, as led by their outside leader, asserted the full right of public meeting without restriction and without control from headquarters. It was a very proper thing, perhaps, but in the circumstances it was hardly the time of day to demand it. The sorters, by quietly pursuing constitutional methods, were very little behind the postmen in point of outside meeting, only in the one case it was acknowledged as a right and in the other they committed official outlawry, and by so doing injured their own case. The Postmaster-General was severely autocratic in rule, yet, when properly approached, he had gone considerably out of the beaten track of officialdom in granting the right of public meeting conditionally. Only a little while longer and the last shackle was to be knocked off. Yet this did not suit the postmen's leader, and his followers were made to think that it could not be accepted by them. They were led into pursuing the ideal of an abstract

principle in preference to urging their more useful and legitimate demand for boots and better wages.   The boots and
other things to which they were as justly entitled were forgotten in the glamour of the right of public demonstration.
Instead of making do with the farthing rushlight for the time
being, they committed the fatal mistake of running after
the will-o'-the-wisp which was to land them in the morass
of humiliation and disaster.

Finding the leaders of the Postmen's Union could not be
persuaded to return to the slower but surer methods of constitutional propaganda, Clery left that body with the intention
of devoting himself exclusively to the work of his own
organisation.

As the months went by, the threat of the strike as the
final argument became more definite, though there was no
effective machinery and little funds.   There was already
growing some uneasiness over the signs of unrest amongst
the Metropolitan Police, so that the added threat of the
postmen at once alienated public sympathy.   This, like
every other warning, was disregarded by the leaders, till it
seemed like the blind leading the blind.

By the assertion of the right of public meeting and demonstration it was thought to force the Postmaster-General to his
knees.   But it was not to be.   If it was thought that what had
been done by Booth in the case of the famous Cannon Street
Hotel and Exeter Hall meetings might again be done by means
of an outside professional agitator, they were mistaken.   True,
the earlier public demonstrations were in defiance of official
rules and prohibitions ; but those were demonstrations of a
united postal service, of a movement to which scores of the
public men of the day had given their countenance ; and
Booth and his followers adopted such a means as the only
alternative to holding cooped-up meetings on the official
premises.   That was in 1873, and this was in 1890.   Circumstances and conditions had considerably altered since that
period, and the right of free public meeting was already for
all workable purposes an accomplished fact.

There were frequent marches with bands through the
streets, and once they were dispersed by the police.   The
Postmaster-General objected to the manner of open-air

demonstrations by uniformed State servants, and issued an official warning ; but the official " ukase," as it was termed, was, with mock solemnity burned on Clerkenwell Green by Keir Hardie, the future M.P. Some of the postmen who attended one of these forbidden open-air meetings (May 16, 1890) were called on for written explanations, the seniors being punished by the loss of stripes and the juniors with a reduction of pay. From then the friction grew apace.

Instead of continuing as it started, with the purpose of securing those material benefits to which postmen were entitled, the Postmen's Union very imprudently demanded that their grievances should be laid before the Postmaster-General by Mr. Mahon, their secretary, personally. As they ought to have anticipated, this request was refused or ignored ; and it was then that they determined to publicly assert their right to open-air demonstration. Their meeting-place was again Clerkenwell Green. From there they fired their shell into St. Martin's-le-Grand. The response was prompt, and a number of men who had made themseleves conspicuous, or whose names were secretly reported, were suspended, and had to be maintained by the funds. The postmen's leader sought to open negotiations with St. Martin's-le-Grand, and wrote to the Postmaster-General that the men who had attended the prohibited meeting would apologise on conditions. The conditions that Mr. Mahon wished to impose were that all restriction on the right of public meeting should be withdrawn ; that the suspended men should be reinstated after tendering their apology ; that the Postmaster-General should immediately obtain the sanction of the Treasury to increase the pay of both established and unestablished postmen, and that the permanently employed auxiliary staff should be placed on the establishment. Mr. Raikes replied, but refused to recognise Mr. Mahon as the postmen's representative.

It was decided further to assert the right of public meeting, and a monster Hyde Park demonstration was organised for Sunday, June 19. The postmen, in mufti, turned up in considerable numbers with their friends ; Mr. Mahon and some others made some strong utterances. An official note-taker, attending by official instruction, was recognised and rather roughly handled. In consequence of this meeting, and the disturbance that ensued, another thirteen men were next day suspended from duty.

But the agitation continued to progress, the men being supported in their demand for the free public platform by a section of the press and a few public men. It appeared that the leader of the Postmen's Union now thought that he was in a position to dictate terms to the Postmaster-General, and repeated the demands of the men in an ultimatum despatched one afternoon by special messenger. The inclusion of the request that the Postmen's Union and its secretary should be officially recognised induced Mr. Raikes to ignore it entirely.

That was the strong official objection every time. And Mahon, as the selected leader of the Postmen's Union, was under the special disadvantage of not being of their " cloth " and not personally sharing their grievances. He, therefore, could not fully appreciate that the postal servants' occupation approximates to no other class outside. If Mahon himself could have been dismissed for his action, possibly events might have been directed differently. The right of public procession, with the passing luxury of following the big drum and open-air meeting seemed for the moment to overshadow all other claims, and the lesson of Booth's 1873 attempt was forgotten. Mahon, not being a Service man, was placed in a false position from the outset without realising it ; and, furthermore, it appears probable that his lead was influenced by fictitious reports and alleged promises of support from other bodies in the Service, while the tense atmosphere was loaded with false rumours from day to day till the climax was reached. No wonder that Mahon felt stronger than he really was ! This much helps to explain why the Postmen's Union was driven along unconstitutional channels.

No reply being forthcoming the same day, a meeting was held in the evening at the Holborn Town Hall, Mr. Conybeare and Mr. Cunninghame-Graham giving their support. Nothing definite, however, was decided on, as meanwhile a rumour had been disseminated that the suspended men were to be reinstated without loss of pay. The next day, July 8, was thought by the authorities to be a critical one, as it was rumoured that the men had separated from the Town Hall meeting with the understanding that if additional hands appeared for duty at any one of the offices in the morning, the Union men were not only themselves to turn out, but to turn out the new men also. This information had been hastily conveyed to the authorities by a confidential reporter the same night. Preparations for an emergency were made accordingly, but the day proved uneventful beyond a few protests against the introduction of strangers at some of the outlying offices. The City men, however, exhibited a somewhat stronger feeling against the emergency men. There were excited gatherings in the kitchens, and on one or two occasions the officials found it difficult to persuade the men to return to the sorting-offices. No reply being forthcoming from the Postmaster-General to decide the point immediately in dispute, a few of the men demanded that he should be sent for. On one of these occasions three or four of the sorters, carried away by the excitement of the moment, very mistakenly, it was alleged, promised the postmen the support of their class. This reaching the ears of the officials, they were immediately suspended from duty ; and of those suspended four ultimately were dismissed. Two of the sorters so dismissed, who had made themselves prominent in agitation, Stevens and Baylis, on leaving the service prospered fairly well ; Stevens emigrated and became a Canadian farmer, and Baylis a local celebrity and a hard-working parish reformer in the south-east quarter of London.

The Controller, to avoid a more serious disturbance, withdrew the emergency men for the time. The postal authorities, nevertheless, felt that they were trembling on the brink of war, and while strong bodies of men drawn from all classes outside were posted out of sight wherever they might be required in the event of a sudden open rupture, almost equally large bodies of police were in readiness to afford them protection if need be.

The first engagement of the ill-advised and ill-planned campaign was begun at Mount Pleasant Parcel Depot on the morning of July 9. There the Union men made an onslaught on the newcomers, and after a short sharp struggle turned them out of the place. It was but a momentary victory, however, for which they were to pay dearly by the suspension and dismissal of a large number during the next few hours. The news of the outburst at Mount Pleasant heightened the excitement among the men at the Chief Office, and the discovery that a number of relief men had been drafted in intensified the feeling. A telegram was sent by the postmen to Mr. Raikes, stating their intention to suspend work until the interlopers were dismissed. They were, however, persuaded to proceed with their duties pending a reply. No reply being forthcoming, the demand for the dismissal of the objectionable relief men and the withdrawal of the police was repeated by means of several deputations to the Controller, but the demand was not acceded to.

Meanwhile, as it was generally understood that the Postmen's Union contemplated the madness of a strike, Clery and Fawcett Association did all that was possible to bring their fellow-servants to a better understanding. Clery had called together about 150 of the postmen, and suggested that the Postmen's Union should definitely abandon the strike policy which they had tacitly adopted in favour of some means of arbitration afterwards to be settled on, and a formal proposition embodying this suggestion was duly seconded, recommending that the executive should consider it. Clery's motive in putting forward this idea was twofold : one, and the principal one, being an earnest desire to save the postmen from pursuing such a suicidal course as they contemplated ; and the other to disabuse their minds that the letter-sorters intended to join with them. It had been circulated among them that Clery's followers were falling away ; that both Clery and Williams had failed to prevent the sorters from joining with them in large numbers. To dispose more effectually of such misstatements, a meeting of the sorters was on July 9 hurriedly called in the Foreign Branch, General Post Office, and over a thousand men being present, a resolution was passed expressing sympathy with the just demands of the postmen, but entirely repudiating and deprecating their strike policy. A deputation of postmen were invited to be present, and they left to attend a meeting of the Postmen's Union held at ten o'clock at Clerkenwell Green the same evening. Yet the same misstatement was persisted in, and

P

the newspapers the next morning announced that the post-men's leader had informed his audience that, at a meeting of the sorting force held in the General Post Office that evening, a resolution pledging those present to join with the postmen was unanimously carried.

At this meeting, which had been called to decide the next step, a huge crowd assembled to listen to fiery denunciations of the Postmaster-General, and it seemed the looked-for hour had arrived. A formal demand on which the strike was to be declared had already been decided upon, and unless the suspended men were reinstated forthwith and the " blacklegs " discharged, the postmen were to refuse to go out on delivery the following morning. The leader anticipated that the postmen in a body would simply obey the call as one man.

Needless to say, the authorities were kept well informed of every utterance and every movement of Mr. Mahon, and almost as quickly as if he had himself telephoned his uttered intention to St. Martin's-le-Grand, the Postmaster-General and his advisers knew the decision come to by the men. Accordingly, the higher officials spent the whole night and early morning in deciding on their plan of action. At three o'clock in the morning, the Permanent Secretary and some other officials presented themselves at the Mount Pleasant Parcel Depot, and as the men hurried in to sign the attendance books, called them up, and dismissed nearly a hundred of those who had made themselves prominent in the previous day's disturbance. Sir Arthur Blackwood went and mounted a table in the sorting-office and addressed the assembled staff in the most earnest and impressive manner ; and then in the name of the Postmaster-General expelled the dismissed postmen from the premises as well as from the Service.

A similar but less serious outbreak at Leicester Square office was followed with the same result, a number being dismissed on the spot.

By this sharp and decisive measure it was hoped that the postmen of the Chief Office would be deterred from taking the step they had the previous evening decided on, for it was felt that the attitude of the London postmen generally would be largely decided by those at St. Martin's-le-Grand. Arrangements for meeting the emergency were made accordingly.

The impressive moment arrived for their appearing on duty in the early hours of the 10th only a short time after the *coup* at Mount Pleasant. The majority of the men on their way to work had learnt by various means, from night policemen and from some of the dismissed men themselves, what had occurred. Those who had not already learnt of the summary dismissals at Mount Pleasant an hour or so before were now informed by an official notice confronting them at the entrance. This notice informed them that similar suspension or dismissal would follow in the case of men at other offices who, either by refusal to obey orders or the molestation of those employed under direction of the Postmaster-General, impeded the public service. The men who, it seems, had been expected to act automatically in accordance with the decision arrived at, having no one near them to inspire them, or to strengthen them in their wavering, and confronted on the one hand by the official proclamation, and on the other by a strong detachment of City police, one by one, silently and sheepishly, went in and took up their various duties. Besides the strong detachment of City police prepared to deal with them summarily at the first sign of disorder, there were the relief men ready to take their places. The postmen themselves felt like a regiment of irregulars without a leader, and there was no General Mahon present to give them the word of command. And perhaps it was as well for the general himself and all concerned. The head officials, who were unseen watching from a distance the entrance of the half-hearted and demoralised men, drew a sigh of relief, for they felt the real and graver danger was over.

The news rapidly spread that the City men had gone in to work ; and the effect was spontaneous almost everywhere throughout the districts, except at the Eastern District Office. The Northern men and the South-Eastern men, who had taken up a very firm attitude, almost immediately went in. But at one or two other places, Finsbury Park and Holloway, the men refused to go out on delivery, and were promptly suspended. The only important contingent who took the extreme step in a body were the Eastern District men. These, reinforced by driblets from other sources, made up a body of about three hundred, who by a woeful misunderstanding and want of information had refused to take up their duties. They marched in order to the General Post Office, expecting there to find the various other districts assembled in triumphant defiance. These misguided men marched in a solid body towards the City, and instead of being greeted as they expected by the welcoming shouts of the whole of the district and City postmen in possession of St. Martin's-le-Grand, found the grim grey General Post Office standing amidst solitude and silence. Except for the police on duty, and the few wondering pedestrians, the streets were deserted at that early hour ; and then, after standing still and wondering for a few seconds, they understood. It was now close on six o'clock in the morning ; they could hear the steady clank, clank of the stamping machines within the great crowded hive, and to these men who had risked all for an ideal, it seemed like intended mockery at their foolishness. They began to realise that they had grasped at the shadow, and lost the substance. Impelled by mingled feelings of hope, despair, and rage, they, as with one accord, wheeled into regimental order, and circled in a moving body round the General Post Office. Round and round they circled, again and again breaking forth into soulless and dispirited cheers to attract those safe within. Nothing more pathetic can be imagined than those cheers, which were but as a voice crying in the wilderness, and flung back to them in echo from the granite walls towering above them. With the police at their heels, and ruin confronting them, they despairingly kept on the move for one weary hour or more, threading the narrow thoroughfares which irregularly surround the General Post Office ; and the cheers, at first of simulated defiance, now died away in almost a piteous groan. Then at last the City police, taking stern action, prevented them from demonstrating any further ; and the wretched heartbroken remnant of the strike army gradually melted away towards the East, whence, in the sunrise, they had emerged so hopeful and so triumphant in anticipation.

During the day the number of men who paid the inevitable penalty of their folly reached nearly three hundred. In the evening there was an attempt at a muster after the battle, and several hundred men again assembled on Clerkenwell Green. Mr. Mahon addressed them, and endeavoured to reanimate them by announcing that the real Waterloo was to be fought on the morrow, when the whole of the London postmen would be called out on strike. Every postman within the Metropolitan area was exhorted to obey the summons.

The morrow came, however, and instead of the general rising and the consequent paralysing of the commerce of the country as was predicted, the postmen, realising the extremity to which they had been pushed and the failure of it, unconditionally surrendered by going about their duties as usual. The whole movement had collapsed, and the Postmen's Union was broken up. During the next two days the authorities were inundated with applications from the suspended and dismissed men for reinstatement, and therewith offering abject apology.

In all 435 men were either peremptorily dismissed or suspended with almost the certainty of dismissal. Of these 263 belonged to the unestablished, and 172 to the established class. Mr. Raikes triumphed, but it brought him almost as much worry and bitterness of spirit as a defeat would have done.

The postmen's strike had ended in even more ignominious failure than had the telegraphists' strike of twenty years previously. Everything that mattered, pensionable service, and all they claimed, had been practically staked against the right of open-air demonstration. The opportunity for presenting the strongest case for redress was thereby utterly wrecked. Once more the lesson had been forced home that it was moral suicide for any single section of State servants to attempt to fight a Government with inexhaustible resources with the weapon of a strike, and without the assistance of an enlightened public sympathy on their side.

CHAPTER XVII

DURING the several years following the introduction of the Fawcett scheme in 1881, the telegraph service had remained in a state of sullen discontent. The formation of the Postal Telegraph Clerks' Association, in the December of the same year in which Mr. Fawcett introduced his measure, did much to keep alive, for the next ten years, the memory of their wrongs. The grievances of the telegraph clerks, notwithstanding Mr. Fawcett's intention, were still so numerous and so genuine that on the face of it it seemed questionable whether it had brought them any benefit worth speaking of at all. The same measure of relief which the sorters were clamouring and agitating for, because, as they thought, it was being withheld from them, was, from its very inadequacy to meet the justice of their demands, the main cause of discontent among the telegraphists. What the sorters thought it would be a boon to get in its entirety, the telegraphists were now discontented with ; and not only were they discontented with the scheme itself for the reasons already shown, but that discontent was still further promoted by the systematic manner in which its few benefits were minimised in their application. The majority of telegraphists were still compelled to bolster up their meagre incomes by means of extra duty, and they were still, after all their agitation, face to face with the hated system of classification and all its attendant evils, irregularity and stagnation of promotion. Since the introduction of the Fawcett scheme the quality and value of their work had greatly improved, while their duties had become yearly more arduous and responsible. Their hours of duty were longer and far more irregular, the pay was insufficient, and daily growing more so when the cost of living and rent was considered, and their privileges were fewer than ever. The few prizes offered by the Fawcett scheme, the few higher promotions from their ranks to the supervising and superintending staff, brought no comfort or satisfaction to the hungry and underpaid army of the lower ranks. Even the overtime, the one means by which they could set up a barrier between themselves and actual want, which, indeed, they were forced to accept to preserve their respectability, was badly paid for and unjustly distributed. Owing to the constant fluctuation in the amount of work, the telegraphists were frequently required to perform overtime at a minute's notice at almost all hours of the day and night. Overtime became morally and officially compulsory, and it was only by means of it that they could earn a respectable income. In the same manner that the postmen's Christmas-boxes were used against them as a means of keeping down their wages, so was compulsory overtime, paid for at slender rates, forced on the telegraphists in extension of their nominal eight hours' day. The confining of a day's work to eight hours, even had it been allowable, would for the vast majority have spelt privation and poverty. So that a decent week's earnings, representing what is now known and accepted as a decent living wage, meant for the telegraphist, not the working week of eight hours' days, but a week of twelve, fourteen, and more hours daily. The extensive and increasing use of code and cipher messages requiring the most delicate discrimination in transmission, the many added responsibilities, the strain on the mental faculties and nervous system continued and sustained during these long working hours, caused in many cases premature breakdown and too early superannuation. An analysis of the superannuation report for 1885-86 showed that of the total number of telegraph clerks pensioned during that period no less than fifty per cent. were compelled to retire at a comparatively early age, owing to affections of the brain and nervous system induced by the constant strain. These facts alone were sufficient to notify the existence of discontent among them. But there were other grievances too numerous to be catalogued. Generally speaking, although Mr. Fawcett had enunciated the principle of payment for work according to its quality, the adoption of the Fawcett scheme was made the medium for greatly adding to the responsibilities of juniors, while imposing on the seniors supervising duties hitherto paid for at a higher rate. They felt that the value and quality of their work was far from accurately measured by the Department. Whether their work consisted of transmitting ordinary messages in the ordinary manner, or the selected duties appertaining to special events, such as race meetings, political speeches, etc., in which rapid and accurate manipulation was essential, they were all too poorly recompensed and too little regarded.

These things are mentioned to show that it was not merely a love of agitation for itself that animated the telegraphists at this period. To recount fully their grievances, it would be necessary to go into a mass of technical detail that would only confuse, and no better convince than the few general facts recorded. Added to all this, there was much dissatisfaction regarding the holiday question. The annual leave was distributed throughout the year, so that many went for years without a summer holiday, while for the loss of Bank holidays there was no equivalent given. Then, again, the conditions and environments of their work were not everything to be desired. There was, too, such a thing as " telegraphists' cramp," analogous to writers' cramp, which the growing pressure of telegraph work had introduced among the operators. True, it was not of very frequent occurrence, but it was something to reckoned with, and no man knew when his turn might come. Telegraphists' cramp is a nerve-wringing, brain-torturing malady, varying in degree of intensity. In one individual it may be confined to the nervous inability to signal particular letters, in itself a fatal defect in a telegraphist. Whatever be the pathological explanation of this very curious nervous phenomenon, it undoubtedly affects telegraphists more or less, and is something to be feared, more particularly in its ultimate results. It is a malady of such a peculiar nature that those who to the eye are physically able, yet may be absolute wrecks as regards their nerves.

Such, then, were the grievances under which the telegraphists laboured between 1881 and 1890. During the interval of that eight or nine years there was, of course, a plethora of petitions and applications for interviews ; there were public meetings, a few suspensions here and there, inflammatory speeches, annual conferences, and more or less sympathetic notices in the press of their doings. But there was nothing actually achieved by the agitation so far. Some splendid individual efforts were made, however, meanwhile ; and the names of Hughes, most prominent during 1884, North, Norman, and others, will long be remembered as men who fearlessly led the van when it was a perilous and delicate task to do so. The individual efforts of these men did much to secure the co-operation of Parliamentary friends and public men, and among those whose services were so secured may be mentioned Sir John Puleston, Mr. Henry Broadhurst, and Mr. Charles Bradlaugh. Mr. Charles Bradlaugh, it will be remembered, did much to promote the earlier postal agitation of 1872-74, and he once more came on the scene to help the telegraphists as he had helped the letter-carriers. He later identified himself particularly with the question of payment for Sunday labour for telegraphists. It was left to Mr. Charles Bradlaugh in the House to take the ballot for a direct motion, and it is not too much to say that it was owing to the number of promises procured by him to vote for this special motion that it was prevented from becoming a very close one. He procured the promises of many Conservatives as well as the bulk of the Liberal party. The Postmaster-General, after previously declining to grant this Sunday concession, as the result gave in, and the victory of this question was complete. Altogether too much gratitude cannot be given to Mr. Bradlaugh for the manner in which he worked for the telegraphists at this time.

There was a deal of work, a laying-in of stores and ammunition for future use, a deal of speech-making, letter-writing to M.P.s, and a general tightening-up of the telegraphists' forces. But there was no immediate and actual benefit secured, and nothing of an exciting nature worthy of being recorded as an event till 1889-90. The telegraph staff, in common with the rest of Government servants, had been cajoled into the belief that the Royal Commission on Civil Establishments would come to afford them some relief, or at least listen to their plaint. Much of the work in which they had latterly been engaged was occupied in the preparation of evidence for this expected inquiry. The disappointment that ensued only gave a stronger impetus to the agitation, and from theorising and pursuing debating-society methods they adopted a firmer and more aggressive attitude. As with the letter-sorters, they found that the evidence they had prepared and the weight of facts they had accumulated, so far from being waste material and a deadweight, came in very useful now for powder and shot with which to enforce their demands.

What was regarded as an unduly harsh interference with the right of combination at Cardiff some little time afterwards, tended very considerably to arouse the fighting spirit in them, and to bring things to the climax of an open struggle. It was only necessary at this juncture to give the telegraphists a few martyrs to emphasise their grievances, and arouse them to action.

In the August of 1889 a disgraceful state of affairs appears to have existed at Cardiff, telegrams being frequently seriously delayed owing to want of sufficient staff. A paragraph appeared in a local paper, the *Western Mail*, complaining of the delay. On this editorial peg, numerous articles, leaders, and letters were hung, till the whole correspondence assumed voluminous proportions. The Cardiff telegraphists, from this realising a sense of their injustice, commenced agitating by meetings and petitions. They complained of the under-manning of the staff and consequent overworking ; the insanitary condition of the office itself ; the fact that Cardiff was one of the worst classified offices in the kingdom ; that supervisors had to perform instrument work to the neglect of their proper duties ; that they were punished for errors unavoidably due to lack of supervision ; favouritism, non-payment of Sunday duty, and sundry minor grievances.

In consequence of representations made by Sir John Reed, M.P., a revision took place, and most of the cause of complaint was removed. So far, so good. But there was to be a sequel. In the following November, the Postmaster-General, Mr. Raikes, was announced to attend a Church Congress in the neighbourhood, and he telegraphed to a certain colonel at Llandaff, stating his intention to arrive at a certain time. Through the medium of the acting postmaster, so it was alleged, this piece of news found its way into the *South Wales Daily News*. The Postmaster-General on learning this took a very severe view of the case, and in consequence the official was compelled to retire from the Service. While the Postmaster-General was in the Principality a number of the Cardiff staff requested him to receive an interview on the vexed question of Sunday work at that office. This resolve was communicated to several provincial offices, and the result was that some thirty telegrams were received, asking him to receive the deputation on the general question. The Postmaster-General promised the Cardiff staff that he would consider. Mr. Raikes, however, left the town early next morning, and the Cardiff men were left disappointed. Further, the various provincial offices, which had sent the telegrams in all good faith, were soon afterwards called on to apologise for their conduct. Appointments becoming due at the Cardiff office, eight of the men eligible were informed by the surveyor that they would receive the higher appointments only on the condition that they proved that they did not write the paragraph which had appeared in the *Western Mail*, complaining of the delay of telegrams. Failing this negative proof of their innocence, or their inability to name the person who made public what was now held to be a secret communication, the promotions would be withheld, and they would be transported. As this punishment of transportation to other distant towns where they were strangers meant the breaking-up of their homes, and the severance of family ties and friendly relationships, the telegraphists concerned felt they were the victims of injustice. They were informed that the transference would be made within eight hours ; and in this short time were compelled to make what arrangements they could for the future, not even knowing to what distant part of the kingdom they would be severally deported. They, against whom nothing more than a suspicion rested of having communicated an innocent item of news, were actually transferred, with little time for leave-taking, next day. They were sent away to various offices. On the night that the first two were ordered away the staff held an impromptu meeting, and the places of the eight men who formed the secretaries and committee of the local branch of the association were filled up. But these officers were also, as soon as it was known, promptly given orders to hold themselves in readiness for transference. It has to be noted here, that Sunday pay was at the time an important item in the general programme, and these men at Cardiff had prepared to urge it strongly ; for it was not till some months later that, through the instrumentality of Mr. Bradlaugh in the House of Commons, the question was settled in their favour.

The despotic treatment meted out to the Cardiff men induced Sir E. J. Reed, M.P., to take up their case in real earnest. For the supposed dereliction of duty they were to be penalised by the loss of a £25 increment, besides being packed off to unknown regions within a few hours. Besides Sir E. J. Reed, other influential public men took the matter up, and the case of the Cardiff " exiles " commanded some attention in the House. But the Postmaster-General was not to be moved by any argument, and contended that it was not intended as punishment, and was ultimately for the men's own good.

Yet while it had been stated that the men were transferred for no other reason than that of communicating this piece of information to the local paper, the First Lord of the Treasury, in reply to Mr. Hanbury in June, 1888, distinctly stated that such communications could not be considered as an offence against Departmental regulations. So that if Mr. Raikes's treatment was not arbitrary, it was inconsistent.

The case of the Cardiff " martyrs," as they were called, produced a very strong feeling against the Postmaster-General amongst the telegraphists ; and principally because of this they could not be induced to share that good opinion held of him by the sorters. And in truth it must be said that the Post-master-General's conduct towards both the letter-carriers and the telegraphists at this period contrasted somewhat strangely with the leniency and indulgence shown towards the sorting staff, and the facilities offered the latter for promoting a constitutional agitation. Certainly the sorters' agitation was conducted with great caution and very little heat, while it has to be allowed that, however Mr. Raikes may have been convinced of the existence of grievances generally throughout the Service, the over-zeal of the letter-carriers, and the importunities of the telegraphists in some quarters, may have caused him to draw invidious distinctions.

All the evidence and all the circumstances of the Cardiff case tend to show that Mr. Raikes, by some unaccountable means, was induced to commit an unworthy blunder, which helped to render him extremely unpopular with the telegraph service. The ebullition of feeling, openly and widely expressed by public meeting everywhere among the London and provincial telegraphists, and sympathetically reported by the press, so far convinced Mr. Raikes that he had made a mistake that he afterwards modified his charge against the Cardiff men.

This incident, in conjunction with other things, helped very considerably to tighten the sinews of the organisation. And in the meantime, while indignation at the Inquisitorial treatment of their Cardiff brethren was at its height, the London telegraphists, who hitherto had been but loosely hanging on to the skirts of the Postal Telegraph Clerks' Association, closed up their ranks, and on December 17, 1889, went over in a solid and enthusiastic body. Great was the rejoicing when the London men definitely joined hands with the provinces. The accession of 7500 Metropolitan men was certainly something to be jubilant over.

With the fresh reinforcements everywhere, the tide of indignation and dissatisfaction spread over the United Kingdom. For two months nearly, each day saw some expression of the feeling which had taken possession of the telegraph service, and some of the papers discerned all the preparations for an early strike among telegraphists everywhere. It became not a question of Cardiff particularly, but one in which the whole telegraph service was involved and identified. From Land's End to John o' Groat's there was an eruptive unrest ; and the whole press of the country— Liberal and Tory, Radical and Independent—was kept busy in recording the utterances and commenting on the doings of telegraphists in meeting assembled everywhere. The Postmaster-General was inundated with a flow of petitions from every quarter ; and besides being heckled from within the Service and without, in the press and on the platform, Mr. Raikes experienced a very lively time of it in the House of Commons.

There can be little doubt that during this busy and exciting period, with newspaper censure hurled at him from everywhere, and threats and prognostications of direful postal strikes filling the air, the Postmaster-General must have been far more severely punished than the victims of his mistake, the martyrs of Cardiff. This kind of thing lasted unceasingly till April 15, 1890, when the whole question of telegraphists' grievances was ventilated in the House of Commons by Earl Compton. Earl Compton minutely traversed the ground of their grievances, and was ably supported ; but Mr. Raikes defended his administration to the satisfaction of the House, and the motion was in due course lost by thirty-nine votes.

But although the telegraphists' case was defeated, it was manifest that the matter could not long rest where it was. The feeling by this time was too strained and too acute to be allayed by an official refusal. All the dormant energies of the telegraphists were put forth, and grievances which had remained quiescent and unexpressed for years now loudly demanded redress and readjustment.

Immediately after the defeat of Earl Compton's motion in the House, Mr. Raikes promulgated a new order restricting the right of public meeting outside the Post Office. The acute stage at which the telegraphists' agitation had now arrived was contemporaneous with the trouble among the postmen.

The growing aggressiveness of the two postal bodies, the telegraphists and the postmen, and the free use they were making of public meeting, induced the Postmaster-General to restrict their freedom in this respect by reviving Lord Stanley's order of 1866. What, however, was a restriction in the case of the telegraphists was a distinct concession to the sorters of the London Postal Service, who had hitherto been compelled to meet inside Post Office buildings, and greatly appreciated the wider liberty. What in the circumstances was regarded by the sorters as a boon and a concession was, after the wider liberty enjoyed by the telegraphists, regarded by them as a direct attempt on personal rights, and the introduction of terrorism and espionage. And after the assertion of the right of outside public meeting by the postmen, this view was fully shared by them. Indeed, it was the introduction of this restrictive rule that afforded a further excuse for the Postmen's Union resorting to extreme methods. In so regarding it, the postmen and the telegraphists were at the time greatly upheld by the press, and the Post-master-General was subjected to a deal of sharp criticism for his action.

The question of free public meeting for all postal employés and other matters arising out of the new Post Office order, so strenuously objected to by the telegraphists, were brought under the notice of the House of Commons on April 24, 1890, Mr. Pickersgill, himself an old postal servant, and other members, strongly urging on the Postmaster-General the desirability of modifying the regulation. Mr. Raikes, however, was firm in his attitude, and maintained that the new order was really to relax the stringency of a rule which for nearly a quarter of a century was absolutely prohibitory in its effect.

The day following this discussion in the House, April 25, a deputation of telegraphists waited on the Postmaster-General to urge that he would not only modify the rule as to public meeting, but also that he would give immediate attention to the many grievances of which they complained, and on which they were agitating. Mr. Raikes promised he would refer the whole question of their grievances to the Departmental Committee then sitting for the purpose of assisting him to come to a decision. The telegraphists had therefore to accept his word for it that their case should receive attention in good time.

But meetings still continued to be held in different parts in spite of the presence of the official reporter. His presence was objected to at Leicester in a characteristic manner by the suppression of the names of the speakers, so that Mr. Raikes might know all that was said of him, but not the identity of the speakers.

The new regulation became so notorious throughout the country that, in one instance at least, the police authorities in Bucks. actually became imbued with the idea that these gatherings were of the nature of proclaimed meetings as in Ireland under the Coercion Act, and thought it part of their duty to keep a watchful eye on all such meetings of telegraphists. Such was a case specially referred to in the House of Commons by Mr. Bradlaugh in a question put May 20.

The question of compulsory overtime was soon afterwards forced to the front by an admission made by Mr. Raikes in the House, June 12, in answer to Earl Compton, that officers of the telegraph department were not compelled against their will, but were asked to volunteer for overtime. For some time after that the telegraph clerks in London and Dublin decided to take their stand on that admission, but the evil still continued with irritating regularity. Numerous were the published contradictions to the Postmaster-General's statement in the House, and the press with striking unanimity, excepting *The Times*, which consistently stood by Mr. Raikes throughout, strongly denounced the system of enforced overtime and Mr. Raikes's incorrect denial of its existence. After the authoritative declaration from the official head the " no overtime " movement was taken up enthusiastically among the men, and spread rapidly, not only in London, but throughout the leading provincial offices. At the Central Office in London about 90 per cent. of the male staff pledged themselves to decline to work overtime, and it was decided to put this pledge into force on a certain date unless the Postmaster-General meanwhile announced some measure of relief for their various grievances. It was alleged that the total number of overtime hours worked in the Central Telegraph Office alone reached the enormous weekly total of from ten to twelve thousand, or 30 per cent. on the day's ordinary work, so that the sudden withdrawal of this amount of work would have meant a serious public inconvenience.

In connection with this attitude a somewhat curious and sensational method of protest was used by the telegraphists on the occasion of the Post Office Jubilee. Arrangements were made by the authorities that, at a signal sent by the Duchess of Edinburgh from the Jubilee conversazione at South Kensington, the whole of the postal and telegraph service on duty at the moment should burst forth into simultaneous cheering for the Queen. The intended pleasing tribute of loyalty was, however, spoilt in a manner that made Mr. Raikes exceedingly indignant with the telegraphists especially. At ten o'clock, the precise moment having arrived, some four hundred telegraphists being assembled in the central galleries at the Chief Office, the superintendent called for three cheers for the Queen. But silence was steadfastly maintained for some moments, and then with one accord, instead of the cheers expectantly waited for by royal ears at the other end of the telephones, the clerks, to show their resentment, burst out into a deep groan. Three cheers for Mr. Raikes were then asked for, but this was met with a volume of groans deeper than before.

The telegraphists, who were afterwards officially interrogated as to the meaning of the demonstration, strongly repudiated any intention of disloyalty or disrespect towards her Majesty the Queen, and explained that the demonstration was spontaneously made as a protest against the manner in which their repeated petitions for redress of grievances had been treated by the higher officials surrounding Mr. Raikes. Their explanation was not deemed satisfactory ; there was much writing and further questioning over the incident. A number of representatives were asked wholly to dissociate themselves from what took place, and were called on to sign a paper to that effect. The matter was discussed, and the official memorandum was rejected by eight to three. The names of the eight clerks who voted against the suggestion were asked for, but they unanimously declined to give the required information. The official memorandum of dissociation was circulated and a number of signatures obtained, chiefly from female telegraphists, but the large majority of the staff declined to sign the document.

The incident was reported in most of the papers, and served as a big advertisement which had the effect of turning closer attention to the nature and extent of their grievances. The telegraphists were not applauded for their action, but the Postmaster-General was in some quarters mercilessly taken to task for what seemed like giving countenance to a silly piece of snobbery on the part of toadying officials.

Q

The " no overtime " agitation continued among the telegraphists, and so intense did the feeling become that a large
proportion were for striking against the enforcement of the
obnoxious overtime at a certain date. The feeling had gained
headway so far that a large number had actually signed a paper
set in circulation promising to obey the call to arms when the
moment arrived. But before the dramatic moment arrived
the Controller suddenly sent for a few of the more prominent
ringleaders to discuss the situation. After some parrying and
courteous preliminaries the official suddenly confronted them
with the question whether they would promise then and
there to use their influence with their followers to restrain them
from adopting the course decided on. There was some demur,
and the question was objected to as unfair in the circumstances. The official gave them half-an-hour to decide and
left them, turning the key in the door as he went out. They
were virtually held prisoners in the official's private room.
After some consideration the leaders of the agitation thought
discretion the better part of valour, and decided to give the
required promise in writing, and this was done. They were
then released and went back to their duties. One of the men,
however, was rash enough to telegraph the news to Newcastle,
with the intimation that the promise given was not seriously
intended. The message, as might have been anticipated, was
immediately " tapped " and conveyed to headquarters, with
the result that the operator was on the spot suspended from
duty. He was accordingly dismissed, and though it was not a
case in which the victim could be made either a hero or a
martyr, the telegraphists, with the generous impulse of comradeship, rallied round him and raised a subscription, which
in a short time realised the sum of £500. The incident gave
a set-back to the " no overtime " agitation for the time, but
the feeling against the Postmaster-General was by no means
modified by its remembrance.

With the hostile criticism of the press and a section of the
House, and engaged in driving a pair of spirited steeds, the
telegraphists and the postmen, that threatened every moment
to break away and overturn the chariot, Mr. Raikes's position
was no enviable one. In the circumstances too ready compli-
ance with the demands on either hand would probably have

been interpreted as weakness, if not by the men themselves, by Parliament, and still more probably by the Lords of the Treasury. Mr. Raikes was an able man, but pride generally overrules conscience and sometimes wisdom. He was but human ; and most men in a position of power would prefer to be accused of tyranny rather than weakness. So the tension continued and increased till, reaching the breaking-point in the case of the postmen, as has been shown, it almost seemed as if the telegraphists must follow their desperate example.

CHAPTER XVIII

THE PROVINCIAL SORTING CLERKS—THEIR POSITION—THE RIDLEY COMMISSION, AND EVIDENCE PREPARED—THE FORMATION OF AN ORGANISATION—THE RIGHT OF PUBLIC MEETING.

THROUGH a long course of years the postmen, the letter-sorters, and the telegraphists had cultivated each their fertile patch of ground, and produced a plentiful crop of the thistles of discontent. But there was one other widely distributed and important section of the postal community who, while feeling most of the grievances of which the others complained, yet took no combined action. While the letter-carriers and the telegraphists especially assumed a more or less aggressive attitude in the maintenance and furtherance of their rights and privileges in the service, the provincial postal clerks, as important a body as either of these, remained passive till the year 1886. Through the whole of the stormy and exciting periods, the strike of the telegraphists in 1870, the upheaval of the postmen and sorters two or three years later, and the recurrence of fierce agitation among all other postal bodies during the few years following, the postal clerks, undisturbed, pursued the even tenor of their way. That they had grievances goes without saying ; but there were influences that held them in check ; and they did not realise the grievances they suffered from so acutely as a body that they could be drawn easily into the vortex of agitation. They agitated more or less for the removal of restrictions and the redress of local grievances, but their efforts were too tentative and sporadic in their character to be of permanent value or make any lasting impression. It was not till 1886 that an awakening was to come. The postal clerks as a collective body were content to sow their wild oats on the Ridley Commission of 1886-87. That commission, on which had been centred the hopes of many thousands of men in the postal service, proved abortive. In spite of the distinct promise held out and express invitations made to prepare and tender evidence before it, the Ridley Commission on Civil Establishments dashed every hope to the ground by prematurely disbanding. The effect of this on other postal bodies has already been seen. The abortive Ridley Commission has had much to answer for, and became in itself the most fruitful source of that discontent it was originally intended to allay. When it became evident that it would not after all reach the doors of the Post Office, a groan of disappointment went up from the overworked and underpaid multitudinous army of malcontents which made up the rank and file of the postal service ; and that groan of disappointment presently deepened into cries of execration at what seemed so like a wilful betrayal. That deep disappointment was shared by the postal clerks everywhere throughout the kingdom ; and in common with other bodies similarly duped, they came to recognise that the very cause of their disappointment might be turned to advantage. After all, the Ridley Commission came as a blessing in disguise. It had provided an opportunity and an excuse for collecting evidence and preparing the strongest possible indictment against the Department. The evidence thus so laboriously gathered and industriously prepared was not to be wasted now. The investigation and the experience had taught them many things ; it had familiarised them with bodies and branches which had hitherto been held apart ; it brought about an affinitive and friendly cohesion of particles ; and small bodies which had revolved in their own distinct circumscribed orbits were now given a place and a relationship in a more or less orderly system. In point of fact it was the means of introducing among them one cardinal principle, a law, that of combination.

Previous to the Ridley Commission the postal clerks had been little heard of as a combined body, but now, on this occasion, with a unanimity that was as commendable as it was remarkable, they showed the necessity by setting the example of forming an association. It has to be borne in mind that the telegraphists were already combined, but their combination proceeded from a different origin, though the effect of the failure of the Ridley Commission was to strengthen their already existing organisation considerably. It was on the purely postal side of the service, however, that the most marked effect was to be produced. In response to the call for evidence of grievances, men hitherto unheard of leapt into the breach, and took up the duties of representatives and collectors of the required evidence most cheerfully. The disappointment that ensued produced the inevitable result where no combination had previously existed, and the ruins of the Ridley Commission were to become the training-ground for a new army of agitation. The same influence operated everywhere. The same effect exactly was produced among the London sorters and the provincial postal clerks. These two uncombined classes had no intercourse with each other ; and though there was a kinship between them it had never been recognised. For all practical purposes they were almost ignorant of each other's existence. Yet the London sorters and the provincial sorting clerks without any preconcerted signal, and unknown to each other, spontaneously gravitated towards combination, where no combination existed before. The provincial postal clerks, however, took the initiative, and it was not till some years afterwards that the Metropolitan letter-sorters, almost unconsciously following the example of their country cousins, formed the Fawcett Association on similar lines. The formation of the Postal Clerks' Association was preceded by the familiar secret gatherings and more or less successful attempts at belling the cat at the various offices. To engage in such forbidden enterprises in those days was, to say the least, risky ; and the promoters stood to pay the penalty of their rashness at any time they might be called on.

As Liverpool had taken a prominent, if not the leading part in the first telegraphists' agitation, and again in 1881, so once more, in the case of the postal clerks, was Liverpool to produce the man and show the way. The deplorable condition into which the postal service had fallen, so far as their working environments, their prospects and pay were concerned, roused one or two individuals among the postal clerks here to seek about for a remedy. The cries of discontent, and the calls for redress from other distant places, came to their ears like inarticulate voices in the night. From various sources it was conveyed to them that the same injustices and the same hardships they suffered from, also afflicted thousands of others of their own widely-distributed class throughout the country. The invitation to lay before the Ridley Commission evidence as to conditions and prospects immediately produced a thrill of expectancy among postal servants everywhere. From Liverpool the threads of sympathetic communication were carried to the different centres of existing discontent all over the United Kingdom, and the threads were gradually strengthened each day till they vibrated in unison.

Telegraphic communication did much, and circular letters did much towards establishing an understanding as to their aims and desire. Much of the groundwork for their plan of future action was thus roughly prepared, and it was in these circumstances that four or five of the Liverpool postal clerks one day met to discuss the situation, and decide on the methods of collecting evidence. With the object of fully ascertaining the feelings of the Liverpool men themselves, and to judge whether the future movement would be likely to be led from there, and Liverpool sustain its character for leading the van, a notice was put up in one of the retiring-rooms calling a meeting of the postal clerks to discuss more openly the matter. A meeting was held December 5, 1886, thirty only attending, however ; but it was decided to form a committee of thirteen. George Lascelles, one of their number, who had actually set the little movement afoot, was elected secretary. More meetings followed in the usual course of things, and the new combination gradually became fixed and determined in its principles, shape, and character. Its dimensions and its name were from this time the only things that remained to be decided. Circulars were speedily got out inviting the co-operation of other offices, sixty-three of the larger towns being thus circularised at first. But so unknown were they to each other that these circulars had to be posted blindly, and addressed simply to the " Sorting Clerks at ――." Gradually the responses came in, the identity of men willing to work in the new mission was revealed, and a human sympathy and a relationship as between new-found brothers all at once sprang into existence. Truly, the Ridley Commission had not been called in vain. The men thus newly brought

into touch with each other were invited to send a representative from each of their offices to a general conference. The
conference was to be held at Liverpool, January 21. The
strangers came out from the darkness ; and those who at
first were but names now met face to face in flesh and
blood reality, the hopeful pioneers of a movement.

The conference was held, and proved an unqualified
success. There was an interchange of views, and a mutual
understanding of their wants, on which they were enabled to
formulate a series of resolutions ; and on the lines of these
resolutions George Lascelles, the secretary, was authorised to
draw up a general statement of evidence for the Commission
then sitting.

It was decided to band themselves together in the
form of an association for mutual support, to be known as
the " United Kingdom Postal Clerks' Association." Like a
gathering snowball the new postal organisation increased in
dimensions, and rolling onward from Liverpool, presently
included Manchester, Birmingham, and similar towns of
importance, picking up the smaller places like crumbs by the
way.

Within a year the Postal Clerks' Association had gone over
the whole length and breadth of the land, and extended
from the north to the south, and from the west to the east.
Besides this their association was now represented in four
or five of the most important towns in Ireland. The only
parallel to this extraordinary response to the call for
combination was that among their. fellow-servants, the
telegraphists, when the Postal Telegraph Clerks' Association
was formed in 1881.

The hardships suffered by the postal clerks at this period
were as real and as acute as any that beset either of the other
bodies of the service. Their grievances were general and
particular. The hardship of compulsory Sunday labour
pressed on them severely. This question of enforced labour on
the Sabbath had been one which affected the service throughout, and had been made the grounds of the first agitation and
the first public protest against postal administration. Postmen,
telegraphists, and sorting clerks alike were the victims to this
compulsory system ; but with the sorting clerks, especially in

some districts, the evil had grown to exaggerated proportions. In some offices, for example—Limerick, Cork, Aberdeen, Norwich, Worcester, and many other places—the clerks, in very large numbers, were regularly employed on duty every Sunday, and without receiving any remuneration. In a great many offices they were kept on duty three weeks out of every four, and only in a few instances were they off duty more than two Sundays in every month. It was a grievance with them that they were compelled to relinquish their day of rest, but it was doubly a grievance that they were denied payment for the time and work given. In many of the leading provincial offices the evil became accentuated, and at Manchester, Leeds, Exeter, York, and numerous other places where the staff of postal clerks represented in the aggregate 400 or more, they were graciously permitted, if the duty allowed, to take a Sunday off once in every four weeks. When it is remembered that these men, whatever their religious convictions or conscientious objections, were compelled to give this time for absolutely no remuneration, it certainly seemed monstrous in a Christian land.

This grievance of Sunday duty, however, was only one among a long catalogue, which had lengthened still with the progress of time. The system of promotion created a feeling of irritation and discontent throughout their ranks, though this was by no means a grievance peculiar to them. As with other branches of the service also, the gravest discontent prevailed among them in regard to the scales of pay, but as aggravating this there was the unequal system of classification, whereby a clerk in one office might be, and very often was, placed at a disadvantage in respect to pay and promotion, as compared with another at a similar office. The average wages of the second-class sorting or postal clerks were 22s. 8d. a week ; but in many instances their work involved the very highest responsibilities, including the care and despatch of money-orders, stamps, registered correspondence, besides payment of pensions, Savings Bank accounts, and similar duties. Not only this, but junior clerks having, as was often the case, to perform the duties of others above them in grade, had no allowance of any description for so acting ; and thus it frequently happened that juniors were constantly kept, on the shallowest pretext, on more responsible duties than their poor salaries would justify.

At this time it was the general practice to deduct one-half of salary when away on sick leave ; and this was regarded as a distinct hardship, as in no other section of the Civil service, so far as was known, was so large a proportion of salary forfeited through enforced absence from causes of illness. They very justly claimed that a deduction of one-third only would more adequately meet the case of unavoidable sickness. Another cause of annoyance to them was the extremely slow rate of promotion, ten and twenty years being a fair average of the period of waiting for dead men's shoes. The analogous question of superannuation affected them very keenly. The Playfair Commission of a few years before had recommended that when a man had given thirty consecutive years of service and wished to retire, ten years might be added to his time in calculating the allowance due to him, and that he should be allowed to resign without either being sixty years of age or wholly incapable from infirmity. But among the sorting or postal clerks there had occurred many cases of infirm men being harshly treated in this respect, and not allowed to retire either through passing the age limit of sixty years of age or through being broken down in health. They were in a position to allege that men had been compelled to attend to their duties when in truth they were physically incapable of properly attending to them. Another sore point with the postal clerks was that a very large proportion of them were unestablished, though they were compelled to perform all the duties of permanent officers better paid, and while they had no guarantee that their years of service would not be peremptorily dispensed with by the whim or caprice of an individual supervisor. Those who were established further complained that promotions to postmasterships which more rightly belonged to them as postal servants were unfairly distributed to telegraphists, this practice seriously diminishing their legitimate outlet of promotion. These were the principal and salient features of their indictment against the Department at this period. But there were many other points, such as proper remuneration for Christmas duty, Bank holidays,

Queen's Birthday, etc. ; the inadequate period of annual leave ; " split " duties, or duties being spread over a large proportion of the day and necessitating several attendances ; the severity of night duty ; and other things quite as familiar to the telegraphists, the postmen, and sorters elsewhere.

It was to find a remedy for this state of things as they affected them that the United Kingdom Postal Clerks' Association was inaugurated.

Then like a thunderclap came the announcement that the Ridley Commission, whose approach they had so confidently looked forward to, did not intend to visit the Post Office at all. It was a staggering blow to the postal clerks, as it was to every other body in the service. But so far from demoralising them, it put them on their mettle the more. Their organisation, which the illusive Ridley Commission had been the means of calling into existence, they still had ; and they determined to stand by it, and use it for purposes of defence and the furtherance of their claims.

For a few years longer the Postal Clerks' Association, still growing and consolidating, pushed its claims in the many various ways known to men who want their wrongs redressed. But they never departed from strictly constitutional lines ; a few members of Parliament were induced now and again to take up their case as included in the common postal cause ; they had their conferences, their meetings, their joint petitions, and their memorials to the Postmaster-General, just as did the telegraphists, the postmen, and others at this period ; still, as an association, they remained an exemplar to the rest of the postal service. Their pursuing such strictly constitutional methods, and their attitude as a combination being practically beyond reproach, was in no small measure due to the personality of their secretary, George Lascelles, who was the real leader.

There was an enormous amount of work done one way and another ; but their efforts towards obtaining any real material benefit were as fruitless as were those of the other organisations.

Soon after Mr. Raikes became Postmaster-General, as has already been described, a crusade of agitation beset him from all quarters, growing fiercer every day. But the Postal Clerks'

Association was not formed for purposes of agitation as agitation ; and it contented itself with remaining as an interested and perhaps a sympathetic spectator. The great wave of industrial agitation following in the wake of improvement in trade everywhere at the beginning of 1890 aroused the telegraphists, the postmen, and the Metropolitan letter-sorters to further exertion in their various ways. And when Mr. Raikes reintroduced the old regulation of 1866, limiting the freedom of public meeting, the postal clerks were not behind in lodging their indignant protest, in common with most other combined bodies. They emphasised the indignation they shared in holding a mass meeting at Liverpool, their centre. Their good manners had so far not been corrupted by evil communication ; but adversity makes strange bedfellows. There were partial jealousies between the sorting clerks and the telegraphists, and both to an extent felt themselves superior to postmen ; but in this they were as one. The Cardiff case gave them no good opinion of Mr. Raikes ; while their minor difference with the telegraphists was forgotten in their sympathy with them. And, added to this, about this time they were given an axe of their own to grind, and the telegraphists in turn looked on with a sympathetic eye. At the Liverpool Conference of Postal Clerks, held April, 1890, the shadow of the official reporter obtruded itself across their threshold. He was introduced to the chairman of the meeting by an official letter, which contained what was tantamount to a demand in the name of the Postmaster-General. The official reporter had to be admitted to take notes, or they had to disband the conference. They were as helpless as was the official reporter himself, who was also a paid servant of the Department. The chairman of the meeting, in his opening statement, referred to the fact that for the first time in their history a meeting of officials called for a praiseworthy object were compelled to receive in their midst an unwelcome intruder sent in the name of discipline. Though there was nothing in the constitution of their society that was antagonistic to departmental authority, they had to accept this humiliating and Russianising condition, or forfeit altogether their right of free speech as Englishmen and Britons. This new restrictive rule became particularly hard of digestion to the postal clerks, who had hitherto prided themselves on the absolutely constitutional lines on which their organisation was run.   The introduction of avowed trade unionism could no longer be regarded as a crime in the Post Office, since Sir Arthur Blackwood, the Permanent Secretary, himself some little time before had publicly stated that there was a growing spirit of trade unionism which must be made allowance for and taken into account.   The postal clerks had so long remained loyally constitutional in their attitude, that the application of the restrictive rule to them they regarded as supererogatory.   However, justified or otherwise, they were compelled to accept it in common with the rest of the service.

Only a few days after this the postal clerks were given a still more serious cause for complaint by the manner in which some of the officials of their organisation were slighted in the matter of promotion ordinarily due to them.   Mr. Henry Labouchere put forward the question in the House of Commons, April 25.   The chairman and secretary of the Liverpool branch of the Postal Clerks' Association, Messrs. Thompson and Clucas, were, it appears, unjustly superseded in promotion by junior men.   The fact in itself was not so unheard-of in the service as to call for public comment ; but the circumstances suggested that these officers had been so treated because of their connection with the association of their class.   The Postmaster-General in the previous March had given an undertaking in the House of Commons that connection with an association or union should not detrimentally affect any officer's official career ; yet in face of that assurance this seemed as clear a case of intimidation as that of Cardiff.   The Postmaster-General denied that their being officers of that union had anything to do with their treatment, and maintained that their position in this respect was neither known to himself nor taken into account.   Possibly it was so, so far as he himself was concerned, for at this period, with the bewildering number of claims and counter-claims put forward from a thousand points at once, the Postmaster-General had necessarily to trust very largely to the permanent advisers for information, and doubtless even for guidance to a ruling in some cases.

Although at this time represented by two distinct associations, there appeared to be much in common between the
Metropolitan sorters and the provincial sorting clerks. Their
entrance into the service, the similarity of their pay prospects,
and the character of their duties, entitled the London sorters
to class themselves with their provincial brethren. They had
urged that they were in reality sorting clerks, and were referred
to as such by Mr. Fawcett in his 1881 scheme. But it was just
on this point that the " Luminous Committee " settled the
whole matter against them. The equality that existed
between the provincial sorting clerks and the provincial telegraphists, it was thought, should find an analogue in the
Metropolitan telegraphists and sorters, and that was the whole
ground of the difference, as already reviewed. Still, if there
were not equality in one case, there was in another, for except
in title the pay and prospects and conditions of sorting clerks
and sorters were almost identical ; while their grievances were,
except on the enforced Sunday duty question, also similar.
Seeing that there was so much in common between these two
bodies, it would therefore not have been surprising had they
made common cause for the purpose of getting their grievances
redressed on a similar basis. It was not so, however, and the
connection between them never went beyond a friendly intercourse, and the ordinary amenities of unionism. There was,
however, a journal started at this period in Birmingham,
intended mainly for circulation among sorting clerks, but to
which Metropolitan men were invited to contribute. The
sorters already had the *Post*, which had now become the
property of the association ; but the new *Postal Review* was
taken up with some enthusiasm among them. The *Postal
Review* might have become a permanent link of friendly
connection, and a handy vehicle for the intercommunication
of ideas leading to more important results, perhaps, but for a
slip that occurred. At the inaugural meeting of the Fawcett
Association, February 10, 1890, a leaflet was distributed
having for its object the promotion of the sale of this monthly
journal, and two of the sorters were advertised as its wholesale
and retail agents for the London postal service. The leaflet,
after announcing that the *Postal Review* had over 300 contributors in different parts of the country, representing so many

distinct offices, referred to many of these contributors as "being in confidential positions, and having access to the most important and valuable information, which," the leaflet went on to say, "when occasion arises or exigencies demand, will be laid before the readers of the *Postal Review.*" The leaflet in question, so far from carrying out its purpose, was the means of abruptly breaking off negotiations with the provinces ; for there was an immediate official inquiry, and the two sorters whose names were mentioned as agents were promptly called on to repudiate all connection with its publication. The matter became the subject for special reference in the Post Office Circular, and the two innocent men who had inadvertently allowed their names to be printed on the incriminating leaflet, were made to renounce connection with it publicly and to disavow all implication in the heinous design set forth.

After that the two organisations went their separate ways, and they were not to meet again for some years afterwards. But though they went their separate ways it was always in the same direction and along almost parallel roads, and often so near to each other that they could occasionally catch the glimpse of their raised banners as they marched towards the common goal.

CHAPTER XIX

THE AFTER-EFFECTS OF THE POSTMEN'S STRIKE—THE
RAIKES SCHEME—FRESH DISSATISFACTION—AN ESTIMATE OF
MR. RAIKES.

IF Mr. Raikes' cautious nature made him slow to convince,
he nevertheless at last came to realise that the rampant
discontent throughout his domain called for some effective
remedy other than coercion. It was not only the continual
heckling in the House, or the numerous public meetings of
postal servants themselves ; but, as Sir John Puleston, M.P.,
himself a personal friend of Mr. Raikes, pointed out to the
telegraphists at the Foresters' Hall meeting at which he
presided, the Postmaster-General was himself inwardly convinced that there were defects in the postal service which
called for a speedy and effective remedy. But while the
continuance of postal agitation everywhere must have hastened
the conviction that something was radically wrong, it somewhat retarded the application of the remedy.

In the case of the sorters' agitation, an inter-departmental
inquiry, known as the " Luminous Committee," sat to decide
on the merits of their claim, and in the case of the telegraphists
particularly a committee of officials investigated and reported
on their grievances. But it was impossible, owing to the
eruptive state of the service, and the enormous amount of
responsibility and detail work involved, to settle all these
conflicting claims simultaneously and immediately. The after
effects of the postmen's strike fully occupied Mr. Raikes for
some months. Another man perhaps would have made lighter
work of it, and allowed the regrettable incident to drop into
oblivion. Not so Mr. Raikes. Physically run down as he was
with the strain of his great responsibilities and the stupendous
load of work this trying time brought him, even when he

should have sought a holiday, he decided to do all that was consistent with his dignity as a minister to repair the losses to the penitent postmen. He early received a deputation of their body, and promised that he would carefully weigh every extenuating circumstance which could be urged on behalf of each individual of the strikers. The same assurance he gave to the House of Commons during the debate on the Post Office Vote, July 23 ; and despite the warning of his medical adviser, immediately set to work to redeem a promise which meant so much to so many. He left England for a short holiday at Royat, but it was a holiday full of work for him ; for the voluminous papers in connection with the postmen followed him daily. There is no reason to think that his inquiry into each painful case was not as conscientious as he promised it should be, but some doubt seems to have been raised by Mr. Pickersgill, M.P., and some correspondence was published between them. The Postmaster-General mentioned that he had devoted one whole week unceasingly to investigating and comparing all the appeal letters and reports bearing on each particular case, " with the earnest desire of finding grounds which might in any individual instance warrant a mitigation of the punishment which all the men had been warned must follow such an offence." In the result somewhere about fifty were restored to duty shortly afterwards, and several others, by the further influence of members of Parliament, were one by one reinstated.

These were certainly the most serious but not the only matters occupying the Postmaster-General's time and attention. For almost side by side with his investigations into these cases, and while he was meeting other troubles, he was preparing a scheme for revising the scales of pay of sorters, sorting clerks, and telegraphists, in accordance with his earlier promise. After the adverse decision of the " Luminous Committee " he had been prevailed upon to see another deputation of the sorting force in June, when once more the whole ground of their claims in regard to improved pay, holidays, compulsory extra duty, split attendance, etc., was carefully gone over and considered point by point by himself and the official advisers. Partly as the result of those investigations, and partly as the result of evidence gathered from other

R

quarters as to the position and prospects of sorting clerks and telegraphists, on November 11, 1890, the long-waited-for scheme appeared. It must, however, be mentioned that the telegraphists' portion of the scheme had appeared in the previous July.

It came as a golden argosy that had braved many storms ; and hopes beat high as they proceeded to unload the cargo. The sorters realised exceptional benefits, adding as it did a considerable number to the first class, which meant so many immediate promotions, and increasing the maximum to 56s. a week, while it also increased the maximum of the second class to 40s. a week, and the annual increment of 2s. A concession already personally made by Mr. Raikes, that of increasing the annual leave of the first class to three weeks instead of two, was now fixed and ratified, and the first class, with its additional benefits, was now extended to the districts which had hitherto had no such promotion to look forward to. The anomalies connected with the payment of extra duty were by this revision done away with, and an equitable *pro rata* system introduced which could not fail in the long run to give satisfaction all round ; while in addition it accorded Sunday pay for Christmas Day and Good Friday. Another concession which was much appreciated was full pay during sickness, " with restrictions." These were the material benefits of the Raikes scheme so far as it covered the London sorters. They perhaps were the most benefited by it ; but except for the material benefits they were not slow to discern certain disadvantages to which they were to take further exception later on.

The privileges of payment for Bank holidays, special pay for Christmas Day and Good Friday, and full payment for sick leave, were, it was understood, from this time to be applied with general impartiality throughout the postal and telegraph services. The sorting clerks generally shared in these advantages, while those of Dublin and Edinburgh were placed on an equal footing with their *confrères* at Manchester, Liverpool, and Glasgow.

The application of the Raikes scheme to the London and provincial telegraphists, however, was not proportionately beneficial in point of pay, and fell far short of their demands.

The maxima for provincial male telegraphists under the new revision were, according to the class of office: 56s., 54s., 52s., 50s., 40s., 38s., 35s., and 32s. a week, as against 50s., 38s., 36s., 32s., and 30s. The maximum of the London men, which was £190 a year—enjoyed, however, only by a limited and exclusive class—was not affected ; and the only benefit accruing to them was that the annual rise of £5 was increased to £6. But apart from the question of pay, the scheme left other considerations almost wholly untouched. Classification still remained to taunt and cheat them. The banality of winter holidays still oppressed them, while they complained that they were not treated fairly in the matter of full pay in sickness.

And the curious irony of this mixed and complicated situation was that the sorters envied the telegraphists, and the telegraphists envied the sorters.

On the whole, however, considering the time and the circumstances in which it was drafted, it was a fairly good scheme ; but it was far from a perfect one. Not even the sorters, who benefited most, could regard it as a perfect scheme, and the less so when they came to closely examine it. The consideration of the very kindly treatment they had received from Mr. Raikes, and the desire he had expressed to them to give them some pleasing souvenir by which to remember his term of office, took the edge off their criticism. They remembered, too, that he had strongly urged that their maximum should be raised to 58s. a week instead of only 56s., and that he had been supported in this by the then Controller ; also that he had shown a desire to give them practical equality with the telegraphists. That the scheme did not meet with their entire approval, or cover all their just demands, Mr. Raikes was not wholly responsible for. All things considered, it was a good scheme, and a generous one for the sorters, at any rate.

The telegraphists thought otherwise, and were not slow to express their deep sense of disappointment. They could not easily forgive Mr. Raikes for what they regarded as a wanton and unnecessary interference with their right of public meeting, and perhaps a far more generous scheme would hardly have compensated and atoned for the imposition of the official reporter. The retention of compulsory overtime was a grievance in common between the telegraphists and the sorters; but the sorters, who were more satisfied on the whole with the scheme for what it had brought them, had, if anything, much stronger ground for dissatisfaction for what it had not. But when the many varied interests of a vast army of men had to be considered, perhaps it was well-nigh impossible to produce a remedy that should fit and satisfy all alike. It left many things untouched both sides of the service; but there is little doubt that Mr. Raikes did all that was then possible, and put himself to enormous pains to understand and find a final remedy for this well-nigh hopeless problem of chronic discontent. Having done perhaps all that it was possible for one Postmaster-General to do for the sorters and the telegraphists, he felt that something had yet to be done for the postmen. Almost simultaneously with the introduction of the scheme for the former, a deputation of postmen was received to take evidence from them with a view to constructing some remedial measure for their class. The postmen were not yet held to have purged their offence; but the Postmaster-General, after reinstating about fifty of the dismissed men, decided that, apart from all considerations of the strike, there were grievances among them which as loudly called for redress as those of the sorters and telegraphists.

There was one other class, however, which at this time claimed to have been overlooked and neglected, the Savings Bank sorters. There was some amount of combination among them, and they had joined in the general agitation. They complained of certain anomalies of classification; loss of prospect owing to departmental alterations; the fact of the introduction of female labour displacing them, and minimising the value of their work; females in receipt of better pay than men with more service, and engaged on the same class of work; the smallness of the minimum and maximum, and numerous other things. They had been altogether overlooked in the recent scheme, and while the other little Jack Horners of the service were more or less congratulating themselves on the plums they had each secured, the Savings Bank sorters were left entirely in the cold. Added to this, they were experiencing in an acute degree the compulsory overtime grievance, having to supplement their wages with more or less extra duty—this extra duty being however forced upon them, whether they liked it or not, often at most inconvenient times. This grievance on the overtime question was, after their exclusion from the recent scheme, so strongly felt that at the beginning of 1891 there was an indignant outburst among them. They had tried every legitimate method of ventilating their grievance by petition, by requests for an interview, and through the House of Commons, but their plaint fell on deaf ears. The feeling rose so high that at last, as a concession to their demand, there was a slight addition to the staff to reduce the amount of compulsory overtime complained of. But it was by no means effective, and on February 2, two hundred and fifty of them declined to accept the summons for extra duty. The result was that nearly the whole of them were promptly suspended. But they were a small body and standing almost alone, so that the struggle was of short duration. The Postmaster-General did not take a very severe view of the case, the whole of them being allowed to take up their duties on expressing regret, and promising never again to offend in a similar manner. The fluctuations of their work, it seems, precluded the possibility of abolishing compulsory extra duty altogether ; but in April some arrangement was made, with a further slight increase of staff, by which a number of permanent volunteers were enrolled to meet emergencies as they arose.

The position of the postmen had for some months after the strike been engaging the attention of Mr. Raikes, and on July 17 he announced in the House of Commons that he had at last found a means of doing something for them. The cost of his new proposal would be over £100,000 a year, but it was to cover a vast area, so that the benefits accruing would not amount to much in each case ; but it was better than nothing, and more than many expected after recent happenings. The two classes of London postmen were to be amalgamated in order to enable the men to progress without interruption from the lower to the higher scale. The maximum was raised by two shillings a week for the suburban divisions of postmen. The auxiliary postmen obtained a slight increase in pay per hour and a little more extra leave. In the country, as in

London, the two classes were done away with, and the maximum raised by two shillings. Extra pay was allowed for Sunday work, and each hour was reckoned as one and a quarter. Perhaps the most appreciated concession of all was an allowance for boots; which till then had not been included in the uniform.

Some organs of the press regarded these concessions as all the more magnanimous in a Postmaster-General whose official path had been so strewn with thorns.

It was the last thing he was to do for the service. His career as Postmaster-General, so brief, yet so full of vicissitude and labour, was approaching its close. The enormous amount of work which the generally discontented state of the service entailed daily upon him was more than could be sustained by any one man for long. Even after the repeated warnings of impending breakdown, he had stuck to his work. He was now to pay the penalty, and the country was to lose a capable and a dutiful servant. Henry Cecil Raikes, Postmaster-General, passed peacefully away on August 24, 1891.

As Postmaster-General, he passed through an exceedingly trying time ; and though it was by some said that he himself was largely responsible for the troubles in the service, if he committed some few human mistakes in administration he hastened to repair them manfully ; his bearing as a minister throughout was dignified and correct. No Postmaster-General was ever subjected to such sharp criticisms from every side at once ; but no other had ultimately proved such a benefactor on so large a scale. His remedy for prevailing discontent was not all-sufficient nor without flaws ; but in the circumstances—and it is the circumstances which have to be considered, particularly in this connection, considering the vast area it had to cover—it was judicious, and it was not his fault that it was not more generous. He lived just long enough to know that, despite previous estimates of his conduct and character, he was at last to some extent appreciated for the efforts he had made to do justice, even at a time of trying and painful ordeal. The sorters especially were sad at his premature departure ; and the secretary of the Fawcett Association, W. E. Clery, it was who wrote the lengthy, touching tribute to his memory which appeared in the *Telegraph* the day following the Postmaster-General's death.

Henry Cecil Raikes was democratic enough in principle, though inclined to be autocratic in rule. He was a capable man, and a leader born ; but the restrictions of his office kept many of his higher qualities in abeyance. If his administration could not always be considered strictly just, it was in part probably owing to influences over which he had little control. Being in the position he was, he was often compelled to identify himself with and take responsibility for the actions of others. Nor was this due to any weakness in the man so much as to the adamantine and tapebound rules of officialdom's etiquette and to other causes and relations which may not here be mentioned. His son, in his " Life and Letters of Henry Cecil Raikes," points out that, so weary of it all—the cares of his office and the curbs on his independence of action—did he become that he was strongly inclined to resign his position, till a higher sense of public duty restrained him.

The telegraphists and others, who felt they had so little cause to esteem him, could not at the time fully appreciate his difficulties ; but they were to learn later that the Post Office could be ruled by worse masters. In his lifetime it seemed his peculiar fate to fail to win full appreciation either from those above or below him. But if Henry Cecil Raikes had been a less honest man, a less conscientious and a less painstaking man, he might have lived long enough to secure his due share of that public recognition and reward which is too often bestowed less worthily.

CHAPTER XX

BENEFITS OF THE RAIKES SCHEME—A MARTINET POSTMASTER-
GENERAL—A NEW PARLIAMENTARY POLICY—A PARTING OF
THE WAYS—POLITICAL RIGHTS OF POSTAL SERVANTS—A BLOW
AT COMBINATION.

LOOKING at all the circumstances impartially, it must be acknowledged that the late Mr. Raikes had bestowed very substantial benefits on the postal service. In the face of opposition to his proposals, and despite hostility from several sides at once, he had manfully tackled the complex and bewildering problem, and had set himself the task of adjudicating on the thousand divergent and multifarious class interests. It was a labour worthy of an intellectual Hercules to seek to cleanse such an Augean stable as the Post Office, but he had done as much as it was possible for one man to dare to attempt, meeting with the growls probably of the watch-dogs of the Treasury, and with little gratitude from those who benefited by the result. The late Postmaster-General had, though chary of it at first, at last set himself to the stupendous task of satisfying the wants and serving the conflicting interests of the discontented army under his control. He had set himself to the task, but he had materially shortened his days for his pains. Both the London sorters and the provincial sorting clerks were fairly well satisfied with the result of the Raikes scheme, but the telegraphists and the postmen were but little satisfied with their measure of relief, and remained hardly less discontented than before. The flowers had scarcely faded on the grave of their departed chief before the mutterings of discontent were again heard, from the ranks of the postmen and the telegraphists particularly. It was not so much that they were guilty of ingratitude as that their grievances as Government servants so far out-measured the well-intentioned remedy.

Shortly before his death Mr. Raikes had outlined in the House of Commons the revision he intended to bring in for the London and provincial postmen. But when the scheme came to be applied it was found that the London town post-men did not fairly participate, that in fact there was no rise in wages for them, their action in regard to the ill-starred Post-men's Union and the strike period being considered deserving of punishment by exclusion from benefits. The discontent consequent on this had brought about, just before Mr. Raikes's death, the suggestion for another experiment at organisation, and on August 15, 1891, a large and enthusiastic gathering of postmen met to condemn the revised scales of pay recom-mended by the Departmental Committee and recently adopted by the Postmaster-General. At this meeting a resolution was carried which led to the immediate formation of a Postmen's Federation of town and provincial men, C. Churchfield being appointed general secretary, and A. F. Harris treasurer. The provisional committee at once issued a manifesto to all post-men, inviting London offices to send delegates to a meeting on September 19, 1891, to elect an executive. The conference was held, and the executive formed. The executive of the newly-formed Postmen's Federation worked with a will, and obtaining for themselves the right enjoyed by the sorters, that of free meeting outside Post Office buildings, a series of meetings was started in every part of London. Having as yet no organ of their own by which to establish a means of communication with the various branches, they approached the Fawcett Association with a view to the *Post* being placed at their disposal. The monthly report of progress among the postmen appeared in the *Post* regularly up to June 1892, when the *Postman's Gazette* was started. On September 16 of the same year the first annual conference of the Postmen's Federation was held, W. Rouse, an E.C. postman, and long known as a powerful advocate of their claims, being elected president. Thirty-three London and thirty-eight provincial men attended this conference. They adopted a programme which consisted of a claim for a 20s. minimum, with a yearly increment of 2s. and a maxmium of 40s. a week in all towns where fifty or more postmen were employed ; three weeks holiday ; eight hours work within a twelve hours limit ; and the abolition of stripes on condition that the maximum rate of pay be raised to 40s. A national petition was soon afterwards drafted, which contained in addition a claim for exemption from parcel-post work as then combined with ordinary letter-carrying duties ; unestablished auxiliaries and rural postmen to be merged into the established force ; citizen rights ; and an improved Superannuation Act for all postmen. This programme was distributed to over five hundred towns. About two hundred and fifty towns adopted the programme completely and subscribed to the national petition based thereon. The new Postmaster-General's reply was unequivocal refusal to all the points raised. That, however, was not exactly the first move in the game of postal chess which Sir James Fergusson, as Mr. Raikes's successor, had sat down to play.

Meanwhile the sorters already had come to realise that, whatever the benefits vouchsafed to them by the provisions of the Raikes scheme, they still suffered disabilities sufficient to entitle them to make a further effort to gain their removal. Sir James Fergusson had come to them with the reputation of a stern disciplinarian, but that did not accuse him of want of justice. As the result of much deliberation and a general meeting, a memorial was drawn up and presented February 18, 1892. The memorial, in pleading for an interview, stated that the object was to urge (1) that the London sorting force may be placed in, at the least, an equal position as regards scales of pay, etc., with the telegraphists at the Central Station ; (2) that they be designated " sorting clerks " instead of " sorters " ; (3) that they may be eligible for promotion to higher positions, including clerkships ; and (4) that the number of higher appointments be regulated strictly according to the number of duties corresponding. Sir James Fergusson's reply was in the negative on every single count, nor would he grant an interview on any pretence. He issued an official circular, March 25, 1892, to the staff reminding them of the benefits already procured to them by Mr. Fawcett and Mr. Raikes, and expressing a regret—clearly intended as a rebuff—that they should reiterate their claims, which were so fully answered by his predecessor.

To the refusal of the Postmaster-General the Fawcett Association drew up a reply, respectfully expressing dissent from the view taken of their case, reiterating their claims, and urging that, while they were not unmindful of the material advantages lately gained by many of those they represented, they were none the less convinced that many of those concessions, with the additions they now asked for, should have been conceded years earlier. They trusted that their renewed request for investigation would not be thought unreasonable, or other than in the interest of the public service. This was signed and forwarded, May 6, by the committee of the Fawcett Association on behalf of the London sorting force. This met with scant courtesy, and a few days afterwards it was intimated to them that Sir James Fergusson directed that they be informed that his previous reply was to be taken as final, that the reiteration of requests which after full consideration had been refused, and the objectionable tone adopted, presumably because of that, was an abuse of the privilege of presenting memorials to the head of the Department.

The uncompromising attitude taken up by the Postmaster-General caused the sorters to strike out a new line of policy from that moment. Clery had become impatient of the slow and unsatisfactory methods of pressing their claims on the attention of the Department. The methods had availed them well with Mr. Raikes, but in Sir James Fergusson they soon had to recognise a master of a different calibre. It was not only the slowness of the hackneyed method of seeking redress with almost the certainty of refusal that decided them on their course of action. There were other things in addition. The general attitude of the officials towards them and their organisation had undergone a marked change almost from the moment that Sir James Fergusson set foot in St. Martin's-le-Grand. One of the first acts was to prohibit the distribution of the *Post*, their official organ, within Post Office buildings, and there was a growing and well-grounded suspicion that it was the first expression of a desire to smash the union of postal employés. There were, indeed, a hundred different influences in evidence everywhere about them which decided the most impulsive of their members to urge the immediate adoption of a vigorous Parliamentary policy and to press for a Committee of Inquiry into the Post Office. If such a policy was not novel, it was a bold one. Clery himself, three or four years before, had advocated such a policy, and it was only owing to the conciliatory treatment meted out to them by Mr. Raikes that its further consideration was so long shelved. There were serious differences of opinion between the chairman of the association, J. H. Williams, and a section of the committee in regard to this question. William's colder, more cautious nature put him in opposition to the more daring line of policy, in which he discerned strong possibilities of personal risk to those adopting it. No man could suspect Williams of want of nerve ; he had proved his high courage sufficiently ; it was only that he thought the old and more familiar methods the safer, and probably the surer. Clery, the more impetuous, eventually gained over by far the greater following to his own way of thinking, and in the result the question was definitely settled at a general meeting, June 15,1892. At this meeting it was resolved " that immediate action be taken to secure from Parliamentary candidates a pledge to support a motion for a Parliamentray Committee of Inquiry." This was carried with enthusiasm, and practically unanimously.

The association had now entered on one of the most important steps in the history of postal trades unionism. Clery on this occasion for the first time occupied the chair, Williams being absent. After the general meeting there were but few dissentients to the policy ; and Williams, with deep regret, though with firm resolve that his view was the correct one, felt constrained under the circumstances to relinquish the leadership. On the adoption of such a policy, to which he was opposed, his position as chairman was no longer possible, and much as the members shared his regret at the necessity of it, Williams laid down the epaulettes he had worn with so much distinction, and resigned his commission. From that moment the chairmanship was by unanimous approval filled by W. E. Clery, and the recognised leadership fell into his hands, while the secretaryship vacated by him was taken up by W. B. Cheesman of the Western District Office. Clery was now the recognised leader of the association, but as a matter of fact for a considerable time previously his strong personality had marked him as the virtual leader when the moment arrived for more decisive action.

In view of the impending General Election, presumably the Postmaster-General took the association's adoption of the new line of policy as a challenge to his administrative authority, for almost immediately afterwards a Post Office Circular, dated June 17, 1892, was issued as special information for postal servants. The Postmaster-General desired to warn Post Office servants that it " would be improper for them, whether in combination or otherwise, to extract promises from candidates for election to the House of Commons with reference to their pay and position." No small amount of curiosity was at first felt at its introduction on the notice boards of the General Post Office, but immediately a whip was issued to the members of the association by W. E. Clery, the newly-elected chairman, which was as decisive as it was prompt. If Sir James Fergusson's new order was intended to intimidate, it did not have the desired result. The Postmaster-General had only just stated in the House of Commons that " there is no Act of Parliament regulating such a matter," yet he had suddenly made a law unto himself. Within an hour or so of the appearance of the Post Office Circular containing this order or instruction from the Departmental head, the following whip was sent the round of the association :—

" The notice in the current number of the Post Office Circular does not affect the policy of the association.

(Signed) W. E. CLERY, *Chairman*."

Accordingly within the next few days, the General Election being now close at hand, a letter as from the Fawcett Association was addressed to Parliamentary candidates all over the country. The circular-letter stated that, in accordance with the resolution passed at the general meeting of their members, they begged to lay before the Parliamentary candidate a brief statement of facts in explanation and support of the position they had adopted, and soliciting an early and definite reply to this question : " Will you, in the event of your being elected a member of Parliament, support a motion for the appointment of a Parliamentary Committee of Inquiry into the Post Office, such as was advocated by Earl Compton, and largely supported during a recent session of the House of Commons ? "

The circular went on to disavow any intention on their part to act otherwise than as ordinary citizens in the enjoyment of the franchise ; and to offer the assurance that it was only because they believed such inquiry would put an end to discontent in the postal service that they felt it their duty to thus ask for Parliamentary support.   This circular was signed by W. E. Clery, as chairman, and W. B. Cheesman, as secretary.   The circular was at once a means of canvassing public support and sympathy, and a protest against the interference with their public rights and public duties as citizens. It was a protest against being taken back to the days when Mr. Monk, the member for Gloucester, fought for them a strenuous uphill battle of years to obtain what was now so lightly to be taken from them.   In thus exercising their right as citizens in approaching Parliamentary candidates, they were doing so not only on their own behalf but in the interest of every other class in the postal service throughout the United Kingdom, embracing the telegraphists, the sorting clerks, the Savings Bank men, the postmen, themselves, and others.   And they were doing so totally irrespective of party bias or motive. Within a few days replies from candidates, for the most part favourable, poured in by the hundred ; and presumably not one of the politicians thus replying saw anything reprehensible in their being thus approached by postal servants in search of a legitimate inquiry into their alleged grievances.   Among the successful Parliamentary candidates who favourably replied were the names of many who were to undertake much work in the future in furtherance of postal claims.   These included Sir Albert Rollit, Mr. James Rowlands, Mr. Naoroji, Mr. Cremer, Mr. Keir Hardie, Mr. James Stuart, and that sturdy veteran of previous postal campaigns, Mr. Geo. Howell ; while occurring in the list were the names of Mr. John Burns, Mr. Thomas Burt, Mr. Pickersgill, and a number of other eminent and equally well-known public men.

The provincial male telegraphists had in the meanwhile issued a precisely similar circular to Parliamentary candidates, and Sir James Fergusson marked his disapproval of such action by specially calling attention to it in the House on June 14. The circular emanating from the telegraphists he quoted at some length, and, referring to the fact that the sorting branch of the service had adopted the same proceedings on the eve of a General Election, he strongly condemned their action as improper. He appealed to the members of the House to decline to give any such pledge as was solicited, and stated that he had the member for Midlothian (Mr. Gladstone) and the member for Derby (Sir William Harcourt) in full agreement with his observations. Mr. Geo. Howell strongly criticised the attitude taken up by the Postmaster-General, and stoutly contended for the right of postal servants to combine, and further to carry out all the legitimate functions and obligations of combination. He was supported by Mr. Lawson and Mr. Story.

It was hoped by the rank and file of postal servants that the Postmaster-General, Sir James Fergusson, would sustain a defeat at the poll ; but North-East Manchester sent him back to the House of Commons, and for a time to his place at St. Martin's-le-Grand, by a narrow majority of 110. Sir James Fergusson temporarily resumed his position as head of Post Office affairs on July 18, immediately after the result of the election was known, and he as immediately made his presence felt. The very same day he re-assumed office he called on the chairman and secretary of the Fawcett Association to explain their action in regard to signing and sending out the circular to Parliamentary candidates. In explaining their conduct, they took up the very natural position that they were simply carrying out the instructions of a general meeting, and had acted in a representative capacity ; that they had been careful not to transgress the official warning as expressed by the Postmaster-General ; and that they had been careful not to solicit pledges relative to their duties and pay. They thought that in the absence of any official order, and in view of the fact that they had been allowed to carry out the behest of their constituents, they were justified in thinking they had not contravened any official rule, since no intimation of such had been conveyed to them. On July 22 the Postmaster-General gave his decision on their case, which was that for their "insubordination" they be dismissed the service. This was a direct blow at the very root of representative principle, and the strongest rebuff that the spirit of trades unionism had yet sustained ; besides, it had in one moment reduced the franchise for postal servants. to the flimsiest mockery. The blow was regarded as so. unnecessary and so unjust that there was an immediate outcry against it both from within the walls of the Post Office and from without. To have been consistent, the Postmaster-General should have dismissed the whole body of sorters who were responsible for the instruction acted on. In twenty-four hours practically the whole of the London sorting force, Chief Office men and District men, had signed a memorial to the Postmaster-General, asking his reconsideration of the dismissals on the ground that they fully identified themselves. with the policy adopted and the instruction given Clery and Cheesman as two officers of their association. Not only from the class directly affected, but from the postmen, the postal clerks all over the country, the telegraphists, and others, came an almost unanimous cry of indignation and disapproval. And this indignation was echoed with surprising unanimity by the press, both Tory and Liberal joining in condemning Sir James Fergusson's action as intolerant and unjustifiably severe. Even the few organs that were induced to say a word in favour of the Postmaster-General's action, based their conclusions for the most part on the supposition that insubordination had been committed ; whereas there was no insubordination, and no contravening of any known existing rule of the Department in asking merely for a public inquiry. Others, while opining that discipline must be maintained in a great public Department of State, nevertheless agreed that it was neither fair nor constitutional that the political rights of citizens should in this free country be at the mercy of official caprice.

The Fawcett Association promptly carried the question one step further, and obtained counsel's opinion that the action of Sir James Fergusson was illegal and unconstitutional, a view in which Sir Charles Russell, the then Lord Chief Justice, fully concurred, as did also Mr. S. D. Waddy, Q.C., M.P.

Yet despite all appeals, all arguments, and all criticism, Sir James Fergusson stuck to his position with the dogged pertinacity of an old-time soldier and a martinet. Rightly or wrongly, he had taken the step, and he owed it to his pride and his reputation to stand by it. And he stood by it, a solid rock of obstinacy against which the waves of protest splashed in vain.

The dismissed chairman and secretary of the Fawcett Association remained in their respective offices, and the members of the organisation rallied round them stronger than ever. There was a feeling that they had been made the martyrs of an injustice for their sakes and for promoting their cause, and they stood by them to a man.

The case of the dismissals, involving as it did the question of the right of combination in the Post Office, occasioned no little public comment at the time, and the interest was to an extent kept alive by the publication of a brochure by W. E. Clery, entitled "Civil Servitude," containing a full and detailed statement of the facts. The General Election by this time was over, and political fate had given her decision in favour of the Liberal party. Sir James Fergusson, therefore, was now reduced to a passing shadow ; but it was still hoped by many that, like a repentant political sinner, he would use his last few hours of office in retrieving the great mistake that had certainly damaged his popularity with the service for evermore. But Sir James Fergusson chose to leave office with the cry for justice still ringing in his ears, and pursuing him even in the House of Commons. On August 9, Mr. Sam Woods took up the matter of the arbitrary dismissals by asking the Postmaster-General if it were not possible on reconsideration to reinstate the two officials. Sir James Fergusson was most aggressive in his replies, and stated amidst the cheers of his own party, that he did not intend to reinstate the two dismissed representatives of the sorters ; nor would he withdraw the warning to Post Office servants on the subject. Mr. Cobb, M.P., bearing on the same subject, put questions which implied that higher officials of the Inland Revenue had been guilty of circularising candidates on personal matters, but Sir James Fergusson was possibly saved from awkward admissions by the ruling of the Speaker

B

that the question could not stand. The trades unionists of
the country were particularly strong in their sympathy
towards the two dismissed leaders of postal combination ;
and expressions and resolutions of sympathy poured in upon
them from every part. There were resolutions expressive of
sympathy with the Fawcett Association, and of condemnation
of Sir James Fergusson ; and amidst a perfect shower of such
trades union condemnations the Postmaster-General in the
middle of August departed from the stage to make way for
his Liberal successor. If the villain had now been cut out of
the piece, all hopes were centred on the newcomer as the hero.

CHAPTER XXI

REORGANISATION OF THE POSTMEN—THE PROVINCIAL POSTAL
CLERKS—GENERAL CONDEMNATION OF THE DISMISSALS—THE
NEWCASTLE INTERVIEW—AN M.P. AND THE POSTAL AGITATOR
—THE RIGHT OF COMBINATION—CORRESPONDENCE WITH
MR. GLADSTONE ON RIGHT OF FREE MEETING—ANOTHER
BLOW AT COMBINATION—RIGHT OF FREE MEETING CONCEDED
BY MR. GLADSTONE—THE GRANTING OF AN INQUIRY.

THE closer relationship between the postmen and the sorters,
which it was hoped would become stronger and permanent,
was broken off in June, 1892. The postmen, besides not
being in full agreement with the sorters on the Parliamentary
policy, had now become strong enough to walk alone without
any assistance, and struck out an independent line for themselves. They were fast recovering from the terrific blow
sustained by the strike, and many of their dismissed comrades,
had been one by one reinstated through the indefatigable
efforts of Mr. George Howell, M.P., who, both in the House
and privately, worked hard for this end. It was owing to a
vigorous attack on Sir James Fergusson in relation to his
obduracy in this particular that he was caricatured in *Punch*
for his pains. The postmen continued to make headway with
their organisation. They were no longer beholden to the
columns of the *Post*, having started an organ of their own,
the *Postman's Gazette*, June, 1892. The *Postman's Gazette*
immediately proved of great assistance in disseminating the
principles of their union among county and provincial men,
and within a few months the gratifying result was shown in
a membership of over seven thousand.

While the postmen's organisation was thus pursuing the
course laid down, and waxing prosperous now that it had
once more got on the smooth metals of a constitutional line of
action, the postal clerks and the telegraphists were not idle.

Soon after the introduction of the Raikes scheme, their disappointment with its provisions found vent in the preparation
of a petition to the Postmaster-General ; but his unlooked-for
death, of course, prevented its being carried forward at the
time. But shortly after Sir James Fergusson's appointment
application was made that he should receive a petition from
the executive of the Postal Clerk's Association on behalf of
their class generally. In reply, a request was sent from the
Secretary for a statement of their grievances, and this was duly
submitted the day following. They were then met with the
refusal of the authorities to receive petitions from an organised
association not recognised by the Department. For a while
the postal clerks strove to obtain official recognition of their
association, but to no purpose. The original petition was then
printed and forwarded from each branch individually.

The postal clerks, like the postmen, had by this time recognised the necessity for a representative organ, and accordingly,
in the same month, the *Post-Office Journal* was started, June
20, 1892. Owing to its similarity in title to the official Post
Office Circular, the Department lodged an objection, so that
the organ of the postal clerks had to be altered to the *Postal
Journal* in March, 1893. The postal clerks were prompt to
recognise the blow that had been delivered against combination in the Post Office by the dismissals of the chairman and
secretary of the Fawcett Association, and one of the very first
uses to which they put their new organ was to protest most
strongly against what appeared to be an attack on the funda-
mental principle on which all postal organisations based their
existence.

With the advent of the Liberal Postmaster-General,
Mr. Arnold Morley, it was confidently expected that the wrong
done by his predecessor would at once be righted. Preparations were immediately set afoot, therefore, to acquaint
Mr. Arnold Morley with this their principal demand, the
reinstatement of their wrongfully-dismissed leaders.

In the meantime W. E. Clery was making hay while the
sun shone, and making the most of his new-found release from
bondage by ventilating his own and the sorters' grievance
before the public. To this end he went to Newcastle on the eve
of the election there, and arranged for a meeting of postal and

other civil servants; and it was sought to obtain the Postmaster-General's sanction for the meeting to be held. Mr. Arnold Morley, however, merely sent a stereotyped telegram to the effect that those of the Newcastle staff who desired the meeting must forward an application to him through the local post-master. It had been hoped that the required answer to Sir James Fergusson could have been given in a public meeting of civil servants. The Postmaster-General's reply and the manner of it were the first indication that it was not a change of methods but only of men. The public meeting convened by Clery was held August 31, 1892, and the late Postmaster-General and his successor in office came in for some free criticising. Mr. John Morley was the Liberal candidate for Newcastle in this election, and it was as much with a view to buttonholing the party chief as of holding the meeting that Clery had come down from London. He met Mr. Morley by appointment to discuss two points indicated by him in his request for an interview; the question of civil rights for civil servants, and the means of dealing with discontent in the Post Office. Mr. John Morley expressed himself very fairly and very freely on the two vexed questions, and promising to support the demand for inquiry, led his interviewer to believe that he had no sort of sympathy with the action of the late Postmaster-General. This attitude of the Liberal leader was taken as setting a good example to his namesake at St. Martin's-le-Grand; and a manifesto to the civil and postal servants of Newcastle was issued the same day by W. E. Clery, in which he urged that they, as Govern-ment servants, had no option but to vote for Mr. Morley and do their best to secure his return. There were five hundred Civil Service voters in Newcastle, and in Civil Service circles it is held that this manifesto secured the return of the author of the famous " Newcastle programme." It should be stated here that Mr. Pandeli Ralli, Mr. Morley's opponent, declined Clery's request for an interview.

The question of the dismissals was now becoming widely public, and Clery himself spared no pains to advertise the fact of the harsh and unmerited dismissal of himself and Cheesman from that " civil servitude " which they were only seeking to improve up to the level of model employment. The London Trades Council adopted a resolution urging the new

Postmaster-General to reinstate the chairman and secretary of the sorters' organisation. But the Liberal Postmaster-General evidently felt himself bound by the decision of his Tory predecessor, and declined to reinstate in the service officers who had been dismissed for "conduct directly subversive of discipline." At the same time the Postmaster-General claimed to reserve "to himself the right of considering on its merits the general question of the rights of civil servants in regard to the electoral franchise." Clery immediately seized on this as an opportunity of approaching Mr. Gladstone, and drew his attention to it in a letter. The dictatorial attitude taken up by Mr. Arnold Morley over this question of the franchise was by many interpreted as a menace. Postal and civil servants had hitherto been under the impression that no electoral disabilities now remained which any minister desiring to hamper the freedom of election might take advantage of legally. And as this was a vexed question concerning at least 200,000 electors in the Government service, Mr. Gladstone, as Prime Minister, was asked to give some information. As the important concession of free and unrestricted public meeting for postal servants afterwards granted by the Prime Minister was undoubtedly resultant on the action taken by W. E. Clery, the text of his letter to Mr. Gladstone is here given :—

"8, EAGLE COURT, ST. JOHN'S LANE, E.C.,
August 31, 1892.

"SIR,—I beg to draw your attention to what purports to be the reply of the Postmaster-General to a resolution adopted by the executive of the London Trades Council. In this letter, written by the secretary to the Post Office, it is stated that Mr. Morley reserves 'to himself the right to consider on its merits the question of the position of the servants of the Post Office in respect to the Parliamentary franchise.' I beg to ask if, in your opinion, Mr. Arnold Morley has any right of interfering with the exercise of the Parliamentary franchise by his subordinates ; if so, from whence he derives his power, and what are the limitations, if any, of his interference? I need hardly remind you that the removal of the electoral disabilities of civil servants was effected by two measures. One, which was passed in 1868, removed all disabilities, and a supplemental

Act in 1874 removed all remaining disabilities. Many, like myself, are under the impression that none remain now under which Mr. Arnold Morley or any other minister who may desire to hamper electoral freedom, may derive the legal power of doing so ; and as this is a vexed question which immediately concerns at least 200,000 electors in the Civil Service of the United Kingdom—because the Acts for the removal of electoral disabilities of civil servants are common to all departments—I hope that you will be able to favour me with some definite information on this constitutional problem.— I am, sir, your obedient servant,   W. E. CLERY."

To this a reply was received in the following terms :—

" 10, DOWNING STREET, WHITEHALL, S.W.,
September 10, 1892.

" SIR,—In reply to your letter of the 31st August, Mr. Gladstone desires me to say that he will take an early opportunity of consulting his colleagues on the question raised by you.—I am, sir, your obedient servant,
SPENCER LYTTELTON."

While they were awaiting Mr. Gladstone's definite reply, the Postmaster-General carried his pretensions one step further. A general meeting was arranged for on November 23 to consider the status and pay of the London postal force, and in connection with this they forwarded a petition to be allowed to have their exiled chairman and secretary present. To this request a refusal was given, and the meeting was therefore abandoned. From this it was evident that the Liberal Postmaster-General was determined to drive home Sir James Fergusson's sentence of excommunication as far as possible. But with a view to testing still further the Postmaster-General's attitude of mind towards their association and its two ostracised leaders, the sorters in December, 1892, forwarded a petition asking for an interview to discuss the matter of their civil rights and reinstatement, at which Messrs. Clery and Cheesman might be allowed to be present. This was signed practically by the whole of the London sorters, but in vain. Mr. Arnold Morley would not budge an inch towards conciliation.

The policy of reinstatement was from this time pursued more strenuously than ever, and it indeed became accepted as the middle plank in their platform. They obtained sympathy and support in unlooked-for quarters, numerous public men and public bodies giving encouragement in various ways, and their persistency in the prosecution of their central claim elevated them to a position of respect among all trade union bodies.

The question of civil rights arising out of the dismissals was accepted by the Metropolitan Radical Federation for discussion at a public meeting held in January, 1893. It was at this meeting that the long-waited-for reply from Mr. Gladstone anent the Postmaster-General's attitude in regard to electoral rights was read. But the missive was so unsatisfactorily Gladstonian in its evasiveness that, beyond implying that nothing was to be apprehended from Mr. Arnold Morley's pretensions, it was difficult of ordinary understanding.

There had been a wait of four months before Downing Street remembered its promise ; and it was only then remembered when the indefatigable postal agitator Clery rapped at the front door with another postman's knock. He wrote again to Mr. Gladstone, and on January 11 received in reply the following communication :—

> "10, DOWNING STREET, WHITEHALL,
> *January* 11, 1893.
>
> " SIR,—I am desired by Mr. Gladstone to acknowledge the receipt of your letter. He is not at present aware of any intention to change the legal status of civil servants, or that public opinion has opened the question of such a change, which is quite apart from the discussion of ordinary administrative improvements.—I am, sir, your obedient servant,
> "SPENCER LYTTELTON."

Mr. Gladstone's reply to the questions put was at the time regarded as unsatisfactory because of its vagueness, but the concession of free meeting granted in the following August showed that he contemplated the act of justice.

Some strictures having been passed on Mr. Cremer, M.P., for his alleged refusal to attend this meeting, and the matter

being brought under his notice, that gentleman sent an
invitation to Clery to attend a forthcoming meeting of his
constituents in Shoreditch, so that he, Clery, might repeat his
original charges against him of neglect of duty, etc., bringing
with him " as many postmen as he was capable of influencing."
Clery promptly replied to the letter accepting the invitation
with all becoming gravity, and enclosing a copy of the resolution he wished to move at the meeting. The meeting, which
was held at the Shoreditch Town Hall, found Clery present ;
and Mr. Cremer, seeing the matter had passed beyond a joke,
introduced him from the platform and expressed the hope
that they would accord him a fair hearing. The resolution
proposed by Clery was " that in the opinion of this meeting of
the electors of Shoreditch, Mr. Cremer should have attended
the public meeting recently held in the Memorial Hall, to
advocate the political freedom of civil servants, or have given
a satisfactory reason for his absence." The moving of this
resolution in a crowded meeting of the M.P.'s constituents
was the signal for an uproar which was maintained throughout
the subsequent proceedings, opinion and feeling being pretty
equally divided. Whether the resolution was lost or carried
was never accurately known.

But there were other matters also demanding the attention
of the sorters ; there were workaday conditions to be improved, and the growing danger of sweating and over-pressure
to be combated. Mr. Arnold Morley, with all the fair pro-
fessions of Liberalism, had in November, 1892, been pleased
to receive a deputation from an organised committee of the
unemployed, requesting him to abolish overtime, and to pay
fair wages to all classes of employés, and on that occasion he
had expressed himself as desirous that " the Post Office should
set an example to other large employers of labour." As the
Postmaster-General had been known to father such a liberal
sentiment, it engendered the hope that at least in matters of
internal economy and working surroundings, he would not
refuse to make improvement where it could be shown that
need for such improvement existed. The enormous increase
of business in the Post Office of recent years had given rise
to new and peculiar grievances and hardships not contemplated
or made allowance for sufficiently in any previous remedial

scheme. It was not so much insufficiency of pay, the method of promotion, or the pension prospect, but more immediate and more pressing were the questions of inadequacy of staff, unhealthy conditions of work, and harassing hours of attendance. Added to these were the growing necessity for medical department reform, and the scandal of secret and confidential reporting. Neither of the schemes of Mr. Fawcett or Mr. Raikes had done more than touch the fringe of these matters. True, the telegraphists and sorting clerks suffered from similar grievances, but it was a question of degree of intensity. No other class of the service suffered to such an extent from pressure and overcrowding as did the sorters at this period. Based on these considerations, a memorial was prepared and forwarded to the Postmaster-General in March 1893. But they had to wait some months for a reply ; and in the meantime it was thought desirable to strengthen their Parliamentary policy, and to foster their Parliamentary friends. Mr. Cremer, M.P., had forgiven the Shoreditch incident, and promised to join in with their other pledged supporters in the House, Sir Albert Rollit, Professor Stuart, Sir Charles Russell, Lord Compton, Mr. John Morley, and the rest.

Of all their alleged Parliamentary advocates, however, perhaps Mr. Murray Macdonald was at this time the most painstaking and consistent. Mr. Macdonald had sought every opportunity to bring on a discussion of postal claims generally, but had several times been defeated in his endeavour. It was then arranged through him to hold a conference of M.P.s and postal representatives for a full discussion of the case, which it was anticipated must presently be brought before the House. With this end in view, Mr. Murray Macdonald asked the Postmaster-General privately if he would guarantee that postal representatives might take part in this conference without risk to their prospects or position. But Mr. Arnold Morley squelched the intention by replying that such a course would be " contrary to the regulations."

Sooner than they expected came the Postmaster-General's reply to the March memorial dealing with pay, pensions, hours of duty, conditions of work, etc., and the extra promptitude of the reply was perhaps explained by its containing a refusal on every single point.

The uncompromising attitude of the Postmaster-General served only to stimulate postal servants generally to the adoption of a vigorous Parliamentary policy, and sorters, sorting clerks, and telegraphists were now more than ever coming to join hands on questions of common interest. This feeling of relationship was perhaps fostered not only by a sense of common adversity, but by the fact that the telegraphists' friends in the House were also, for the most part, the friends of the sorters and sorting clerks. The Parliamentary friends of the postal cause were now representative of every shade of party politics, and included men of widely divergent views. The question of Civil Rights for Civil Servants was one that enabled men like Sir Albert Rollit, Professor Stuart, Mr. William Saunders, and Mr. Keir Hardie to stand side by side on the same platform ; and this was actually the case on the occasion of a meeting held at the Memorial Hall, June 8, 1893. With such advocates as these and many others in the House to champion their cause, it seemed that the coveted Royal Commission could not now be far off, or at any rate the existence of such a solid phalanx of Parliamentary support must surely overcome all the objections that could be centred in a single Postmaster-General, even with a more powerful personality than that of Mr. Arnold Morley.

A year's experience of Mr. Arnold Morley's administration was sufficient to convince all postal bodies that they had little generosity to expect at his hands. While in opposition he had consistently voted for Earl Compton's motion for inquiry into postal grievances, but as soon as he assumed the reins of office he as steadfastly opposed it, as perhaps was only to be expected.

The provincial postal clerks, perhaps, least of all had cause to think of Mr. Arnold Morley as an indulgent master ; for an attempt to petition the Postmaster-General was the means nearly of bringing about the downfall of their association, while it was seized on as a sufficient excuse for suspending an annual increment of the whole executive. The executive of the Postal Clerks' Association, acting for and in behalf of certain offices, desired to draw the Postmaster-General's attention to the fact that irregular methods were in vogue, and prayed for an independent inquiry. Mr. Arnold Morley threw doubt on the allegations, and called on the signatories to the petition to substantiate the truth of the charges by giving specific instances of the " local maladministration " referred to. The executive promptly supplied the demand for particulars. Then, to their astonishment, the allegations were judged to be untrue. The executive were considered in fault for allowing these charges to go forward, and it was decided that they must be punished by stoppage of increments. The case of the association's secretary, Lascelles, was considered more serious : he was compelled to resign the secretaryship of the association, and his increment was suspended in spite of further overwhelming evidence immediately forthcoming that the original charges were in point of fact true.

It was, perhaps, unfortunate for Mr. Arnold Morley's popularity in the Post Office that two previous Postmasters-General had in a measure dealt with the grievances of the various branches of the service. His economical spirit as an administrator would not admit of the necessity for further revision, and he early came to the conclusion that postal agitation had no longer any justification in fact, and was only being promoted for personal ends by a few individuals. That he honestly induced himself to believe so there can be little doubt, though subsequent events were to prove, possibly to his own surprise, the utter falsity of his view and the precipitateness of his judgment.

It is necessary to make the same allowance for Mr. Arnold Morley in this position as for Mr. Raikes or any previous Postmaster - General, but the sympathy and kindliness of nature which in Mr. Raikes went to retrieve most of his earlier mistakes, and the rare quality of tact which went far to rehabilitate his popularity at last, were utterly lacking in Mr. Arnold Morley. His freezing coldness of demeanour towards the staff who sought to approach him with their grievances begot the conviction that if he were not actively hostile to their interests, he had no real desire to understand their difficulties, because he was instinctively prejudiced against their claims.

Circumstances, however, were to conspire to bring about that which Mr. Arnold Morley was from the first opposed to. As the result of Clery's persistent correspondence with Mr. Gladstone, the last shackle was knocked off the right of public

meeting among postal servants, August 8, 1893. From a
postal point of view it was a great triumph of principle. Much
of the agitation of the last few years had centred round
this principle, and it was mainly as a vindication of it
that the unfortunate postmen's strike was precipitated. It
was round the demand for free public meeting and as a protest
against the presence of the official reporter that the agitation
among the telegraphists took the course it did, and nearly
ended in another strike. What was intended as a safeguard
by the Department proved in reality a further menace to contentment in the service, and a continual source of annoyance.
It was well, therefore, when after that careful consideration
which he promised in a reply to the letter from W. E. Clery as
chairman of the Fawcett Association, Mr. Gladstone at last
saw fit to announce the concession of free speech and free
meeting. As Mr. Gladstone's concession constitutes one of
the main charters of postal liberty, and will become memorable
as such, it may be as well to quote it *in extenso*. The Premier's
decision, delivered on August 8, 1893, was as follows :—

" It is desirable that there should be uniformity throughout
the Civil Service, and that the servants of the Post Office
should be on the *same footing* as those in other Departments.

" That as regards the Parliamentary franchise there can be
no question that its exercise is absolutely free from *internal*
interference, although of course subject to the general obligation which affects the public servant *in common with all other
voters* to use the franchise for the public good. The only
restriction by the custom of the public service is that persons
in the permanent employment of the State should not take a
prominent and active part in political contests, and it is not
intended that in the future any other restrictive rule should be
imposed on the servants of the Post Office.

" As regards public meetings not of a political character,
but relating to official questions, the Postmaster-General has
decided to withdraw the instructions at present in force, but
in the Post Office, as in other departments, it must be understood that the right must be exercised subject to a due regard
to the discipline of the public service."

It was held by the Liberal members of the House to be a
concession of civil rights almost without restriction, and it

removed with one stroke of the pen the reproach that postal
servants were not to be trusted in the same manner as other
civil servants. Hitherto it might be an offence of the greatest
magnitude to invite on their platform any but those still in
the service ; thus not only were the dismissed officials of their
associations banned and banished from such public gatherings,
but they dared only at their peril permit the presence of
any one of their numerous Parliamentary supporters. Mr.
Gladstone's concession now removed this anomalous state
of things, and in respect to the right of holding public
meetings they were, nominally at least, as free as other
British citizens.

The recognition of this right could not but have the effect
of bringing the various postal movements in closer touch,
while at the same time it enabled each body to perfect their
internal organisation. As a further means to this end, the
sorters affiliated to the London Trades Council, January, 1894,
and thus for the second time in postal agitation a postal
organisation was gathered into the embrace of the general
body of London trades unions. During this time there was
being established a *modus vivendi* for future Parliamentary and
public action between the telegraphists and the sorters
especially.

Following closely on an interview reluctantly granted
by the Postmaster-General—at which, however, the concession
of full pay in sickness was more definitely granted—there came
a conference of members of Parliament in the House of
Commons to discuss ways and means for inducing the
Government to appoint a Royal Commission on the Post Office.
A deputation of members waited on Mr. Arnold Morley to
urge on him the desirability of his promoting the appointment
of such an inquiry, but the Postmaster-General steadfastly
declined.

The Postmaster-General's attitude towards postal combination was interpreted as becoming more and more hostile, and
it was feared in some quarters that he would act on the
injunction of the *Standard* in dealing with agitation among
postmen at this time, and dismiss the leaders. The brutal
frankness of the *Standard* on the occasion of a public meeting
of London postmen called forth some indignant protest on

the part of postal officials generally, and the postmen and sorters in particular.

But agitation in the Post Office was becoming familiar to the public mind, and the organised labour of the country had declared sympathy. The affiliation of one postal body to the London Trades Council had in a measure been a means of drawing the attention of all trades unions to the merits of the postal case for inquiry, and was likely to give postal servants an immense advantage, in London particularly. The London Trades Council prepared a report for adoption in which the restrictive system of discipline in the Post Office was condemned, and a deputation to the Government recommended ; while, in addition to this, W. E. Clery, the chairman of the Fawcett Association, interviewed the Parliamentary Committee of the Trades Union Congress, by invitation of Mr. C. Fenwick, M.P. With these influences at work, it did not seem possible that they could remain persistently ignored in their demand for the searchlight of a public inquiry.

As one result of the co-operation of the London Trades Council, a deputation from that body waited on the Chancellor of the Exchequer, Sir William Harcourt, to discuss the rights of civil servants. W. E. Clery, who had now become a postal representative on the London Trades Council, was one of the deputation, and stoutly contested several important points with Sir William Harcourt. But beyond the publicity given by the press, little was gained from the deputation. Sir William promised to consider the points raised and give a reply, but never did so.

Among the Parliamentary friends who had rendered themselves prominent in the furtherance of the demand for inquiry were Sir Albert Rollit and Mr. Keir Hardie, and their services were recognised in illuminated addresses presented at an annual dinner of the Fawcett Association, January 10, 1895. But there was also another supporter in the House, Mr. Sam Woods, who was to render a signal service, and effectually carry through what Mr. Murray Macdonald had been only partly successful in doing.

On February 8, 1895, Mr. Sam Woods, true to his promise, but contrary to the expectation of many, withstanding every insidious influence and all overtures from behind the Speaker's chair, pushed forward his amendment to the Address. He had been requested to carry this to a division by the Fawcett Association, and in spite of the strength of the Government opposition actually lost only by eight. By the narrow majority of eight the Government was saved, and from a postal point of view it was something of an achievement. In whatever other light it might be regarded, it was distinctly a moral victory for postal politics. The Liberal press were naturally very wrath at pushing the joke so far, while for the same reason the Tory journals were jubilant. The postal movement was given credit by members of the Government for a desire to wreck the Liberal administration, and the leaders of postal agitation were not slow to accept the impeachment.

At this time the fellow-feeling and community of interests prevailing between them induced the postmen and the sorters once more to try the experiment of federation. The telegraphists were not included, but the tracers—a small body of tracers of telegrams, attached to the telegraph side of the service—were embraced, and the new Postal Service Federation was formed, February 26, 1895. Simultaneously with this event came one which was to prove of far greater importance and significance, the publication of a remarkable letter from the Postmaster-General to the Eleusis Club, affirming the right of combination among postal servants. The Eleusis Club, Chelsea, had passed a resolution calling on the Government to recognise postal employés and all servants in its employ as citizens, with the right to combine to protect and further their interests without any dread of departmental rules and regulations to the contrary ; and, further, it was deemed the duty of the Government to reinstate those who had suffered in performing their citizen duties.

The reply of the Postmaster-General through his Assistant-Secretary was calculated to affirm and emphasise the right recently accorded by Mr. Gladstone, but better still, it removed any suspicions that the Liberal Postmaster-General was only waiting to swoop down like the wolf on the fold to destroy their various combinations. As this, in conjunction with the Gladstone proclamation, was regarded as a valuable pronouncement on liberty in the Post Office, it is necessary here to reproduce it. The following is the reply.

" GENERAL POST OFFICE, LONDON,
February 14, 1895.

" SIR,—I am directed by the Postmaster-General to acknowledge the receipt of your letter of the 8th inst., and to inform you, in reply, that the political committee of the Eleusis Club appears to be under a misapprehension in believing that the rights of combination or citizenship are denied to Post Office servants. On the contrary, *I am to state there are no official regulations restricting the right of Post Office servants to combine or to meet, when not on duty, when and where they like.* In the same way, with certain exceptions not material to the present purpose—such as the situation of process-server, rate-collector, and such like—*they are not* precluded from serving in any office the duties of which do not interfere with their official duties, *or from taking part in politics.* As regards the latter part of the resolution, expressing the opinion of the Eleusis Club that it is the ' duty of the Government to reinstate those who have suffered in performing their citizen duties,' I am to state that Mr. Morley is not aware who those persons are.—I am, sir, your obedient servant,

(Signed) " H. JOYCE."

Forgiving the pretended ignorance of the recent notorious dismissals, to say the least it was reassuring, and was the more unexpected from Mr. Arnold Morley, who had all along been credited with a ravenous desire to swallow up everything in the shape of trades unionism in the Post Office. It is possible that had the concession been offered by Mr. Raikes, it would have been offered by him in such a manner as would have won him simultaneous and unanimous applause. Mr. Raikes would have offered it with a genial smile, as if it gave him unbounded pleasure to render this little service, but somehow coming from Mr. Arnold Morley's hand it was accepted differently ; it was offered without the smile, and with a cold and impassive air that indicated official boredom kept in check only by mechanical good breeding. The Postmaster-General was too indifferent or too indolent to make a good actor, so they merely accepted this new concession to principle as a something thrown to them by an unsympathetic hand. But no matter how they came by it,

T

or whatever it came wrapped in, it was thought none the less a gem, and they came to prize it accordingly.

W. E. Clery, now that he was free from the trammels of Post Office life, devoted himself almost exclusively to the promotion of postal interests through public and Parliamentary channels. He contributed numerous articles to the press on postal grievances ; he daily interviewed M.P.s both in the House and at their private residences ; delivered a long series of lectures on the need for postal reform ; and generally did all those things which no postal servant still in the service dared openly do.

By this time, having become well known as a writer and an enterprising young journalist, he commanded no little influence with the London press ; and numerous articles that created a stir were either from his pen or inspired by him. There had been some allegations of wrong treatment of a patient by the postal medical department, to which the premature death of a popular young officer was ascribed. An account of this appeared in the *Sun*, and immediately there followed quite a shoal of correspondence on postal maladministration generally. This was continued for a considerable time, and the grievances of postmen and sorters were reviewed from every possible standpoint. Following on this, W. E. Clery delivered a lecture on the subject matter of the correspondence at the South Place Institute, one Sunday morning in March ; and a report of the proceedings appearing in the press next morning, the Postmaster-General was stirred so far as to direct a denial of the truth of the allegations. Unfortunately for the Departmental case this denial only provoked still further criticisms, and brought forth an abundance of fresh evidence, which elaborately proved that Mr. Arnold Morley had been at least a little too premature in his denial of facts.

It could not have been want of evidence that stood in the way of the Postmaster-General's conviction that the postal dominion over which he reigned was suffering from the effects of maladministration. Mr. Arnold Morley may not have been responsible for it, and he might have remedied it to some extent if only he had the power ; but throughout he weakly pretended that there was nothing to convince him, that there was really nothing wrong with the service beyond the imaginary evils produced by chronic discontent fomented by self-advertising agitators. Yet from top to bottom the whole postal service was honeycombed with discontent, and moth-eaten with the most squalid grievances. It was not only the letter-sorters, the telegraphists, the postal clerks, and the still more familiar postmen, who were now engaged in this battle for the betterment of the service. These had now been reinforced by the postmasters and sub-postmasters ; and the *crème de la crème* of the service were united with the despised and outcast mailcart drivers in a demand for better pay, better hours, and better conditions generally. In the face of this, Mr. Arnold Morley chose to put his fingers in his ears and shut his eyes. The Postmaster-General appeared to think that by affirming and reaffirming the right of combination among postal employés, there his moral responsibility ended.

It was gratifying to postal servants throughout the kingdom to learn that on April 2, 1895, Mr. Arnold Morley, in correspondence with Mr. Murray Macdonald, had once again reaffirmed this right to combine. It so far pinned the Department down, and was a contract it could not decently depart from in future ; but where was the real value of this right, when the real and painful grievances from which they complained were to remain ignored? But Mr. Arnold Morley was not the first Postmaster-General who had played the part of Mrs. Partington with her broom. The inevitable was to happen in this case as in similar others ; and at last the growth of discontent, backed by the sympathy of the press and the public, was to bear down the barriers of Departmental opposition ; and the Postmaster-General was forced to capitulate.

The matter was brought to this climax on May 17, 1895, when Mr. Hudson Kearley, M.P., moved for a Parliamentary Committee of Inquiry. Mr. Arnold Morley, as the Department personified, naturally resisted with a brave show of strength, and then pretending to melt into a magnanimous mood, agreed to, as a compromise, a Departmental Committee of Inquiry. The pretence of magnanimity, however, was in serious reality intended as a practical piece of cynicism, characteristic of its author, and introduced solely as a means of contributing to the undoing of the enemy. If the malcontents of the service would have edged tools to play with, Mr. Arnold Morley was not to be blamed if they badly cut themselves. And so it came about that the Inter-departmental Committee of Inquiry, afterwards to become notorious as the " Tweedmouth Committee," was appointed, June 11, 1895.

CHAPTER XXII

PROGRESS OF THE TELEGRAPH MOVEMENT—CONSTITUTION OF
THE COMMITTEE OF INQUIRY—ITS TERMS OF REFERENCE—
FIRST SITTINGS—THE AWARD OF THE TWEEDMOUTH COMMITTEE
—DISAPPOINTMENT AND CONDEMNATION.

WHILE the history of the letter-sorters' agitation was progressing towards the point concluding the last chapter,
contemporary movements in the service were passing through
the same vicissitudes, and emerging from similar difficulties in
their process of development. The Postmen's Federation,
independent and strong, had spread itself over a wide area,
and extended its ramifications throughout all the ranks of
postmen, till it now embraced a vast proportion of the rural
letter-carriers, and numbered a roll-call of 20,000 or more.
The postal clerks had likewise strengthened their movement in
spite of the blow sustained by the deprivation of Lascelles,
their founder and secretary ; and by the importation of new
men and new leaders in the persons of Paul Casey, Leo
Brodie, and George Landsbery, their organisation continued
to flourish and do able and useful work in the direction of
Parliamentary inquiry for the general good. The telegraphists
in the same manner had rendered a good account of themselves. By assiduous lobbying, circularising, and by private
interviewing they had gained over to their side a numerous band
of supporters in the House. The telegraphists had now quite
a respectable literature of their own, their grievances being set
forth in pamphlets and brochures innumerable ; while through
their organ the *Telegraph Journal,* and afterwards the *Telegraph
Chronicle,* the merits of their case were kept well to the
forefront by the most brilliant service-writers among them.
The guiding spirits of the telegraph movement during this
time, and for a considerable period before, were Hall of

Liverpool, Scott of Manchester, and Nicholson and Garland of London.

But one of the most remarkable effects of the appointment of the new Inter-departmental Committee of Inquiry was that new postal organisations, of which the rest of the service had scarcely ever heard, suddenly made their presence felt. The Head-Postmasters' Association and the Sub-Postmasters' Association had been in existence some time, but they had conducted themselves with such a studied decorum, eschewing anything that hinted at the dreaded appellation " agitation," that it was confidently expected by many that they would never consent to lay evidence before a Committee of Inquiry that was born of sheer agitation. But they were to come forward none the less. And besides them, in a motley crowd, came associations of postal porters, overseers and supervisors, telegraph linesmen, tracers, writers, and others, a never-ending line of witnesses, all prepared with voluminous evidence on the long-accumulated grievances of their respective classes.

The Inter-departmental Committee on Post Office Establishments consisted of Sir Francis Mowatt, K.C.B., Secretary to the Treasury ; Sir Arthur Godley, K.C.B., Secretary to the India Office ; Mr. Llewellyn Smith, Secretary to the Board of Trade ; and Mr. Spencer Walpole, Secretary to the Post Office.

Thus, with the single exception of Lord Tweedmouth, who presided, the committee was composed of representatives of departmentalism, who, being high Government officials, could not in human nature be expected to have an impartial sympathy with the claims to be laid before them. It was a committee of permanent secretaries of important Government departments, with whom the principle of economy was the guiding and paramount one. It was manifest from the first moment that there was little generous treatment to be expected from a tribunal so constituted. If anything were wanting to strengthen this supposition, it was the fact that Mr. Arnold Morley, as Postmaster-General, in laying down the terms of reference for the guidance of this committee in its deliberations, expressly made it a condition that they should be guided by the consideration that the " Post Office is a great Revenue

Department, and that, in the words of the Select Committee on Revenue Departments Estimates in 1888, ' it is more likely to continue to be conducted satisfactorily, if it should also continue to be conducted with a view to profit, as one of the revenue-yielding departments of the State.' " Thus it was made abundantly clear from the first that sheer justice was not to stand in the way of all-sacred economy. Things had come to such a pass in the Post Office that the Liberal Postmaster-General was bound to make a show of doing something, especially as the days of his party were now drawing to a close. Liberal Ministers had of late made much of the platitudes which were likely to catch the ephemeral applause of the multitude, and they had been mainly responsible for the doctrine that the State should be the " model employer of labour," and that the Government should be in the " first flight of employers." Mr. Arnold Morley had not shirked his share of the responsibility of giving utterance to these mock heroics.   If only for the sake of an appearance of consistency, therefore, it was well to have called the Committee of Inquiry into existence.   By the time it either failed or succeeded in its object the General Election would be over, and the responsibility for the acceptance of its recommendations, whatever they might be, would come as a legacy to the next Government.

The constitution of the Committee of Inquiry, as soon as it became known, called forth a deal of comment from the discontented service it was called on to examine.   The general feeling was one of distrust from the very beginning. Both the telegraphists and the sorters were some time considering whether to trust their destinies into the hands of such a committee, whose only redeeming feature seemed the presence of Lord Tweedmouth, generally accepted all round as honest and disinterested in a judicial capacity.   The leaders of the various associations were especially dubious.   It was not the independent inquiry they had looked for ; but then gradually the feeling set in among the members that, come what may, the inquiry could not result in rendering their position worse. They might get nothing ; but there was a chance of getting something. W. E. Clery, of the sorters' organisation, endeavoured from the start to combat this feeling among his

followers, and warned them that, the committee being constituted as it was, it would be only a waste of time and energy
preparing evidence. He urged that only on one condition
should they accept its authority and its recommendations in
their case ; and that was that the question of civil rights
and the dismissals of their chairman and secretary should be
considered and adjudicated on.

.. At an early stage of the proceedings, it was sought to
ascertain whether these two important questions would come
within the purview of the committee, and also to obtain
consent for their chairman, W. E. Clery, to be accepted as a
witness in respect to this part of their case.

As the result of a meeting held at the Memorial Hall,
May 30, it was decided to put the matter before the Postmaster-General as the subject of an inquiry. This was
accordingly done, and the reply, through the Permanent
Secretary, one of the newly-constituted committee, was to
the effect that as Mr. Clery " is no longer a servant of the
Post-Office, he will not be at liberty to appear before the
committee which it is Mr. Morley's intention to appoint."
The one question which, as a matter of the highest principle,
was of the utmost importance to postal servants, was to be
burked from the outset. The treatment of this question
went far to strengthen the prejudice against Lord Tweedmouth's inquiry. The sorters had, however, meanwhile
consented to accept the inquiry, and accordingly prepared
evidence. The sorters' case was to be taken first. The committee held its first meeting on Monday, June 24, 1895, and
the inquiry was conducted in Committee Room " B," a small
apartment of the House of Lords overlooking the Thames.
The proceedings had all the air of a police court inquiry, and
the court seemed centred in a strong atmosphere of officialdom imported from St. Martin's-le-Grand. But it was scarcely
imposing either in its assembly or its surroundings. There
was little to relieve the sombre dulness of it except the red
splashes of colour supplied by the crimson-leather chairs with
their embossed coronets, and the gliding vision of Thames
steamers and barge traffic beyond, seen through the generous
expanse of window. The grave and reverend seigneurs who
constituted the committee were ranged in a semicircle at a

horseshoe-shaped table, and the enclosed space was occupied by a witness, an arrangement which hinted at inquisitors and a prisoner in a trap. Lord Tweedmouth as the presiding judge, and perhaps the chief inquisitor, was a striking figure. Gaunt and towering even as he sat, the sunlight strongly reflecting on his curious pyramidal-shaped cranium, his visage hawk-like, for the most part silent and grim, he seemed like a great brooding eagle, supported on either side by kindred birds of lesser personality. Sir Francis Mowatt, with his disposition towards making ponderous jokes in a dry croaking raven's voice, pitched curiously enough, however, in a surprisingly pleasant key, was perhaps, next to Lord Tweedmouth, the most striking figure among the committee. The others were ordinary unobtrusive-looking gentlemen ; and the most unassuming-looking of them all was a rather slight elderly man, with grey hair and beard turning white. This was Mr. Spencer Walpole, late Governor of the Isle of Man, and now Permanent Secretary to the Post Office. Courteous, bland, and dignified in demeanour, there was nothing except the mouth, seeming set in a perpetual sneer, to indicate the man ; yet he it was who was to dominate the proceedings from start to finish.

If postal servants indulged the hope that the vexed question of civil rights and the cognate one of the unfair dismissal of trades union officials would be included for consideration, Lord Tweedmouth in his opening address made it clear that it was to be tabooed. There was naturally some disappointment manifested over this, and one of the witnesses for the Fawcett Association, E. J. Nevill, gallantly tried by a manœuvre to get it discussed. Lord Tweedmouth sternly negatived it, and the Controller of the London postal service, as one of the attorneys for the department, with prompt significance demanded the name of the man who had dared to ask so impertinent a question. It was the presence of this official, and the way in which he was allowed openly to influence the proceedings, which largely served to show the real character of the inquiry, and to weaken the men's confidence in its ultimate impartiality. The little incident of demanding the name of a lower subordinate witness, and the manner of it, induced the witnesses present, through one of their number, to get a protective guarantee from Lord Tweedmouth that none should suffer in their prospects for speaking openly. That it should have been deemed necessary to seek such a guarantee was suggestive.

The presence of all the heads of departments arranged in reserve squadron, and commanded by the Controller of the London postal service and other officials in turn, deprived the inquiry of its strictly impartial character. These officials were allowed to sit apart from ordinary witnesses and immediately behind the Permanent Secretary to the Post Office, the departmental representative on the committee, to perform attorneys' work, to make suggestions, provide questions to be put, and to pass written communications innumerable. If Lord Tweedmouth felt ashamed of the unfair latitude allowed in his court, he scarcely betrayed it.

In the meantime, either by implied understanding or by the weak acquiescence of the rest of the committee, the Postal Secretary was quietly but diligently asserting his mastery over it. Mr. Spencer Walpole had a reputation as a man of brilliant parts, and being a descendant of that historic Walpole who so cruelly used the poor boy-poet Chatterton, and who is asserted to have laid it down as a dictum that " every man has his price," it had come almost as a natural heritage to him to be regarded as a born cynic. A little of this inborn cynicism seemed to peep out when asking a witness who and what were his parents, adding, with what was regarded as unnecessary sarcasm, that the witness need not answer the question if he did not like to. The question was supposedly put for purposes of comparison, but it produced a rather sore feeling against the commissioner, and in no way tended to alleviate the growing conviction as to his unsympathetic attitude. They knew that Mr. Spencer Walpole was an important factor to be reckoned with, but they did not realise as yet that he was virtually the committee. It did not become marked for the first day or two. Each member of the committee was allowed to put a fair number of questions to witnesses, but gradually Mr. Spencer Walpole's personality spread itself over the entire gathering, and it became an acknowledged fact that it was the Post Office administration personified in him that was sitting in judgment on itself and moulding the inevitable verdict. The Permanent Secretary, backed up by his silent but industrious force of officials preparing the ammunition that he was to fire off, took the lead with almost every witness. If it was thought he was partial, it had to be acknowledged he was clever ; if he was merciless, he was also artistic to an extent, especially when he forgot his cynicism. The manner of his smartness, his alertness, and directness in choosing the leading question and putting it at every opportunity would have done credit to an Old Bailey lawyer. It seemed gradually to dawn on two or three of the committee that there was little left for them to do, so they accordingly subsided, only to pop up occasionally as if for the sake of appearance. Sir A. Godley from an early stage of the proceedings was either so thoroughly bored with the whole business, or so thoroughly convinced that the verdict could be come to without his active assistance, that he unblushingly dropped off to sleep, commonly for half-an-hour at a stretch. The only commissioner who inspired energy into the proceedings was the most interested party of all, the Permanent Secretary of the Post Office, whose administration it was that had come up for judgment. Not even the occasional laugh, always in such deliberations eagerly snatched at as a welcome break in the oppressive decorum, could deprive the occasion of that air of unreality and insincerity that seemed to pervade it.

The sorters, introduced and led by Groves, the treasurer of the association, stated their case already so familiar, and in one or two instances received the compliments of Lord Tweedmouth for the clear and able manner in which they had made themselves understood. That, of course, so far as it went, was gratifying, and as each representative in turn was questioned as to whether he was not an officer of such-and-such an association, it was calculated to heighten the conviction that official recognition of their organisations had come at last. The hope, however, was only a temporary one, doomed to be obliterated by the growing realisation that this was only too likely to prove a solemn farce. The witnesses came and went—sorters, telegraphists, postmen, and others— and in every case, with wearisome monotony came the iteration of that cold, metallic leading question from the Permanent

Secretary—the spare man with the yellowish-white beard surrounding the cruelly sneering lips—" But is it not the fact," etc.   The question was always so framed that the counsel for the Post Office very often wrung from a witness a reluctant or unwary admission afterwards turned to good account in the summing up.

The rebutting evidence of the officials as witnesses for the department was taken alternately with the completion of statements for each class or section of the service.   The evidence of the Postal Controller was not altogether un-favourable, containing as it did some valuable admissions ; but strong exception was taken by the sorters to his denials of undue pressure in the working conditions, while surprise was felt that he should seek to justify a lately-developed system of petty secret reporting and espionage, execrated and condemned by the staff generally as unworthy of an English Government department.   The evidence of the chief medical officer was in most respects distinctly favourable, corroborating their evidence of unhealthy hours and conditions of labour and the insanitary surroundings of their workaday lives ; and his evidence, so far, in a large measure helped to remove the bad impression prevailing in respect to the medical officials' attitude towards the staff at St. Martin's-le-Grand.   The telegraphists found in their Controller a very friendly witness so far as his utterances went, and they felt they had cause to congratulate themselves ; only they had yet to learn that fine words butter no parsnips.   The hostility of the Assistant-Secretary, Mr. Lewin Hill, nephew of the founder of the penny post, was blunt and undisguised, and especially displayed itself towards the postmen, portions of his evidence being received by them with the strongest signs of dissent.

The evidence of the officials originally intended to minimise the value of that given by the subordinate and manipulative staffs, could not on the whole, however, be adjudged altogether unfair.   The authorities had to play the game according to the rules prescribed for them, and mostly with a view to scoring for the department.   If they did not play the game entirely devoid of prejudice, they played it con-sistently as witnesses for their department on its defence.

The tribunal itself may have been unfairly constituted, but there were few outward and visible signs that it was so during the taking of evidence. The naked truth was as decently draped as possible. And for the artistic arrangement of the drapery there was much credit due to the secretary of the committee, Mr. Bruce, to whose courtesy and considerateness the host of witnesses owed much in carrying through their tasks. Lord Tweedmouth was, as the president of the inquiry, always studiously fair and strong in his judicial capacity ; but he struck one at times as being uncomfortable and pained at the realisation, that had come too late, that he had been betrayed into a false position.

If ever it was a case of " Save us from our friends " it was so with Lord Tweedmouth. Mr. Arnold Morley as Post-master-General had lightly and airily granted this inquiry, apparently with the full conviction that the case of the postal malcontents was so weak and flimsy that examination would only cover them with confusion. That indeed was to be the end and purpose of the whole inquiry ; and Lord Tweedmouth, trusting to the representations of his friend, agreed to risk his reputation on it. However open-minded Lord Tweed-mouth may have been when he approached the problem, the constitution of the committee, the terms of its reference, the restrictions with which it was hedged in various ways, all conspired against a free and impartial verdict. It is probable that Lord Tweedmouth was as surprised as anybody to find how complex, how tangled, and how stupendous was the problem so lightly laid before him by Mr. Arnold Morley. Whatever may have been his chagrin at being thus betrayed into the acceptance of so onerous and gigantic a task, Lord Tweedmouth courageously determined to see it through to the end. And he did ; but he came out of the fearful ordeal scarcely the man he was when he went in, and his public reputation, if not sullied, was certainly not enhanced. If the recommendations of the Tweedmouth Committee were not the result of a prearranged and foregone conclusion, the subsequent discontent was largely based on the suspicion that it was so. The inquiry lasted for some two or three months ; there was an elaborate examination of witnesses drawn from every branch and every section of the lower ranks of the service, there was a very industrious show of getting at the facts of things, there was some amount of patience and tolerance displayed, but considerations of economy were to warp and stultify the verdict to be presently given. If the verdict had only been just in accordance with the promise implied in the simulated earnestness of certain members of the committee, there would perhaps have been little to object to. But it was not to be. Certainly, few held optimistic views of the result of the inquiry, but scarcely any one was prepared for what was coming.

When, after some months of silent and unseen deliberation in preparing their recommendations, the long-looked-for report of the Tweedmouth Committee was, on March 10, 1897, issued, it immediately produced a thunderclap. It was eminently disappointing to the whole service. The mountain, after all its long labour, had brought forth a mouse. The many who had asked for bread were offered a stone, while only to a few were given some small crumbs of comfort. The new scheme was to appropriately take effect on the First of April.

An examination of the scheme revealed it to be full of flaws and omissions ; and what it appeared to so generously offer with one hand it filched with the other. It was regarded by every section of the service as a clever piece of financial thimble-rigging. The only class who appeared to derive any material benefit worth speaking of were the London sorters, their maximum being raised to £160 per annum ; but even this benefit was found to be minimised by restrictions, while certain emoluments and allowances for extra responsibilities and particular duties were to be sacrificed.

The telegraphists, so far from benefiting, were the principal sufferers, their maximum, instead of being raised as they had hoped, now being reduced from £190 to £160 uniformly with the sorters. The postmen, except in the matter of one or two additional good-conduct stripes, were no better off than before ; while the vexed question of Christmas-boxes— a source of humiliation to themselves and an unjust tax on the public indirectly imposed by the department—was left untouched. Altogether the Tweedmouth scheme was a source of still further grievance all round. The provincial sorting clerks were "bitterly disappointed," the postmen were " dumbfounded," the sorters "by no means satisfied," and the telegraphists were simply "overwhelmed with consternation." These were the verdicts of the various bodies who were included in the scheme ; but several of the classes who had tendered evidence, in hopes of getting their grievances redressed, were herein conspicuous by their absence. If there was a little given there was much taken away. If there was a slight increase in the holiday period and other minor advantages, ample compensation was taken in the serious reduction of the telegraphists' maximum, and the abolition of allowances for special and senior duties among other classes, the sorters and sorting clerks. When, indeed, these reductions and abolitions were considered, it was difficult to accept as an actual and literal fact the alleged enormous cost of this scheme, seemingly so hollow and so empty.

The two concessions to sentiment and humanity principally appreciated by the sorters and others were the acknowledgment of the insanitary conditions of the sorting-offices and the proposed reduction of the rigours of middle-of-the-night attendance and split duties. But other grievances almost as pressing were either ignored or glossed over, or wholly rejected as not sufficiently proved. In spite of the representations that had been made on every ground of proof that postal servants were overloaded with work and responsibility ; that the growing strain and stress was a common cause of brain malady and nervous breakdown ; that the conditions of postal life generally conduced to premature decay, and were becoming a prolific cause of consumption, especially among the indoor staffs, the Tweedmouth scheme was to supply no remedy. In spite of the evidence that the conditions of work and the disgraceful overcrowding during the performance of important duties were so largely responsible, it seemed that men were still to be punished and humiliated for errors next to unavoidable. The Tweedmouth scheme, moulded within the narrow groove of a mechanical economy, was to bring no relief for these things. The charges of favouritism in the service had been scouted as not proven ; but if there were few well-defined cases of direct nepotism, there still obtained the kindred evil of the neglect, suppression, and humiliation of deserving merit for no other reason than that it was not accompanied with the prescribed abjectness and self-efface-ment.   These evils, and the thousand and one grievances arising out of them, exhaustively and conclusively pleaded as they were before the inquiry, were practically left untouched by the scheme intended to provide a panacea for all postal ills.   Hence the disappointment of all classes, both those who were included in the too meagre benefits and those who were not.   It was regarded all round as a scheme more for the department than for the force.   If the department had made a few concessions, it had exacted a heavy price for them. It had been confidently thought that if they would not concede they would not take away ; but the result showed that in return for the little that had been given old privileges were to be ruthlessly cut away and old landmarks disturbed. The scheme reckoned so costly was found by this means to partly pay for itself, and even the hours of duty in some cases were so manipulated as to more than compensate the department for the three days' increase in annual leave, the most costly item of the whole.

It is unnecessary here to go into a close analysis of so technical and complex a scheme as that embodied in the report of the Tweedmouth Committee ; but such was the feeling its introduction produced among every class to which it applied, that it was regarded as an insult and a fresh injustice ;   and serious outbreaks of discontent seemed imminent all over the country.   However, whatever the merits or demerits of the Tweedmouth scheme, the serious fact had to be faced that it had met with sweeping and universal condenmation, even those whom it most favoured accepting it only as a Pyrrhic victory for agitation.

CHAPTER XXIII

CONTINUANCE OF AGITATION—ANOTHER THREATENED STRIKE OF TELEGRAPHISTS—THE NORFOLK-HANBURY CONFERENCE—THE " HARDY ANNUAL " OF THE POST OFFICE—POSTAL FEDERATION—THE JUBILEE OF POSTAL AGITATION—CONCLUSION OF FIRST PERIOD.

DURING the deliberations of the Tweedmouth Committee, the attitude of the service had necessarily for the most part been one of waiting and expectancy. But it was not without its record of work in the interim. The vexed question of civil rights and the reinstatement of Clery and Cheesman were urged in Parliament and on the attention of the Postmaster-General whenever there was an opportunity. In the previous session of Parliament, Sir Albert Rollit raised the matter in the House of Commons for the twentieth time, on a motion to reduce the Postmaster-General's salary, but the motion was withdrawn on a promise of a reconsideration of the question. Parliamentary policy was, however, almost of necessity during this while in a passive state, though a hold was still kept on the numerous Parliamentary friends of the movement. The connection between the postal organisations and the general labour movement had by this time become more intimate than ever. The sorters' organisation, the Fawcett Association had, through its chairman, W. E. Clery, been mainly instrumental in bringing into existence the Government Workers' Federation which started with the ambitious project of ultimately embracing all classes of Government workers. Moving along the lines on which it was originally started, it bade fair to become an important and formidable factor in domestic politics ; but differences arose among the leaders on points of policy, and Clery, having so many demands upon his time in connection with postal agitation proper, relinquished

U

the leadership of it, though the sorters' organisation still continued affiliation to it. The chairmanship of the Government Workers' Federation was then filled successively by G. E. Raby, then organising secretary of the Fawcett Association, and by W. B. Cheesman, general secretary of the same body, and under the latter especially continued to exert some amount of political influence. The postal movement particularly, as represented by the sorters' organisation, discharged its due share of work and responsibility in connection with the general crusade of labour, sending delegates to the Trades Union Congress each year, holding a respected position in the London Trades Council, and rendering assistance both moral and pecuniary in most of the functions of trade union and labour politics.

Then came the announcement on March 10, 1897, of the recommendations of the Tweedmouth Committee, and the consequent disappointment of the whole of the postal service. That disappointment became the stronger the more they realised that their confidence and patience, so sorely tried, had been so ill repaid. The voice of discontent broke out with renewed vigour, and found expression in public meetings all over the country once more. There was a general demand that the whole thing should be thrown into the melting-pot and recast. Fiercely enthusiastic and crowded meetings of postmen and telegraphists were held in London, and among the latter particularly there were growing warnings of a renewed disposition to adopt a strike policy.

Certainly among the postmen and the telegraphists the application of the scheme threatened only to make confusion worse confounded. Considering the amount of discontent it had revived, and the manner in which it bade fair to strain the loyalty of postal servants to the uttermost, it seemed that the Treasury and the Government were by no means to be congratulated on their bargain, costing, as it was supposed to, the enormous sum of £275,000 a year. So far from effecting its purpose, it appeared rather to be producing a spirit of open revolt among the very classes it was supposed to pacify. A recognition of this circumstance and the influence of pressure brought by members of Parliament at last induced the Postmaster-General, the Duke of Norfolk, who had now succeeded Mr. Arnold Morley, and Mr. Hanbury, Secretary to the Treasury, to consider the advisability of a further inquiry, presumably with a view to some revision of the scheme so strongly objected to. The fault of the situation lay not so much with the malcontents, or any proneness to agitation on their part, as to the innate defects and anomalies of this costly and cumbrously ineffective scheme ; and members of Parliament, and a considerable section of the press, held to that view in calling on the Postmaster-General to institute a further inquiry. It had been urged from every postal platform throughout the United Kingdom that the scheme, which all servants of the Post Office had looked to to bless them, had produced quite the opposite effect. The scheme, instead of proving the plentiful cornucopia they had hoped for, and felt they merited, had turned out a Pandora's box, full of evils, but without even hope at the bottom.

The tide of indignation quickly gained in strength, till among the London telegraphists their inclination to strike became scarcely any longer disguised. The threatened strike was, it was understood, to take the form of a general refusal to perform overtime, a contingency which, in view of the already undermanned condition of the staff, was likely to give rise to serious complications for both the department and the public, especially with the approach of the busy summer season.

Some of the press in their comments on the situation were ill-advised enough to assure the telegraphists of their support and sympathy in the event of their adopting this course, but there is no reason to think that such assurances influenced the telegraphists in their decision. They boasted of being able to fight the battle on its merits, and with confidence as to the result if they did so decide. There had already been telegraph strikes, and all had ended with more or less success for the men concerned. The first was that of 1871 in England, the second was in France in 1881, and the third was in Spain in 1892. All three were conspicuous examples of what inconvenience to the public could be caused by a stoppage and dislocation of the telegraph service, and in each case the struggle was brief. But that was before the general adoption of telephones. Possibly the telegraphists

U*

who at first contemplated striking against overtime recollected this in conjunction with other considerations.   While they were making a show of preparation, and subscribing to an emergency fund started in Liverpool, the authorities were not slow to take advantage of the warnings, and, none too secretly, were providing against the emergency accordingly.

On June 15 the Duke of Norfolk granted an interview to the aggrieved telegraphists, and by a deputation of the London men was made personally acquainted with the full text of their grievances.   The Postmaster-General promised to give full consideration to the facts laid before him, and to acquaint them with his decision at an early date.   After waiting for five weeks for the promised answer, the telegraphists gave vent to their further impatience by deciding to take a ballot of their members on the question of ceasing to work overtime. The result of this ballot showed practically a unanimous vote in favour of a refusal to obey overtime summonses, the proportion of the whole country being 83 per cent. in favour, or fully 70 per cent. of the whole male staff.   In London the vote showed 94 per cent., in Liverpool 85 per cent., and other provincial towns gave similar results.   The ballot showed that the men were getting angry ; but in view of a promise given in the House by Mr. Hanbury as representing the Postmaster-General, the executive of the telegraphists announced their intention to recommend their members to delay for a while before carrying the intention into effect.   There was an excited mass meeting of London telegraphists, male and female, and it is probable that only the intervention of Sir Albert Rollit averted a threatened strike.

The platform utterances in public meeting during this exciting period were in some cases none too guarded, and, as a result, two Newcastle telegraphists, and Garland, the secretary of the London branch, one of the ablest of the leading agitators, were called on officially to explain certain expressions used by them in reference to the avowed intention of their body to " walk out " from the operating-rooms when the signal came to be given.   Their explanations were, however, accepted a little later on as more or less satisfactory ; and this was done with a tactful exhibition of leniency in a trying emergency that at the time was favourably commented on in the press, and possibly did much towards conciliating the telegraphists as a body and turning them from their intention ; though it must be noted that some little indignation was expressed among them owing to their two comrades at Newcastle having their salaries reduced.

Meanwhile petitions and memorials were being numerously signed and sent in from almost every class of postal servants pleading for interviews with heads of departments, and urging the authorities in various ways to remedy the newly-discovered defects of the Tweedmouth scheme, or to see that its more favourable recommendations were interpreted and applied more equitably ; for during this time it was observable that the department showed a marked reluctance to give postal servants the full benefits the scheme entitled them to, though every advantage on its own side was almost at once rigidly exacted.

Little or no satisfaction resulted from these appeals, and on July 16, 1897, the report of the Tweedmouth Committee being brought on for discussion in the House of Commons, the opportunity was taken to raise most of the knotty points afresh. Sir Albert Rollit was again to the fore, and well vindicated the claims of the postmen, the telegraphists, and sorters, and, to promote discussion on the matter, moved the reduction of the Post Office vote by £1,000. He was ably supported by Captain Norton, Mr. Hudson Kearley, Mr. William Allen, Mr. Pickersgill, and a number of other influential members, the whole ground of the established forces and the rural and auxiliary postmen being once more gone into.

As the indirect result of this debate, a conference was arranged between members of Parliament and the Postmaster-General and Mr. Hanbury, as Secretary to the Treasury ; and to this conference members of the still aggrieved classes in the service were invited to give supplementary evidence. The Norfolk-Hanbury Conference, as it came to be called, occupied several sittings during July, representatives of the numerous classes affected giving further evidence. What was at first hailed as a Committee of Arbitration was, however, found to be presided over and dominated almost entirely by the Postmaster-General, members of Parliament being reduced to the position of witnesses and having no voice in the decisions to be arrived at. Sir Albert Rollit, as the principal advocate of the postal case, strove earnestly and strenuously to convince the Duke of Norfolk and Mr. Hanbury that the Tweedmouth scheme was inadequate ; that where it had not actually introduced fresh grievances it had but imperfectly met the just demands of the service ; and that the short-comings of the scheme were aggravated by the niggardly manner in which the few favourable recommendations were being applied.

An additional volume of evidence on fresh points was put forward by various witnesses called from among the men ; and in many respects it was sought to be shown that the conditions of the service were far from being bettered by the scheme, and that many unfair advantages were being taken by the authorities. At an early stage of the proceedings one more effort was made to discuss the questions of civil rights and the notorious dismissals ; but it was as promptly ruled out of order as before. There was a deal of ammunition expended by the various postal bodies on the Norfolk-Hanbury Conference, but from certain indications in the Postmaster-General they were led to believe that he was not wholly unsympathetic. They had, however, to wait for a period of seven months for the second instalment of their great disappointment.

During this seven months of waiting for the Postmaster-General's final decision on the points raised, there were several interesting happenings.

For the first time in the history of postal journalism, a writer in the *Post* was called on by the department to explain a certain paragraph to which his name was attached. The whole thing was innocent enough and was proved so, but the spirit that inspired the interference was thought to savour of official censorship, and being promptly resisted, the Permanent Secretary, seeing the absurdity of pressing the point against the writer, very sensibly allowed the matter to drop. This ended as a comedy ; but a rather more serious matter was the further trespass on the right of combination on the part of the officials in compelling Groves, the treasurer of the Fawcett Association, to resign from his position as a paid officer of the organisation. He had received a small appointment as a supervisor, and he was given the alternative of resigning his appointment as an overseer or ceasing to be a paid officer of the organisation. Groves had been identified with the movement from its inception, and was regarded as one of the pillars of postal combination. He had either to resign his position as treasurer or be reduced to the ranks. That was the Postmaster-General's decision. Groves put himself in the hands of his constituents, and as it was decided that it would be impolitic and unnecessary for him to martyr himself, he resigned his position as treasurer of the association.

The all-important question of civil rights for postal servants, and the outrage on the principle of combination involved in the dismissals of Messrs. Clery and Cheesman, was once more brought before the attention of the House, this time by Mr. Sam Woods, M.P., who on February 18, 1898, moved an amendment to the Address. The reinstatement question had now come to be known as the " hardy annual " of the Post Office. Sir Albert Rollit ably supported the amendment. Mr. Hanbury, as representing the Postmaster-General, replied to the strictures on postal administration, and in dealing with the particular matter of the dismissals and the question of reinstatement, made some very pointed allusions to the two dismissed officials of the sorters' trades union, Messrs. Clery and Cheesman. After recapitulating the facts of the dismissals, as interpreted by the Post Office, he went on to speak of Clery at some length, quoting a memorable speech made by Clery at Newcastle in 1892. He justified the dismissals, and maintained that postal servants had nothing to complain of in the matter of civil rights, and, while paying a high tribute to the loyalty that distinguished the service, urged that nothing should be done by the House to break down the foundation on which the service rested. The amendment was lost by a majority of seventy-seven.

At length, on March 15, 1898, the long-waited-for decision of the Postmaster-General to the various questions laid before him as the outcome of objections to the Tweedmouth scheme was announced. This decision on the numerous points was nearly as disappointing as the report of the Tweedmouth

Committee itself. There were a few very minor concessions, which affected only a few, but which were said to involve an additional cost of £80,000 per annum ; but the greater number of the questions raised were unceremoniously dismissed in a simple paragraph as " the various other matters which are not mentioned in this paper." After all the solemn pretence of rehearing the case, and admitting evidence that seemed well-nigh irrefutable, postal servants expected something more satisfactory. Indignation meetings were once more held among the various postal bodies, and disappointment and disagreement again found vent in strongly-worded resolutions calling on the Postmaster-General for yet another revision, on the ground that the reply did not adequately deal with the facts submitted, and that in the main the representations had been ignored.

The expenditure of the additional sum of £80,000 on the further concessions did not go very far when spread over such a vast area of postal service, and it was far from satisfying.

The numerous representations made to the Postmaster-General as the result of this renewal of disappointment called forth some months afterwards, in September, what the *Daily Chronicle* described as a " stern message," to be shared equally among the discontented. This " stern message " was conveyed in the Postmaster-General's annual report, issued September, 1898. Dealing with the Tweedmouth Committee and the grievances of sections of the postal staff covered by that inquiry, and the manifold representations that had since been made, the Postmaster-General stated that further concessions had already been made to the amount of £50,000 ; and he added, " Since that time I have declined, and shall continue to decline, to allow decisions which have been considered by the Tweedmouth Committee, and which have been revised by Mr. Hanbury and myself, to be reopened. It is my belief that these decisions have been liberal, but whether they are liberal or not, it is for the interests of all parties that it should be understood that they are final."

The word " finality " was written across the decisions of the Postmaster-General, and the postal service was given to understand that nothing more was to be expected. This did not tend to allay the feeling of disappointment that had taken possession of all bodies of postal servants. There were still more meetings, and still more protests ; but to no effect so far as the department was concerned. The conviction that their claims had not been adequately met, however, obtained a strong hold everywhere, and helped still further to promote that spirit of federation which for some two or three years had been at work among the various associations. It was not so much how little they had gained by the Tweedmouth inquiry that caused this discontent, as what they had actually lost, and the extremely economical manner in which many of the more favourable recommendations were being applied by the authorities, and even in some cases, as was alleged, wholly withheld.

The question of civil rights for postal servants and cognate matters occupied the attention of the Trades Union Congress at Bristol ; and two resolutions were passed urging the matter once more on the attention of the Postmaster-General. The first of the two resolutions in question protested against the persistent refusal of the Postmaster-General to allow the legitimate right of combination and civil liberty to postal employés, and strongly condemned " the repeated attempts to break up the postal organisations by intimidating their officers." The second resolution protested against " the failure of the Postmaster-General to carry into effect the recommendations of the Tweedmouth Committee in regard to split duties (emphatically condemned by the official medical officers as highly injurious to health), and the insanitary condition of Post Office buildings, which were admitted to be in a most dangerous condition, and a standing menace to the life and health of the workers." These two resolutions were forwarded by the Parliamentary Committee, through Mr. Sam Woods, M.P., to the Postmaster-General. The Postmaster-General, November 15, 1898, replied to this impeachment of the Trades Union Congress ; and, admitting much of its truth, pledged himself that " every effort was being made " to remedy the objectionable working conditions, and at the same time repeated his assurance that he had " no wish to curtail the privilege of combination in the Post Office," but he wished it to be distinctly understood that he was " unable to condone insubordination in any rank of the service, merely because it is disguised under the cloak of civil liberty." The reply of the Postmaster-General was regarded with some slight satisfaction by postal servants, though it was not accepted as covering all the facts alleged.

The long-standing hostility of one of the higher officials towards the principle of combination again manifested itself in an unexpected manner not long afterwards. In the following month of December some severe animadversions on postal servants and postal combination from Mr. Lewin Hill, the lately-retired Assistant Secretary, reported in the *Daily Graphic*, provoked strong resentment generally, which, however, gradually subsided in amusement on the attacks becoming several times repeated, and as often replied to in other organs of the press.

In the prosecution of Parliamentary policy the postal movement had gained strong reinforcements, both in the service and in the House of Commons. Members of Parliament had come and gone, but the number of their advocates had not fallen away. Among the new adherents to their cause was Mr. W. C. Steadman, M.P., whose return for Stepney had been secured by the turning balance of the postal vote there. Among all the members of the House who had beaten their brains against the granite walls of St. Martin's-le-Grand, Mr. Steadman from the first moment of his election proved the most persistent and the most pushful in his advocacy of postal claims. On the opening of the February session, 1899, he moved an amendment to the Address, and once more recapitulated the sins of omission and commission for which the Tweedmouth Inquiry was responsible, and strenuously urged for a Parliamentary Committee of Inquiry to complete the work left undone, being ably supported by other friends of the postal cause. Mr. Hanbury, as representing the Post-master-General, resisted further inquiry by the adoption of the official arguments which had served their purpose so well on former occasions. As strengthening his argument, the Postmaster-General's representative took the opportunity of importing into the discussion a personal attack on W. E. Clery, who had, since his dismissal for furthering the right of combination, become notorious as the arch agitator of the postal movement. Mr. Hanbury made the damaging assertion that "the battle rages round Mr. Clery, the man who is responsible for the agitation." Yet very illogically, as it seems, he tried to prove that the agitator round whom this battle was raging had not the confidence of trades unionists, inasmuch, as he averred, he was refused admission to the Trades Union Congress, "because he was neither a working member of the trade he represented nor a paid permanent official."

It was an absurd misstatement, as the chairman of the Sorters' Association had never been refused admission at any Trades Union Congress, but had represented his society there for several successive years. If he was not literally and actually a working member of the craft he represented, he was so in the meaning of the Congress rules, and in any case it was a weak and unworthy argument. In conclusion, the Postmaster-General's advocate, in paying an unintentional tribute to the postal agitator by allowing that Clery was the pivot on which the whole agitation turned, and that but for him there would be no organised discontent, used an argument which was most calculated to strengthen the hands of the agitator whom it was desired to efface. This speech for the defence on the part of Mr. Hanbury on this occasion was also rendered a cause for remembrance to the telegraphists, whose work he contemptuously described as only "superior type-writing." The insult thus levelled at the telegraphists was pointed with a comparison with the sorters' duties, which were described as requiring "more skill than telegraphic work."

But neither the attack on Clery in the House of Commons nor the compliment to postal work at the expense of the telegraphists availed beyond the momentary triumph. The interests of postal servants were wedded and welded in a new comradeship, which neither insult nor flattery were likely to dissolve.

The best answer to these strictures was the successful institution of Postal Federation throughout the service. (1898) The federation of postal associations was already an accomplished fact, and at last telegraphists, postmen, sorting clerks, sorters, and nearly all classes were united in one homogeneous whole for the furtherance of common interests. There had been several tentative attempts at this in the years gone by, but misunderstandings had forbidden its culmination till now. One result of the universal disappointment following on the Tweedmouth Inquiry and the Norfolk-Hanbury Conference was the burying by mutual consent of all class feeling, and the cementing of classes and sections which till now never fully realised that they had so much in common to strive for. The aim of the federated associations was to be at once simple and comprehensive. Unitedly they were to set about it as their first and primary duty to obtain an unofficial, impartial, and disinterested, yet authoritative, Committee of Inquiry into the remaining grievances of postal servants. This they apprehended would comprehend, if not all things, yet most. The vindication of full rights of combination, which could never bring its logical benefit to the men or to the department until it was coupled with official recognition, was another important matter which was to be accepted as a foremost plank in their platform.

Of equal importance to every postal servant, whatever his grade, was the claim to full recognition of the liberty of the individual in his leisure time, and the abolition of paltry and unnecessary restrictions on a postal servant's freedom to engage in any enterprise or undertaking of an honorable nature, according to his fitness or desire to better his prospects outside the service. Related to and closely following on this was to be the claim for citizen rights and all that it involved, including the reinstatement of the unjustly-dismissed officials of the Fawcett Association. They were to insist on more humane treatment as servants of the State, and all those better conditions of hours and work which even the Tweedmouth scheme had left them unprovided with. A better minimum wage for the juniors, the question of deferred pay and pensions, promotion, favouritism, harsh medical restrictions, and numerous other matters were to be included in the programme which should facilitate their hopeful journeyings in search of the postal Land of Promise and a contented service. The general adoption of this programme by the combined associations at the first Congress, held at Derby, September, 1899, marked an epoch in postal history. It was a fitting celebration of the jubilee of postal agitation. Now, with the purpose of achieving these ideals by the way, they steadfastly set their faces towards the time-point when the State should in very truth become the model employer and the great exemplar to the labour market of the world.

.   .   .   .

Such concisely supplies the first period, covering 50 years, of the history of a remarkable agitation. Whatever its lesson, and whatever the ultimate verdict upon it from a strictly impartial standpoint, postal agitation is a fact that bears recording in the general history of organised labour. Whether it may be deemed wholly justified or not in all its varied phases, it has its value as an episode.

Agitation in the Post Office may not always have been studiously correct in attitude and demeanour, but perhaps it has committed no more and no greater mistakes than have the officials in their dealings with it in the past. It might almost be said that it represents, if only in miniature, the people's fight for freedom and the gradual extension of popular liberty ; for the Post Office has seen its pre-Chartist days, when to dare openly to organise discontent would have been to make men amenable to the Law of Conspiracy. It has represented a continuous conflict between the spirit of exaction on one side and the natural desire for betterment in pay and conditions, in just accordance with the improving value of labour everywhere, on the other. It has, indeed, been but a reflection and an analogue of the earlier struggles between capital and labour outside, and generally a protest against that fixed and fossilised scale of pay and that Procrustean standard of conditions for all time which have been shown to be no more possible here than in the broader arena of the labour market. Right or wrong, but always sustained by the conviction of right nevertheless, with the self-same tenacity with which their efforts have been repelled, the men who have from time to time engaged in this movement have persisted till they have beaten down the barriers, and gained some proportion of those advantages they laid claim to as their just dues.

It is in itself of small consequence to the world

outside the Post Office, perhaps, but it is significant as a consequence and an outcome of that free, powerful, and independent public opinion which safeguards and promotes our liberties ; it is only one of the natural results of that dominating spirit of democracy which has so broadened our boundaries morally and materially as a nation.

END OF BOOK I

INDEX.

CPSIA information can be obtained at www.ICGtesting.com
Printed in the USA
BVOW04*1038020914

365169BV00011B/371/P